ACTUALLY, IT'S NOT EASY

ACTUALLY, IT'S NOT EASY
ESSAYS ON OUR NOT-SO-SIMPLE HEALTH POLICY, GOVERNMENT, AND OTHER CHALLENGING TOPICS

So good to see you back in the neighborhood — it wasn't the same without Cafe Martin.

— N

NICHOLAS COHEN

Lulu Press, Inc.
627 Davis Drive, Suite 300
Morrisville, NC 27560
www.lulu.com

ISBN: 978-1-387-64356-1
First Edition, 2018
14 13 12 11 10 / 10 9 8 7 6 5 4 3 2 1

For my mother, who wanted me to write a book.

TABLE OF CONTENTS

PREFACE

I never set out to write a book. When I sent a few words to seven highly indulgent friends, writing a book wasn't a thought in my mind. But if you are reading this, it has apparently become a reality.

My writing career has a genesis story that bears telling. Knowing that I had something to say about government, some friends asked me to explain how Social Security works. My narrative-based explanation and questionable attempts at humor must have hit some high points because I was informed (to my surprise) that they found my analysis interesting. They thought others would as well. I decided to write another piece. More people stopped by to read what I called my Commentary. This cycle continued. Before I knew it, I had built a platform, albeit still a small one.

I soon learned I had a luxury that other writers lack: time. News outlets spend every 24-hour period reporting on what happened in the previous 24 hours. They often want to help their audience understand the news but are limited by a market that demands real-time reaction to today's events. Because my goal for the Commentary was reach rather than revenue, I could ignore the commercial rules that others must follow. When the history of a government program is relevant to understanding today's events, I'll write the piece of history and let others focus on the current event. I'm not going to beat the professionals to a scoop, but I can help explain why what they've written is important to you.

There was another distinction my writing could have: an analytic approach to every topic. I'm a math guy. I mean a for-real math guy. I literally have a degree in theoretical mathematics (admittedly, from a few years ago). In your everyday life, if you are lucky, some of what you read will contain a few figures. These are usually quoted with little context and no explanation of "what they mean." Now, don't worry—this is not a textbook. You don't need any background in mathematics to read this book. I don't use math for its own sake. But I try to differentiate my writing by using a consistently analytical approach to help explain complex topics. I've included many charts and graphs to help you along the way. But I want to challenge you to not be afraid of mathematics. Many people like this approach, including those who didn't expect to. I think it helps that I don't take myself so seriously and I follow a strict joke-to-math ratio.

After the Commentary was born, six months passed quickly, and there were more than 100,000 of my words sitting out there on the Internet. But I came to realize another fact about writing in the information age: the half-life of Internet content is astoundingly short. Something you post will have 75% of its readership in the first day. After a week, it's so far down the feeds on Facebook and Twitter that it may as well have been carved on a stone tablet. This was a problem. The whole reason I was doing this was to provide information that didn't have to be timely. But my words were quickly fading away into the dark reaches of cyberspace. I wanted a more permanent format in which to preserve and distribute the project. Compiling and improving what I'd written, and releasing it in a book format, would be both a challenge for me and an interesting product for my readers.

If you look at the news but get lost in the terminology, I hope this book will help you. If you want to know the history of how we got here, I hope to provide the context. If you see reporting of what happened yesterday, but want to know what it means for tomorrow, this should show you the possibilities. However, this book is at best a jumping off point, highlighting areas where you might be interested in learning more.

The LobbySeven Commentary project wouldn't have happened without a lot of help from a lot of people. Tony Kim and Pedro Arellano first pushed me to get something down on paper. Tony helped to expand the early audience, while Pedro graciously loaned me the name LobbySeven. Without either of them, it wouldn't have gotten off the ground. Benjamin Wang was another early reader who provided a lot of constructive criticism and encouraged me to go further.

Several people joined in as subject matter experts. TJ Wilkinson and Manoj Viswanathan helped me get my act together on taxes.

A lengthy discussion with Nicolas Hernandez greatly improved my knowledge of nuclear weapon development and proliferation. My sister, Laura Cohen, advised me on legal matters, especially about voting rights. This was more helpful when her advice came *before* I published, but hey, I'll take what I can get.

As the Commentary developed into a book format, I engaged another group to provide friendly comments and spine-stiffening encouragement to go forward. Manoj Viswanathan, Shari Cohen, Chris Johnson, Jason Poff, and Joe Sikoscow all volunteered to keep me on message and ensure that I made my point. Benjamin Texier's help was critical; he provided comments on nearly half of the manuscript. A few others asked to help anonymously; you know who you are.

Dan Fisher, my father's first cousin, became strategically involved with the project just as attempts to repeal Obamacare picked up in the summer of 2017. Since then, he has done an enormous amount to help me prepare and publish: approving topics and outlines, providing information sources, and checking for flow and accuracy (and occasionally for spelling). His background in the insurance business has been invaluable when talking about health insurance markets. Without his forced rewrites, the piece on algebraic topology would have been unreadable. He also provided strategic help as to what the book should be and gave the final assent that it was ready to hit the shelves.

As I began the move from Web to paper, I brought on an editor/research assistant, Brittany Reid. The quality of the book's content and appearance greatly improved after she got involved. My first realization of how much work was involved in writing a book came from her edits. Mengyue Sun was also involved in editing the manuscript, focused on the charts and graphics. To the extent these help you to understand the material, you should thank Meng. Just when I thought I was almost done, Linda Orlando read the entire manuscript, finding 4,000 additional edits. It was a pleasure working with Linda, and her advice played a critical role in the stretch run. The book was laid out by Phillip Gessert. It is because of his work that this actually looks like a book.

My wife, Michelle, handled the lion's share of the early editing. She did this despite having, on average, 1.5 children screaming at her, crawling on her, or demanding food and water—in addition to her own career to worry about! Virtually all the readers that have found the Commentary came from social media. Luckily for me, she is an expert at growing online audiences; I hope I was a good student.

To use a writers' cliché, any remaining faults are my own.

Finally, I wouldn't have started this, and wouldn't have continued to do it, without everybody who has stopped by to read. Seeing traffic on the website, interacting with readers on social media, and receiving other feedback is the reason to keep going. I know you have many choices for your information needs, and I appreciate you choosing the Commentary. I wish you a pleasant read of the following pages, wherever your final destination might be.

—NC
Brooklyn, NY
October 2017

INTRODUCTION

A ll writing is autobiography. It always tells the story of the author as much as of the subject.

After seeing a new publication, readers always ask me, "How much of this did you know, and how much did you have to research?" I obviously don't know each fact and figure by heart, but I also don't choose a topic without having a message in mind. Despite writing what I know, I am always surprised by how much more I have to learn. Misconceptions pervade my thinking about subjects I think I have down cold. The act of looking up the facts and figures makes the work more empirical, but also gives me a better understanding of how and why things happen. The words of others show me new and interesting ways in which to present the material. But I always start writing with an idea of where I will end up; with my thesis in mind from the start, I avoid the trap of just compiling the thoughts of others.

Although the Commentary began as a set of objective discourses about topics like Weimar Germany, I was surprised by how personal the experience of writing became. Not a single event in my life is described in this book, and yet it is very much "about" me—how I think and what I think about. Don't take this analogy too far; health insurance regulation is not the primary concern of my day-to-day life. However, when you complete this literary voyage to the bitter end, you will come to understand my view of the world. You'll understand me.

MY POINT OF VIEW

When writers purport to have a basis in fact, they should communicate the point of view that they bring to their writing. Everything you read is colored by who wrote it and what they have experienced in their lives. Bias is a word that has developed a negative connotation but rest assured: everybody is biased. The best a writer can do is to take stock honestly and explain where they are coming from. Understanding and admitting your biases is a key step toward counteracting them. Similarly, beware falling into the trap of living in an echo chamber. Don't focus all your attention on information that fits your world view. Include for consideration intelligent arguments from those with whom you disagree. Confirmation bias is a universal tendency, and it clouds our judgment.

So, I'll get to it. Here is how I define myself. It is the point of view which, in my opinion, has shaped this book.

I am an Empiricist

An empiricist is one who operates through the scientific method. An empiricist travels around (metaphorically speaking), observing the world. Based on these observations, he or she forms hypotheses about how the world works. These hypotheses are continually tested via further observations and experiments. If the results are as expected, hypotheses become stronger; if not, the hypotheses are refined or even discarded. Observations and experiments can also come from secondary sources; I don't need to see a quark with my two eyes to know that they exist. I trust information from sources I view as reputable. But an empiricist doesn't accept information without evidence. An empiricist doesn't "believe" things based on faith alone.

I am a Bayesian

To a Bayesian, nothing is absolutely certain. A Bayesian always accepts some minute possibility that even their strongest hypotheses are wrong. Therefore, if you wait to act until something is certain, you will be too late.[1] The human mind is not wired to think probabilistically. We like to think in terms of certainties, and we are not good at understanding what it means when we hear that something has a "10% chance of happening."

---

1. See Change, Climate.

Being a Bayesian again involves working with hypotheses and refining their probabilities as new information is received. I find Bayesian methods applicable to most decisions that feature risk and reward. For Bayesians, the day is filled with searching for additional information, incorporating it into your hypotheses, and acting despite lack of certainty. If you don't know much about Bayesian theory, don't worry, you will soon.

I am a Democrat

This book is primarily about government, and not at all about politics. We talk about policy goals and the means of achieving them. We talk less about whether they will be popular or how they will affect the next election. However, my political views are obviously a lens through which I view our country and cannot be ignored. I am registered with the Democratic Party.[2]

I am a Democrat because I have analyzed the policies of the two parties, considered how these policies are likely to work, and determined that Democratic policies are likely to lead to better outcomes for the country (and myself). In fact, the core of this book is made up of these analyses.

Beyond policy, I have serious problems with the politics of the Republican Party and its politicians. I think much of their activity is antithetical to the principles of our nation and detrimental to its future. The Republican Party believes that government is incompetent and government itself is the problem. We have strong evidence that this is true—for Republican-run governments.

I am worried

Republics are fragile systems. The more power the executive holds, the more fragile the republic is. The only way I know of to prevent a *would-be* American tyrant from becoming an *in-fact* American tyrant is to not elect one President. The institutional guardrails that prevent a President from destroying our institutions are not as strong as you think they are. A determined President with a pliant Congress would likely be able to end representative government in the United

---

2. This is hardly a secret, since party registration in New York is public.

States. To paraphrase Benjamin Franklin, we must be vigilant if we are to keep our republic.

WHAT IS A VOLUME?

The basic format of my Commentary is the Volume. This word was chosen carefully. It is intended to signify completeness. It may conjure an image of an old, leather-bound book of great length. When you finish reading one, you know everything you need to about its topic. My Volumes are mercifully shorter than these and have no bindings, but each contains its own beginning and end, its own thesis and conclusion. Where one subject has earned multiple Volumes, each is intended to be read independently, to the greatest extent I could manage.

As you read you'll come across footnotes. A lot of them. This is the fun part. You know how you sometimes are in a discussion with somebody and you want to elaborate further on your point, but you just don't have any way to fit it in without monopolizing the conversation? Well, it's too bad you can't use footnotes in everyday conversation. I use them to expound on a point without harming the narrative flow, to mention an interesting tidbit that doesn't otherwise fit in, or simply to add a touch of humor.[3]

When I tell people I'm writing, they always ask, "Is it a blog?" Now, I have nothing against blogs—I read a lot of blogs. But I don't know any blogs that look like my Volumes.[4] That being said, on occasion there was a current event to which I wanted to respond quickly. I began to write some shorter pieces too. These are more like what you would see on a normal blog. Although shorter and less formal, some of these were pretty good; I chose a few of them to include here.

---

3. A thief sticks a pistol in a man's ribs and says, "Give me your money!" The man replies, "You can't do this, I'm a United States Congressman!" The robber says, "Well, then give me my money!"
4. Although some blogs do have footnotes.

Moving what I'd written on the Web to this new format required as much effort as writing the Commentary in the first place. Getting a book printed is easy; getting it right is a chore.

This book is mostly a compendium of what has already appeared on LobbySeven. The information you'll read is based on I knew at the time of each chapter's original publication. Some facts and circumstances will have changed by the time you're reading this, and more will change in the future. I'm not omniscient and don't wish to appear so. Because of this, editing has been mostly for style and clarity, not to project clairvoyance. When events have rendered incorrect something I'd previously written, I've tried to say so in a footnote.

To prepare my writing for this book, the prose was improved, mistakes eliminated, formatting made more aesthetic. I hope it is not undue pride to say that it is much, much better. If you've read some of this on the internet, you'll recognize the titles and some arguments, but little else. Not all the warts have been excised. Where I was wrong, I'll still be wrong and take my lumps. To demonstrate how this book came to be, I didn't even re-order the Volumes; the Weimar Republic and Poincaré Conjecture are jumbled between articles on health insurance and fiscal policy. It's like you sat down to read it on the web, start to finish.[5]

USE OF SOURCES

As I said, I don't claim to be unbiased, because I don't think it's possible. Facts and figures must be enriched with prose if an author wishes readers to remain conscious. Even quoting the Census Bureau can be misleading without proper context. No matter how hard I try, my personal biases—the experiences in my life that inform my thinking—will be incorporated into this book.

But where I can, I stick to verifiable facts. If I quote a figure, I'll provide the source. I use only sources I think are reputable, and I en-

---

5. But in a format that you can repurpose as a doorstop or coaster.

courage you to be skeptical. The sources used for specific information, as well as the way they were used, are listed in the Notes and Sources section at the end of the book. If you want to know more about a topic, or just want to check my math, this is for you. Given that my writing comes from the Internet, most of the sources are available there.

I had one additional way of using sources. Sometimes, a book featured so strongly in my thinking that I felt the need to reference it, even if it wasn't directly quoted. I would know nothing about Weimar Germany and the rise of Hitler if not for *Rise and Fall of the Third Reich*. I wouldn't have thought to touch the nuclear arms race had I not read Richard Rhodes's excellent *The Making of the Atomic Bomb*. These books and others that have informed my writing are listed in the Further Reading, also at the back of the book. We are what we read, and this is an autobiography.

SUMMARY OF THE INTRODUCTION

I've probably pushed my luck as to how much you really care about the process, so I'll finish up. If I were forced to give a message, it would be this: complex problems are solved by making choices. With notably rare exceptions, there is no free lunch. If we want something, we need to pay for it, one way or another.

Free markets are great, and we need to be careful to preserve them. But we also need to remember that individuals are often incentivized to act in a way that harms the group; only a government can prevent these perversions of free markets. Generally, governments do this via regulation. That's why governments exist—to create sets of rules to incentivize fair play, allocate resources and costs, and provide security. The rules are necessarily messy, as they must constantly balance the interests of the many groups that exist in a society such as ours. Politicians, those who make and enforce the rules, have their own incentives, which often conflict with what is best for their constituents. In the United States, all this must come together to deliver food, water, electricity, internet, health care, and myriad other modern necessities to over 300 million people living on nearly 4 million square miles. It's not easy.

SOCIAL SECURITY
THREE TRILLION DOLLARS IN A FILING CABINET

"You really should read the OASDI Trustees Report."
—Anonymous

Like so many pieces of advice I've given to my friends, I would guess this one has never been followed. But Social Security is a critical bedrock in our nation's retirement savings, and its Trustees produce their report for a reason. If you work for forty years and earn $100,000 per year, by the time you retire you will have invested $496,000 into Social Security. I doubt you have any other large investments that you know so little about.

Despite being a constant topic in political discussions and representing annual payments of over $900 billion—24% of all federal government spending—most people have no idea what Social Security is, how it works, or what its future looks like.

- What is Social Security?
- How does Social Security work? What is the trust fund?
- What is the prognosis for the system? Is there a crisis?
- What about the various changes that have been proposed?

Image 1: Bush '43 looks at paper

WHAT IS SOCIAL SECURITY?

Social Security is the common name for the **Old-Age, Survivors, and Disability Insurance** (OASDI) program. Created in 1935 as a key plank of the New Deal, Social Security was designed to combat rampant poverty among seniors, which at the peak of the Great Depression was approaching 50%. The Social Security Administration (SSA) was established to manage the program. An initial check for $22.54, written to Ida May Fuller in 1940, was the beginning of what has grown into the largest federal government expenditure and a major component of the U.S. economy. In 2016, over 60 million Americans received benefits from Social Security.

In the 80 years of its existence, Social Security has been modified many times by Congress. Some of the major events in the program's history are:

- 1939: Spouses and minor children added as beneficiaries
- 1954: Disability program added
- 1965: Medicare created
- 1977-1983: Significant changes to funding and benefit calculations to ensure stability
- 1997: Temporary Assistance for Needy Families and State Children's Health Insurance Program added to SSA's mandate

According to the Center on Budget and Policy Priorities, in 2015, Social Security income raised 22 million Americans out of poverty.

HOW DOES SOCIAL SECURITY WORK? WHAT IS THE TRUST FUND?

Social Security is deceptively simple. Take a look at your paystub. Among the deductions from your gross income you will see a field designated FICA SS Tax. The amount withheld from your paycheck is equal to 6.2% of your earnings, up to a taxable income cap of $118,500. Your employer pays the same amount, but you'll never see this.[6] This money goes to the SSA, which sends out monthly checks to beneficiaries.[7] The amount of the tax withheld and benefits dispersed are set by Congress. Any extra cash generated goes into a **trust fund.**[8]

---

6. For the self-employed, the mechanism is a bit different. The total tax liability is usually the same, but the entire payment is paid by the individual.

7. Interesting aside: the costs to manage the SSA are $6.2 billion per year, or around 0.22% of assets. This is much efficient than private bond funds. And of course, the SSA provides services that private funds don't, such as sending out tens of millions of checks every month.

8. Technically, there are two trust funds, one for Old Age and Survivors and one for Disability. The government treats them as interchangeable, so I will too.

Social Security is a pay-as-you-go system, fundamentally different from how most pension funds operate. In a typical corporate pension fund, contributions are made by or on behalf of current employees, invested until they retire, and then paid out to the same workers. In Social Security, the contributions made today are used primarily to pay today's retirees. At some point around 1980, some nerds[9] looked at the numbers and saw there was a problem. The system was doing well, but demographics down the road looked ominous. Congress made significant changes to the system, increasing taxes, reducing benefits, and delaying the retirement age, to ensure the system would remain solvent. Social Security began taking in significantly more than it paid out, and the trust fund started to grow.

Fast forward to today. The trust fund is going strong, with approximately $2,800,000,000,000[10] in the bank. But of course, the way in which this huge sum is managed is not straightforward. The trust fund used to hold regular U.S. government bonds, but the Social Security Administration couldn't handle the changes in market price inherent to these bonds. They created a new class of securities, **special issues**, which can be redeemed by the trust fund for face value at any time. Surprisingly, these certificates are kept in a plain, old, three-ring binder in a common-issue filing cabinet in Parkersburg, West Virginia. In 2005, George W. Bush went to West Virginia to look at these pieces of paper. After touring the building where the filing cabinet sits, President Bush made a controversial statement about the nature of the trust fund.

There is no trust fund, just IOUs that I saw firsthand, that future generations will pay—will pay for either in higher taxes, or reduced benefits, or cuts to other critical government programs.

The office here in Parkersburg stores those IOUs. They're stacked in a filing cabinet. Imagine—the retirement security for future generations is sitting in a filing cabinet. It's time to strengthen and modernize Social Security for future generations with growing assets that you can control, that you call your own—assets that the government cannot take away.

---

9. I assume.
10. That's $2.8 trillion.

President Bush was wrong, in several ways. While they cannot be sold to the public, the special issues are backed by the full faith and credit of the U.S. government, just like other Treasury bonds. Failure to pay them would be a default on our obligations; there is no reason to think they have more risk than other government securities. Moreover, the $2.8 trillion isn't money that future generations will pay; it's money that past generations have invested. The trust fund did not cause our government to borrow the money; if Social Security didn't exist, somebody else would own the debt. While the government could, in theory, take the trust fund assets away, you can say the same about any other investment. We could find a better plan for storing $2.8 trillion than a filing cabinet in a small city in West Virginia.

We should also note President Bush's prediction about what would happen if the trust fund were depleted. We know what would happen if the trust fund were exhausted, because it's in the law. Social Security has a dedicated funding source, so a deficit must be bridged by reducing benefits. This would indeed be highly unfair to people who had paid withholding taxes and were expecting to receive full benefits.

WHAT IS THE PROGNOSIS FOR THE SYSTEM? IS THERE A "CRISIS"?

The phrase "Social Security Crisis" has been thrown around so much that it's lost all meaning. To reassert context, let's look at where we are today by the numbers.

In 2017, the OASDI perimeter had an income of $957 billion, of which $88 billion was investment income. Total expenses were $922 billion, meaning that Social Security turned a profit of $35 billion. We can agree that no business turning a $35 billion profit is in a crisis. There is therefore no immediate threat to Social Security. But what about the future?

The OASDI trustees project future trust fund balances based on three economic/demographic scenarios: base-case, worst-case, and intermediate. In the worst-case scenario, the trust fund is exhausted in 2029, after which it will pay out 73% of the currently promised benefits. In the most optimistic scenario, the trust fund remains in surplus until 2090, as far out as they care to project. In the intermediate case, the trust fund will run out of funds in 2035. After this, Social Security will be able to pay out just over 80% of promised benefits.[11]

With such a wide range of scenarios, it is difficult to know what to think. But we can boil this down to a sensible qualitative view. At some point in the 2030s or 2040s, the trust fund will probably, but not definitely, be depleted. Were it to be depleted, there would be a significant cut to benefits. After this cut, Social Security should run smoothly for as long as we can project. Merriam-Webster defines "crisis" as "a situation that has reached a critical phase." Projections for the future of Social Security show potential serious problems, but not nearly as dire as its doomsayers are claiming.

WHAT ABOUT THE VARIOUS CHANGES THAT HAVE BEEN PROPOSED?

While I do not subscribe to the Cult of the Social Security Crisis, there is certainly a risk to future benefits. Therefore, I am in favor of taking some actions now to strengthen the system. This is a case of risk management, making moderate changes today to lower the probability of needing drastic action in the future.

To properly consider potential changes to Social Security, we should introduce the term **long-term actuarial deficit**, which I will just refer to as just the Gap. The Gap is the amount of tax increases and/or spending cuts required to balance the system in the long run. It is quoted as a percentage of total taxable income. The most recent projections say that the Gap is 2.66%. This means that if we raised additional taxes equal to 1.33% of wages, from each employee and their employer, actuaries would consider Social Security to be solvent.[12] We have a few choices as to how we proceed.

---

11. Personally, I think the most likely economic path is between the intermediate and best-case scenarios. Of course, I have no track record of successfully predicting macroeconomic conditions over a multi-decade period.
12. This ignores any macroeconomic feedback of tax increases. However, as we will discuss in a later chapter, there is little evidence that these macroeconomic effects of small changes in tax policy are significant.

1. Increase the cap on taxable income

Currently, only income up to \$118,500 per year is subject to Social Security FICA tax. Increasing this cap would increase the income subject to the tax. Doing so would affect only about 20% of households in any given year. There are many ways to change the cap, and the effects vary from plan to plan. Making all earned income subject to FICA would close 90% of the Gap. A more common proposal is to set the cap dynamically so that it covers 90% of all income; this would close 35% of the Gap.

2. Decrease the benefits paid by Social Security

Remembering that benefits would automatically decrease if the trust fund is exhausted, we could reduce benefits today, making future reductions less dramatic. One proposal you may have heard about is to decrease the annual benefit adjustment due to inflation by using something called the **chained Consumer Price Index** (chained CPI).[13] This would close around 18% of the Gap. A more straightforward plan, lowering benefits by 3% for those newly eligible in 2017 and later, would reduce the Gap by 14%.

3. Increase the retirement age

The retirement age is already steadily increasing toward 67 in 2027, due to the changes made in the late 1970s and early 1980s. If the retirement age continued to slowly increase to 68, this would close about 15% of the Gap.

4. "Privatize" Social Security

In 2005, as you may remember, there was discussion of allowing private investment accounts in Social Security. These talks died very quickly when it became clear that it was not a good idea.[14] The exact effect of privatization of Social Security's finances depends on the

---

13. For something that only a small number of economists and actuaries understand, chained CPI gets a lot of attention. Chained CPI is lower than the inflation measure currently used to calculate benefit increases, saving money for the trust fund.

exact proposal. My view is that, generally, adding private accounts is unlikely to improve the solvency of the system. Money would be diverted from current uses to fund personal accounts. You would personally get a better or worse return depending on the market, but the trust fund's future would be largely unaffected.

5. *Combination of the above*

The changes described earlier, if all of them were fully implemented, would get us where we need to go and well beyond. We could enact a portion of each, still leaving the system solvent with room to spare. None of these changes are ones that we *want* to make. But an array of modest tax increases and benefit cuts would eliminate problems in Social Security for decades, maybe forever. It seems there is a political deal to be had, if only our representatives are brave enough to make one.

Trillions of dollars, affecting every portion of our economy, and a critical filing cabinet.

What is the future for Social Security, politically? The uncertainty here is overwhelming, and it is easy to find an elected official who shares any opinion you happen to have. From my perspective, no politician or political party wants to be *seen* cutting Social Security. They want the other guy to take the blame. The strategy of increasing Social Security taxes or cutting benefits, but pinning the changes on the other party, has obvious limitations.

Practically, while Democrats would consider trading small benefit cuts for an increased cap on subject wages, it is safe to assume that the GOP will block any tax increases on top earners. The GOP attempted a privatization scheme during George W. Bush's presidency and may again. I expect it to fail for a second time, as the underlying politics haven't changed.[15] We are likely to continue along in the

---

14. Just because the entire public hated it doesn't necessarily mean it was a bad idea. But privatization doesn't solve problems, while leaving beneficiaries exposed to the market.

short term, with no changes to the program. At least until the next election.

This isn't a bad thing. Those who push the slogan of a Social Security crisis are apt to forget that it is a real program, on which millions of real people depend. Because of this, it is better to do nothing than to do the wrong thing. The policies we set today will affect our ability to keep our citizens out of poverty for the next 50 years or more. Via Social Security, we've managed to nearly eradicate abject poverty among our seniors, a condition that used to be endemic. You know people—parents, grandparents, aunts, uncles or friends—who would be unable to afford basic necessities without their Social Security checks. And as we've seen, the barbarians are not nearly at the gate. Let's have a bit of humility and plan with circumspection. And when the OASDI Trustees put out their next report, you should at least read the summary.

---

15. And, again, because the idea makes little sense. We already have many tax-advantaged savings vehicles that let you bet on the market. For most people, Social Security is the only savings vehicle available that provides a guaranteed benefit.

HEALTH INSURANCE, PART I
1945–2008
A HORSE DESIGNED BY A COMMITTEE

"You can check out any time you want. But you can never leave."
—Eagles

Nobody would have set out to design the health insurance system we have. It has no underlying foundation. Incentives are misplaced, negative externalities abound, and inefficiencies are layered on inefficiencies. The toxicity of health care politics makes any changes difficult, as they will always produce winners and losers. And people who are currently satisfied with their care reasonably fear change.

Many of America's health care problems derive from how we pay for our care. Benefits are haphazard. People are favored or penalized by the system for no apparent reason.

Countries should make informed, rational, and consistent decisions as to how much care they want to provide their citizens; after all, nothing is free. Most developed countries have done this, intentionally allocating health care amongst their populations. The United States did things differently.

- Why did employers start providing health insurance?
- Who is getting their health insurance from the government?
- What did the health insurance ecosystem look like just before the Affordable Care Act?

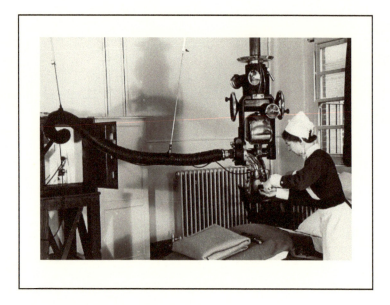

WHY DID EMPLOYERS START PROVIDING HEALTH INSURANCE?

Before World War II, health economics were simple: almost all Americans paid directly for their medical care. It was a time before MRIs, billion-dollar wonder drugs, and soaring levels of joint replacement.[1] We all know how far medicine has advanced in the span of a lifetime, but let's take a minute to imagine a world without:

- Antibiotics (discovered in 1928, not in widespread use until after World War II)
- Chemotherapy (1940s)
- Tylenol (1948)
- Pacemakers (1958)
- Ultrasounds (1953-1965)
- Vaccines for typhus (1937), flu (1945), polio (1955), and measles (1964)

---

1. There are 2.5 million Americans who have an artificial hip and an additional 4.7 million with an artificial knee. For Americans over 80 years old, 6% and 10% of the population, respectively, have had these joints replaced.

I could go on, but the point is that with fewer health services available, the issue of how to pay for them wasn't so critical. It wasn't until the 1930s that Blue Cross launched the first product resembling modern health insurance. But while entities like Blue Cross started us on the road to a system based on health insurance, the market really took off because of World War II.

Throughout history, virtually every war has been accompanied by inflation. In the midst of the largest war effort ever, President Franklin Roosevelt was reasonably worried about the economic consequences in store for the United States. To preserve economic stability and preempt inflation, the National War Labor Board was created. The board was granted powers to prevent work stoppages and control wages in critical war industries.[2] However, its creation included a loophole that is still having unintended consequences: health insurance was exempted from these wage controls. Because companies could no longer compete for workers on salaries, they started competing on benefits. **Employer-sponsored insurance** was also tax efficient. Because health insurance premiums are deductible from an employer's taxes, and not considered income for the employee, it is better for an employer to insure its employees directly than to give them the money necessary to insure themselves. In 1960, the Federal Employees Health Benefit Program was created. Soon, most government employees at the local, state, and federal levels were receiving health benefits from their employer, just as in the private sector.

Fast forward a bit, and health insurance became a de rigueur feature of a "good job." Proud mothers of recent college graduates began bragging that their kid "has a job and it even has health insurance."[3] In 2008, 58.5% of Americans were receiving health insurance from their employers. But while employer-sponsored insurance had become the norm, problems with such a system were becoming evident. First, because the employer chooses the health plan, an employee's doctor might not accept it. Second, changing jobs usually requires changing health insurance plans (and therefore, often, doc-

---

2. The NWLB was created by an executive order without any legislation behind it. Imagine a President today, even in war time, unilaterally creating a board with the power to freeze wages and prevent strikes at private companies.

3. Source: my mother, circa 2001.

tors as well). Third, the self-employed and owners of small businesses are unable to establish plans; this discourages entrepreneurship. Also, as the cost of health care increased, some companies stop offering health benefit plans, while others force employees to pay an increasing share of the costs. And, obviously, an employer-based system does very little for people who are out of the work force, no matter the reason.

If people can reasonably go and buy health insurance on their own (in what is called the **non-group market**), these problems are mitigated. But, as we will see, the individual market started to become highly dysfunctional toward the end of the 20th century.

WHO IS GETTING THEIR HEALTH INSURANCE THROUGH THE GOVERNMENT?

By the 1960s, employer-based plans dominated the health insurance market. However, large groups of people remained uninsured, and Presidents Kennedy and Johnson wanted to take action on behalf of some of these groups. Since 1945, when President Truman stated it was a moral obligation, a governmental role in providing universal coverage has been part of the Democratic Party's platform. Alternatively, the Republican Party has consistently supported a market-based approach, opposing government involvement, especially at the federal level.[4]

In 1960, retirees comprised a large segment of the population who lacked health insurance. Some elderly citizens maintained coverage through retirement plans provided by their previous employers, but about half of Americans over 65 were uninsured. With large

---

4. Recently, the GOP has departed from its position of "no federal involvement" to suggest that the federal government should override the states by forcing them to allow sales of unapproved insurance plans. This means that, rather than your state deciding its own insurance needs, they favor putting other states in charge of what is available.

Democratic majorities following the landslide 1964 election,[5] Medicare was created to provide coverage for this population.

The basic financial structure of Medicare is similar to Social Security. It is funded by a payroll tax and paid through mandatory spending, with the surplus going into a trust fund. Originally, Medicare had two major programs: hospital/hospice insurance (Part A) and outpatient insurance (Part B). In 1997, Medicare was modified to allow seniors to receive coverage through private plans (Part C), better known as Medicare Advantage. Finally, in 2006, a prescription drug program was added (Part D). Over time, it was also expanded to include some disabled persons under the age of 65. Today, approximately 46 million seniors and 9 million non-seniors receive health insurance through Medicare. Virtually no seniors remain uninsured, meaning that Medicare has been highly successful in achieving its primary goal.

The next large group without access to health insurance was, speaking broadly, the working poor. Medicaid, a joint federal and state insurance program for people with limited income and resources, was created as part of the Social Security Amendments of 1965. Figure 1 shows a breakdown of the population enrolled in Medicaid as of 2010.

---

5. The GOP had only 32 senators and 140 representatives in 1965. This Congress passed more consequential legislation than any other in the Post-War Era. Whether or not you like the Great Society programs, it is impossible to overstate the extent to which they changed the nature of our relationship with our government.

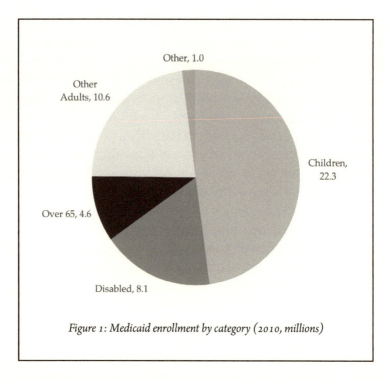

Figure 1: Medicaid enrollment by category (2010, millions)

It's a common misconception that Medicaid is a welfare program, with benefits going to people who are not working. As you can see in Figure 1, most Medicaid beneficiaries are outside the work force: young, retired, or disabled. Among able-bodied adults on Medicaid, 72% are in households with at least one income.[6] They are just in jobs that don't provide health benefits. From 2000 to 2005, the number of adults receiving Medicaid increased from 6.9 million to 10.6 million. This was not due to reduced employment among beneficiaries, but rather fewer employers offering health coverage.[7]

Medicaid operates in a fundamentally different manner than Medicare. Medicaid is a partnership between the federal govern-

---

6. Creating work requirements in order to receive Medicaid is often proposed, but it addresses a problem that basically doesn't exist. The most common reason for otherwise-able Medicaid recipients to be out of the workforce is to care for a dependent. Studies show that work requirements mostly function to increase red tape, and decrease enrollment only among the elderly and disabled, who have trouble completing the paperwork.

7. Adults on Medicaid increased further (to 12.1 million) by 2010. Much of this increase was due to a rise in unemployment during the financial crisis.

ment and each state, meaning that coverage and eligibility vary greatly depending on where you live.[8] In return for meeting certain requirements, the federal government is committed to picking up 50% of the total costs (in wealthier states) or more (76% in Mississippi). States have significant discretion in how their Medicaid plans work and who is eligible. The requirements to gain federal cost sharing allow significant leeway. But states meeting just the strict minimum requirements will leave large populations of the working poor without any options for health insurance. Many states, therefore, offer Medicaid benefits to larger populations than necessary.

By the 1990s, one large, remaining gap in coverage was among minors. While history has labeled Hillary Clinton's 1993 health insurance initiative a failure, it ignores a very significant accomplishment: the creation of the Children's Health Insurance Program, or CHIP. CHIP is a federal-state partnership, like Medicaid. In some states the two are managed as a single program. By 2009, 7.7 million children under 18 were covered by CHIP.

In addition to these programs, government also provides health care directly in its role as an employer, as we discussed. In the sense that it is linked to employment, beneficiaries have more in common with those in employer plans than those on Medicare or Medicaid. But around 35 million people have health care through their government employer—two-thirds as federal, state, or local employees, and the remainder through the military (TriCare or the Veterans Administration).[9] In Figure 2, we can see a complete overview of our health insurance system as of 2008.

---

8. For example, Arizona didn't create a Medicaid program at all until 1982, a full decade after every other state. Up to that point, Arizona taxpayers were paying for every other state's Medicaid program and receiving nothing back.

9. While researching government employment statistics, I was amazed to learn that federal civilian employment was the same in 2014 as in 1966—despite the population growing by 120,000,000.

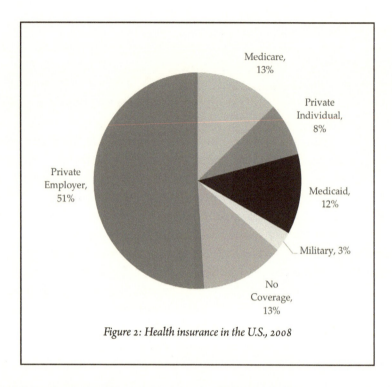

Figure 2: Health insurance in the U.S., 2008

WHAT DID THE HEALTH INSURANCE ECOSYSTEM LOOK LIKE JUST BEFORE THE AFFORDABLE CARE ACT?

We've now covered in fair detail how the U.S. public and private health insurance systems came to exist. But starting around 1995, strains in this patchwork system were felt by more and more Americans.

The driver of these problems was the increasing costs of health care. Since at least 1960—well before the government-based expansions of coverage described above—health spending in the United States has been increasing significantly faster than inflation. Table 1 shows the difference between general inflation and health inflation, as calculated by the U.S. National Health Expenditures (NHE) survey.

Period	Description	NHE Growth
1961-65	Pre-Medicare / Medicaid	7.5%
1966-73	Coverage Expansion	7.2%
1973-82	Rapid Price Growth	5.8%
1983-92	Payment Change; Continued Rapid Growth	6.5%
1993-99	Cost Containment (i.e. HMOs)	4.1%
2000-02	Backlash to Cost Containment	6.2%
2003-07	Slowdown in Spending	4.2%

Table 1: Growth in U.S. health expenditures, above inflation

At the same time, because of increased costs, fewer employers were offering employer-sponsored insurance, as we see in Figure 3. Even for those still receiving health insurance through their employer, out-of-pocket costs were increasing as corporations fought to control costs.

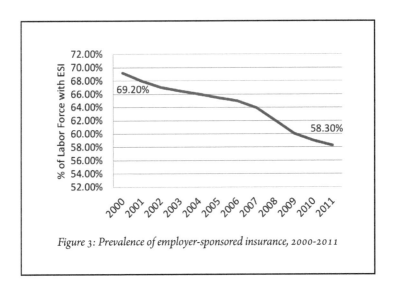

Figure 3: Prevalence of employer-sponsored insurance, 2000-2011

With these changes in the employer-sponsored market, more people were forced to either buy their own insurance or go without. But why did so many people "choose" to go without health insurance?

One reason is that health insurance markets in many states experienced what is called a **death spiral**. We'll describe a death spiral in our first example of the challenges inherent in a private health insurance system.

Let's say that you lose your employer-sponsored coverage. Maybe your employer stops offering it, maybe you are laid off, maybe you leave to start your own company—the reason why doesn't matter. You research alternative health insurance choices, price-check several insurers, and choose a plan that is the best for you, your wife, two children, and dog. Your insurance company places you in a pool of insured individuals who will all be charged similar rates. The pool is closed to new enrollment, but anybody can leave at any time by not paying their premium.

Over time, people in your pool begin to develop ongoing and expensive health conditions. High blood pressure, lupus, diabetes, heart disease—over time, people get sick. The cost to insure the pool starts to increase, so premiums increase for everybody. Suppose your family is lucky, with no major health issues. As premiums increase, you will cancel your current insurance, and join a new, healthier pool—with lower premiums. For those lucky enough to avoid health problems, everything works fairly well as the process begins again.

But for those left in the pool, the withdrawal of healthy families means that the average health of those remaining rapidly worsens. The increase in premiums therefore begins to accelerate. Beneficiaries generally can't be kicked out of their coverage due to health conditions, but no new pool will take them. Given a choice, no for-profit business would willingly offer coverage to people with expensive health problems. Or, they may accept them, but exclude coverage for their **pre-existing conditions**.[10] Therefore, those left in the rapidly sickening insurance pool are faced with an unenviable choice: they can remain, paying premiums that are getting harder to afford. Or they can go without insurance. These are, by definition, people with major medical problems.

---

10. For example, in Tennessee, Blue Cross/Blue Shield regularly turned down one-third of applicants.

To further complicate matters, state governments get involved.[11] Constituents complained about getting rejected for coverage, so some states made it illegal to deny coverage due to pre-existing conditions. This regulation is called **guaranteed issue**.[12] Because insurance premiums are based on the average cost of the people buying said insurance, healthier people went without insurance, which was overpriced from their perspective. This well-intended regulation again caused insurance pools to become sicker, which caused rates to increase, driving out the healthiest remaining members, causing the pool to become sicker and rates to increase...well you get the idea. This is a death spiral, and it is not theoretical. After passing health insurance regulations including guaranteed issue, New York's private health insurance system underwent a terrible death spiral. The number of residents in the market tumbled from 1.2 million to 31,000.[13]

This was the state of the American health care system on the eve of Obamacare. Total health care spending was still increasing faster than inflation. More people were being pushed into the non-group insurance market. This segment of the market was becoming more strained as health insurance companies were forced to screen applicants for pre-existing conditions.[14] The rate of uninsured was increasing every quarter and the factors driving this increase were accelerating. People without insurance were foregoing preventative treatment, which worsened their health outcomes, and often increased overall spending.[15] The financial strain began to show. In a two-tiered pricing system, individuals had no access to the reduced prices negotiated by large insurance networks. Health bills became by far the largest source of personal bankruptcies. The problems in

---

11. Before the Affordable Care Act, almost all health insurance regulation was at the state level.
12. They also prohibited charging more for pre-existing conditions, a policy that is called **community rating**.
13. Some states passed better designed regulation than New York, but they faced the same structural problem.
14. Yes, forced. Had an insurance company chosen not to do so, it would have faced an adverse selection bias as it became swamped by applicants with high expected cost of care.
15. Generally, the earlier something is treated, the less expensive it is to treat.

the system were everywhere, and nobody was making a serious attempt to solve them.

Then, in 2008, Barack Obama was elected President, with a clear mandate to do something about the health care system.

—§—

The health insurance market cannot operate solely on the principles of supply and demand. While more government regulation can be counterproductive, an insurance system without regulation results in inability for many to buy coverage. Increases in competition, price transparency, tax breaks—none of these addresses the core problem. An unregulated system might work well for the rich or the lucky, but not for everybody. It will also tend to be highly inefficient, like the American system today.

Figure 4 is a comparison of health spending and life expectancy, by country, for the developed world. Each point on the graph represents a different country. For every nation but one, there is a strong relationship between health spending and health outcomes. Those that spend more get better results, just as you would expect. In every nation the government has stringent regulation on health insurance and prices.

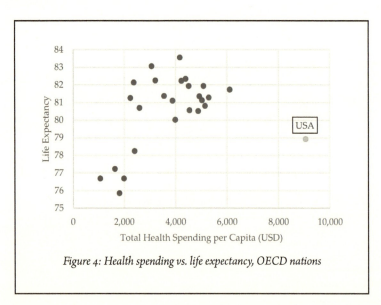

Figure 4: Health spending vs. life expectancy, OECD nations

Despite spending far more on health than any other nation, the United States does not have the best health system in the world. Instead, all that money seems to be for naught, as our outcomes are below the group average.[16] Addressing this imbalance, high costs with low performance, was the primary goal of health reform. The consequences of the new legislation would result in major changes to the health insurance system. And to the political system.

---

16. Other health metrics, such as infant mortality or adult mortality, show similar results.

A TALE OF TWO
ALABAMA GOVERNORS
A CONTINUATION OF POLITICS BY OTHER
MEANS

"Injustice anywhere is a threat to justice everywhere."
—*Martin Luther King, Jr.*

In our nation, the legal system is supposed to promote justice. Courts, civil and criminal, exist to ensure that people receive the reward or punishment that they deserve.

Unfortunately, our system is also capable of horrifying perversion. Among other uses, this perversion can be directed towards the gathering of political power. Immense discretion exists in the hands of investigators, prosecutors, and judges. At its best, this discretion tempers our justice with mercy or stiffens it with resolve. At its worst, it allows for individuals to selectively punish those who challenge their political power.

In recent years, two Alabama governors have stared into the teeth of our legal system. The disparate outcomes of their prosecutions, relative to their alleged crimes, serve as a warning of how easily our judicial system can be manipulated. This manipulation not only destroys the lives of those directly involved, but it can also create a chilling effect on those who would participate in our public debate.

Image 3: Don Siegelman and family

Don Siegelman was the last of his breed: a true progressive Democrat winning statewide office in the Deep South. He wasn't bashful about his politics. He forcefully promoted public education, voting rights, and what we now call criminal justice reform. He was also business friendly, instrumental in bringing Hyundai, Mercedes-Benz, and Honda to Alabama. He spent funds on the infrastructure of his state, rebuilding over 1,000 of Alabama's schools among many other large projects. Fighting corporate abuse was a passion for Siegelman, and he declared war on Big Tobacco.

Siegelman was a fixture in Alabama politics for more than two decades. He first took statewide office at the age of 33, winning the first of two terms as Secretary of State in 1979. He earned three promotions: to Attorney General in 1987, Lieutenant Governor in 1995, and, finally, was elected Alabama's 51st Governor in 1999. He is the only person to have served in Alabama's top four statewide offices.

His personal story is also unique. He paid his way through Georgetown Law School by working for the U.S. Capital Police. He is a Catholic—the only Catholic governor in the history of Alabama. Despite this, his children were raised with Jewish traditions, based on his wife's heritage. Whatever the formula, something about Siegelman was attractive to Alabama voters. He was a force on the campaign trail, winning 57% of the vote in his gubernatorial race.

In his campaign for Governor, Siegelman strongly supported starting a state lottery to help close Alabama's budget deficit. Recognizing that his position was controversial, he pledged to put the issue to the voters via a referendum. After his election, this is precisely what he did; this is where his problems started.

Like many referendums, Siegelman's attempt to start a lottery faced significant opposition. Foremost among his critics were Native American gambling interests in next-door Mississippi. The tribes were represented by the notorious lobbying firm of Jack Abramoff.[1] Abramoff worked with mainstream Republican figures like Ralph Reed, Grover Norquist, and Michael Scanlon. Leveraging on their aura of respectability, he traded campaign contributions for promises to shield his tribal clients' casinos from competition.

HealthSouth, one of the nation's largest providers of post-acute health care services, was—and still is—one of the largest corporations based in Alabama. As you might expect, HealthSouth's CEO at the time, Richard Scrushy, was a major figure in Alabama politics. He had been nominated by each of the three governors who served before Siegelman (all Republicans) to sit on the state hospital regulatory board. This board was an unpaid advisory position, of which our cities and states have a plethora. Any benefit Scrushy received

---

1. Abramoff, you may recall, later went to prison for conspiracy to bribe public officials.

for his service was entirely intangible, he wasn't paid a dime. Like it or not, it is standard practice for CEOs of major corporations to receive such recognition in their home states.

Scrushy was a lottery supporter, and a Siegelman supporter. He made a legal donation of $500,000 *to the campaign* supporting Siegelman's lottery referendum. Siegelman, again, has never been accused of personally receiving a penny. Scrushy's donation was used, with other campaign funds, in a completely legal manner to support one of his publicly stated policy goals. At around the same time, Scrushy's term on the hospital board came to an end, and Siegelman reappointed him to a fourth term. Scrushy didn't even especially want the board seat any more, having served on it for more than a decade already.[2]

In 2002, Siegelman was up for re-election. Given his personal charisma and electoral success, this was a guy who could easily head to higher office. He received occasional billing as "the next Bill Clinton." As a potential national candidate who could marry progressive policies with Southern appeal, Siegelman was a threat to national GOP leaders. Abramoff and his crew were mobilized to defeat him. In his tell-all memoir,[3] Abramoff admitted to funneling $20 million into the campaign to defeat Siegelman. Much of this money was at the very edge of campaign finance laws, and some was certainly illegal. The beneficiary of Abramoff's largesse was Bob Riley, Siegelman's Republican opponent.

The election was close. On election night, it appeared that Siegelman had won a tight victory; he gave a victory speech and went to bed. However, in a single county, the Republican election observers stuck around after the departure of their Democratic counterparts. They removed 6,000 votes from Siegelman's total. Alabama Attorney General William Pryor, a Republican, rejected requests to conduct an impartial recount of these votes and Bob Riley became the 52nd Governor of Alabama.

---

2. Scrushy had his own, unrelated issues. While he was CEO of HealthSouth, the company had major governance faults. While I would never hire him to be my company's CEO, these problems were not Scrushy's direct fault. In any case, with respect to our story, HealthSouth's problems were not known at the time.

3. Which he published after he got out of prison.

Bill Pryor wasn't done. He launched an investigation into the Scrushy "bribe" of Siegelman. The claim was that the $500,000 donation was made against the quid pro quo of Scrushy's re-appointment to the hospital board. Never mind that Siegelman didn't receive any personal gain from the alleged transaction. Nor that Scrushy didn't really want to be on the board. Even if the facts had been different, the statute of limitations had passed to prosecute Siegelman for bribery. Pryor had to find a jurisdiction that was willing to ignore these few minor details.

He was in luck. The newly appointed U.S. Attorney for the Middle District of Alabama, Leura Canary, was married to Bill Canary. You've never heard of him, but Bill Canary was a Republican operative, critical to Abramoff's money funneling operations that defeated Siegelman in the first place. It does not seem coincidental that his wife was willing to prosecute such a dubious crime. The Judge drawn for the trial was Mark Fuller, a George W. Bush appointee whose only qualification for the lifetime job on the bench was six years spent running the Executive Committee of the Alabama Republican Party. I don't think I need to explain how the trial went.

Siegelman's team of tormenters has done well for themselves. Due largely to his role in the prosecution, Bill Pryor impressed Karl Rove and President Bush. He was promoted to his own federal judgeship and is on the shortlist for future Republican Supreme Court nominations. Bill Canary still makes a good living infecting elections with dark money, although his wife is less visible today. After his term as governor, Bob Riley is living a very comfortable life; he occasionally draws coverage as a dark-horse presidential candidate.[4]

Siegelman spent more than five years in prison before being released in February 2017.

Robert Bentley succeeded Riley as the 53rd Governor of Alabama, taking office in 2011. A member of the Alabama House of Representatives and a physician, he was, like Siegelman, a formidable campaigner. His margin in the 2010 election was the largest ever for an Alabama GOP gubernatorial candidate. He broke his own record four years later.

---

4. The Honorable Judge Fuller has had more problems. He resigned his seat in 2015 due to substantial evidence that he had repeatedly committed spousal abuse.

But things began to turn sour for Governor Bentley in March 2016. A fired former staffer accused him of having an affair with his senior political advisor, Rebekah Mason. This was hardly the first time a politician had been caught in flagrante delicto, but to use the old cliché, the cover-up was worse than the crime.

Turns out, good old Bob Bentley had repeatedly used the good old power of his office, given to him by the good old citizens of his good old state to conceal his affair from the public. He conducted the affair with public travel funds. He threatened the staff members who helped his wife (now ex-wife) uncover the affair. He used law enforcement officials and his state-funded security staff to cover his tracks. He also co-mingled campaign funds with his personal funds while all of this was going on. All of this is illegal. Unlike certain other Alabama governors, it involved state tax money in addition to private campaign funds. And Bentley received a direct, personal benefit.

Image 4: Governor Bentley and Rebekah Mason

Even though his party controlled the state government, these indiscretions were too much to ignore. But the investigation went a bit differently than the Pryor-Siegelman affair. Alabama's Attorney General was now "Big" Luther Strange. Strange's investigation moved along quite slowly, despite virtually all of the evidence being in the public record. Even before the 2016 election, it was obvious that Bentley had badly misused the power of his office. Alabama's State Auditor had filed an ethics complaint, and there were bipartisan calls from the state legislature for him to resign. But Strange urged caution. He requested that the legislature hold off on impeachment proceedings while he continued his investigation.

Eventually, Bentley was allowed by Strange to plead guilty to two misdemeanors, admitting only to the campaign finance abuses. He will never answer for his misuse of public funds. He received a suspended sentence and faces only probation and 100 hours of community service. He must repay $9,000 to his campaign and turn over his remaining campaign funds to the state.

But Strange's delay in reaching the settlement had far-reaching consequences. Just as the pressure for Bentley to resign was accelerating, an Alabama Senate seat became available with the appointment of Jefferson Beauregard Sessions III to the office of Attorney General. In one of his final acts as governor, Bentley appointed Luther Strange to the United States Senate. Bentley also used his power as governor to set Strange's first election as far in the future as legally possible, to maximize the value of his incumbency.[5]

Luther Strange received a forceful endorsement from Donald Trump as he sought election to the remaining portion of a six-year Senate term.[6] Bentley is $9,000 poorer and spent a couple weeks as a pro bono dermatologist.

Our judicial system is a fragile thing; in the wrong hands it can easily be subverted for political purposes, destroying lives in the process. What scares me the most is the chilling effect of Siegelman's prosecution on those who would run for office in Alabama going forward. Would you want to run against this cabal, knowing the penalties you could face?

---

5. Bentley's successor, Governor Kay Ivey, changed the date of the special election after taking office.

6. He went on to lose the Republican primary to Roy Moore, who faced numerous credible allegations of sexual assault against minors. This did not dissuade President Trump from strongly endorsing Moore, but it was too much for the good people of Alabama, who chose Doug Jones as their next Senator instead.

HEALTH INSURANCE, PART II
HOW MANY LEGS DOES A GOOD STOOL NEED?

*"Five days from now… millions of Americans who don't have
health insurance because they've been priced out of the market or
been denied because of a pre-existing condition, they will finally be
able to buy quality, affordable health insurance."*
—Barack Obama

It is impossible to write about the Patient Protection and Affordable Care Act (ACA) without touching on politics. Democrats
have favored governmental enforcement of a right to health care for
at least 50 years. Republicans have opposed governmental action at
the federal level, believing solutions are best found by the market.
Health insurance reform, by definition, will have winners and losers.
Any discussion of the federal government actively increasing access
to care will be a political issue.

To avoid the politics as much as possible, we will rely on our usual
method. Look at the data, use it to build a theory, and test the theory. We have convincing evidence that, given a basic set of goals, any
working health insurance system must have certain specific regulations. My goal is to demonstrate this empirically and theoretically.
We'll then look at the details of how the ACA implements these regulations, as well as its other features.

- What is the three-legged stool of a stable health insurance
  market?
- How does the Affordable Care Act create a stable market?
- What else is in the Affordable Care Act?

```
SUMMARY OF CHARGES
R&C SEMI-PR  1DAYS@  2124.00    2124.00  2124.00
R&C PRIVATE 28DAYS@  2141.00   59948.00 59948.00
    PHARMACY                  135870.52
                                        135870.52
    SUPPLY/DEVICES              1618.00  1618.00
    LAB                       24889.17 24889.17
    LAB/PATH                   1799.00  1799.00
    RADIOLOGY/DX                630.00   630.00
    CT SCAN                    6471.00  6471.00
    OPERATING ROOM             1488.00  1488.00
    BLOOD PROCESS FEE          1823.69  1823.69
    IMAGING SERV                631.00   631.00
    CARDIOLOGY                 1869.00  1869.00
    MRI                        6314.00  6314.00
    MED/SURG SUPPLY             250.00   250.00
    OTHER                      3465.00  3465.00


SUB-TOTAL OF CHARGES          249190.38
                                       249190.38
```

WHAT IS THE THREE-LEGGED STOOL OF A STABLE HEALTH INSURANCE MARKET?

Let's start with a simple premise: in the United States, in 2018, everybody has a right to some level of health care.[1] There are several reasons why this is a sound policy. There is an economic argument: better health care leads to a healthier work force, which leads to economic growth. There is a selfish argument: if people don't have access to medical care, communicable diseases will spread, and that is bad for me. There is a moral and practical argument: we have the resources to provide this care and therefore we can and should.[2] We can endlessly debate the level of health care to which we should all be entitled. But my basic principle is that no American should die of an easily treatable condition because of inability to pay. Nor should they go bankrupt. Unless you disagree with these statements, then

---

1. Everybody. This includes visiting foreigners, undocumented immigrants, and other non-permanent residents.
2. All other advanced countries provide this guarantee while spending significantly less than we do on health care.

the imperative is to determine how to provide this care and how to pay for it fairly and efficiently.

The easiest solution is to have the government handle most of the problem. There are two basic ways a government-based health insurance system can work: **single payer** or **single provider**. In a single payer system, the government pays for health insurance for its citizens, but care is provided by private entities. An example of this is Medicare. Canada's health system is single payer.[3] In a single provider system, doctors and hospitals are employed by a government organization. This is what the U.K.'s National Health Service is. Both types of systems have proven successful around the world but transitioning the U.S. system to either model would be difficult, disruptive, and expensive. Our short-term focus should be to make the existing hybrid public-private system better.

As we've already discussed, an unregulated (or poorly regulated) private health insurance system will devolve into a death spiral. However, some countries, such as Germany and Singapore, have had success with systems of well-regulated private insurers; we know it is possible. Using both theory and experience, we know that a stable, market-based health insurance system must have three basic features. Just like any other stool, without three sturdy legs your system will collapse.

The core problem in designing health insurance markets is what to do with people who are currently ill or who have serious ongoing health conditions. In other words, people with pre-existing conditions. Health care usage is highly skewed, with almost half of U.S. health care spending going to just 5% of the population. Care for this group therefore costs ten times as much as the population average. Given a choice, no insurance company would insure these people at any reasonable price; they would lose money. Therefore, if they are permitted to do so, for-profit insurance companies will create screening processes and deny coverage to those most likely to get sick. But what happens to the people who are denied coverage?[4]

---

3. Their system is also called "Medicare." They spend about half of what we do on health care, with better results.
4. Or accepted, but not for treatment of their pre-existing condition (e.g. an asthmatic would be covered for everything except asthma). These were called "exclusions," and insurance companies' use of them doesn't help the system.

First, because they can't afford it, they avoid getting care for all of their medical issues. Generally, early treatment of health problems results in both better outcomes and lower costs. When people don't take advantage of preventative treatment, we all pay for it and people die.

Second, when a medical issue does become urgent, they seek emergency care. When you look at a medical bill, the top of the invoice states an exorbitantly high price for your service. Farther down is the discount that the insurance company negotiated with the provider, and the net price is more reasonable. But the uninsured do not get this discount. Generally, those without health insurance are not wealthy, and are especially unable to afford the non-discounted price. So, when faced with major medical bills, they tend to declare bankruptcy. When patients can't pay their bills, the provider gets no revenue. However, at this point doctors and hospitals have already experienced their own costs for the care provided.[5] To make up for these losses, they raise their prices for everybody.[6] Bringing the uninsured into the system would counteract this effect and save us all money.

This brings us to the first leg of the stool: guaranteed issue and community rating. Guaranteed issue means that applicants cannot be denied health insurance based on medical condition and history.[7] Community rating means premiums depend on the expected cost for the population, not the individual. When a policy maker says they want to have protections for pre-existing conditions, these two regulations are what they mean. But if a system has guaranteed issue and community rating, it will experience a death spiral, in absence of other regulations. Healthy people will wait until they are sick to buy insurance, since it can no longer be denied. The group of people buying health insurance will become more expensive to insure and premiums will increase. As premiums move higher, even more

---

5. Yes, hospitals are usually willing to negotiate their fee, but then they are paid back only a portion of their costs. This doesn't solve the problem.

6. There are some programs where hospitals that experience high levels of uncompensated care can be reimbursed by the government. This is still a cost to the system.

7. Fifty-two million adults under the age of 65 have pre-existing conditions; these people would be severely challenged in obtaining comprehensive insurance in an unregulated market. It represents 27% of the population.

healthy people will go without insurance, and the cycle repeats. We need to find a way to keep the healthy people in the system.

The solution to this is the **individual mandate**, the second leg of the health care stool. An individual mandate requires people to carry health insurance.[8] Out of all the provisions of a successful public-private health insurance system, the individual mandate is the most controversial and unpopular. Why should there be a penalty for not buying health insurance if you don't want it?

An insurance mandate shouldn't be a new concept to anyone. If you own a car, you are required to carry car insurance.[9] The idea is simple. Anybody can get into an accident, even the best drivers. Accidents cause damage to cars, people, and property. Damage costs money to repair. Drivers of cars in accidents are liable for the cost of repairing this damage. Some accidents cause damage with catastrophic repair costs; people can't afford these costs and would go bankrupt if forced to pay them. Therefore, drivers are required to carry car insurance, which solves this problem.

We can spell out the analogue for health insurance mandates, in case it isn't clear. Anybody can get sick, even the healthiest people. Sickness causes damage to your body. The damage costs money to repair. People are liable for the cost of repairing this damage. Some sicknesses cause damage with catastrophic repair costs; people can't afford these costs and would go bankrupt if forced to pay them. So, people are required to carry health insurance, which solves this problem.[10]

This brings us to our third leg. To be able to insure people while preventing anybody from gaming the system, insurance companies are required to accept all applicants, and everybody is required to have health insurance. However, we still need to make sure this insurance is affordable for households of all income levels. The solution is **subsidies**: the government pays some or all of the cost of health insurance. These subsidies are usually designed to decrease

---

8. Or, similarly, attach a penalty for not having insurance.

9. Unless you live in New Hampshire.

10. Yes, there are some differences between auto and health insurance mandates. In theory, medical problems only harm you, while a car accident damages other people's property. But as we've said, the uninsured person who suddenly decides they do want care affects all of us.

for households with greater incomes, but you can envision a system where they are the same for everybody.

This is the three-legged stool of a stable public-private health insurance system: guaranteed issue and community rating, individual mandate, and subsidies. The system will not work if any of the legs are removed:

- A system with community rating but no mandate will enter a death spiral as people wait to buy insurance. Subsidies will slow down the spiral, but not prevent it.
- Community rating and an individual mandate without subsidies will require people who can't afford insurance to buy it. The math doesn't work.
- Mandates and subsidies without guaranteed issue means that people with pre-existing conditions are forced to buy health insurance, but nobody will sell to them. This is nonsensical.[11]

---

11. In theory, if the subsidies are equal to the entire cost of the insurance, you don't need a mandate or community rating, as everybody would be able to get health insurance at no incremental cost. It would be a de facto single payer system.

An Aside: The Fundamental Theorem of Health Insurance

Many disciplines have fundamental theorems. They take a complex topic and distill it to the essence, from which much more can be derived.

Fundamental theorems are often stated for branches of mathematics. For example, in arithmetic, every integer greater than 1 can be uniquely expressed as a product of prime numbers. A simple statement from which much of arithmetic necessarily follows. Fundamental theorems aren't intended to tell you everything. However, if you take each to its logical conclusions, you'll be amazed by how much you know.

Like mathematics, health insurance markets are complex. Can we distill their essence to something that will easily fit on an index card?

> **If it's not required for everybody, it will not be available for anybody. If everybody has the choice, then nobody will have a choice.**

"Not required for everybody" means there is no individual mandate. As we've seen, a health insurance system without a mandate will move towards a death spiral. All insurance becomes expensive, effectively unavailable for anybody to buy.

"Everybody has a choice" means that a benefit is optional. An optional benefit will soon cost as much as its most expensive users—for example, optional maternity benefits will cost as much as a pregnancy. It will again be too expensive to be rational to buy. The so-called choice is available to nobody.

A fundamental theorem never tells you everything but this one tells a lot. Next time a health system is said

> to lack mandates, or to offer choices, you'll know that it doesn't work.

HOW DOES THE AFFORDABLE CARE ACT CREATE A STABLE MARKET?

At its core, the ACA is a straightforward implementation of the three-legged stool. But because the goal was to modify the existing system as little as possible, the actual way the stool was built has a few complexities.

Guaranteed issue and community rating

In the ACA's individual market, insurance companies are required by law to accept all new applicants and renewal requests during the annual enrollment period. It lists the factors that may be considered when determining premiums and limits the extra amount insurance companies can charge. So far, so good.

Individual Mandate

The ACA's individual mandate is structured as a tax, collected by the IRS,[12] against those who do not hold coverage.[13] However, given that the penalty ($695, with adjustments for inflation) is less than the cost of buying insurance, some healthy people will voluntarily remain uninsured and pay the penalty. This is a problem—it worsens the health status of the pool of people with health insurance, raising premium levels.

---

12. One of the strangest ACA myths is that it is run by the IRS. This is nonsense. The subsidies are based on income; the IRS knows your income and is in best position to compute subsidy amounts. The individual mandate penalty is a tax; the IRS checks to see if you owe the tax. That's it. I am amazed I have to say this, but the IRS does not receive your personal health information and has no role in health care decision making at any level.
13. The penalty is waived if a person cannot afford insurance after receiving subsidies. This is defined as not being able to find coverage for less than 8% of household income.

Subsidies

The subsidies in the ACA scale based on household income and size, residency, and cost of plans. Subsidies are available for families earning up to 400% of the Federal Poverty Level (FPL). This means that a family of four living in Brooklyn will receive a subsidy for a household income up to approximately $97,000.

These three provisions are the core of the ACA. It's not perfect—the mandate is somewhat weak, and the subsidies are a bit low—but at first glance it is a stable three-legged stool. It should help us achieve our main goal, providing access to health care, as well as a way to pay for it. While it relies on government regulations, the system is still largely based on private insurance.

WHAT ELSE IS IN THE AFFORDABLE CARE ACT?

As you may have heard, the ACA is a long law—1,900 pages.[14] It makes a lot of changes to our health system beyond the three-legged stool we've described. Some of its features go beyond health insurance and into health care.

Expansion of Medicaid

When determining the subsidies, households that fell below a certain income threshold (138% of the FPL) were going to be subsidized for the full cost of purchasing health insurance (or nearly so). Because Medicaid provides care more efficiently than the private insurance market,[15] it made fiscal sense to add these households to that existing, successful program.

Recall that Medicaid is a state-federal partnership, with Washington paying between 50 and 75% of the costs. The ACA said that if states increased Medicaid eligibility to 138% of FPL, the federal gov-

---

14. This is a lot of pages, but our government is not efficient in terms of printing bills. In word count, the ACA is similar to the longer Harry Potter books. This doesn't seem unreasonable to me, given that it restructured one-sixth of our economy.

15. In a study by the Kaiser Family Foundation, a 1996-1999 survey showed that moving adults from Medicaid to private insurance would increase the cost by 18%; a similar 2005 survey showed a 26% increase. And surveys show that people are at least as happy with Medicaid as with private insurance.

ernment would pay for 100% of the incremental cost initially, declining to 90% after 2020. Astoundingly, 19 states have turned down free money offered to expand their Medicaid programs. Their citizens are paying increased taxes under the ACA, but not getting the benefits. I have never heard a convincing argument for a state not to accept Medicaid expansion. But hey, it's their right.[16]

Tax Increases

Between paying for the subsidies and for Medicaid expansion, the government is going to have to come up with some revenue. When designing the ACA, President Obama and congressional leaders wanted the law to be deficit neutral. Being Democrats, they decided to create 21 new taxes. The only one that is likely to affect most Americans directly is a surtax of 0.9% of earned income and 3.8% of investment income on earnings above $200,000 (individuals) or $250,000 (families).[17] Netting costs and revenues, the CBO predicted in 2010 that the ACA would reduce federal budget deficits by $124 billion over the period 2010-2019. Today, they project that the ACA will reduce budget deficits by $353 billion from 2016-2025.[18]

Creation of Exchanges

To facilitate the purchasing of health insurance, the ACA created exchanges where individuals can shop for health plans. Each state can create its own exchange or rely on the national exchange. The purpose of the exchanges is to have a single location to compare available policies, see their costs, and estimate subsidies. After a disastrous rollout, healthcare.gov is operating well. Some of the state exchanges are excellent, while others are sub-par.

---

16. It is literally their right, per the Supreme Court in NFIB v. Sebelius.
17. The individual mandate, which could affect you, is another one of the taxes.
18. I am taking the cost of repeal to be equal to the benefit of being in place as a good first-order approximation. I use the version without macroeconomic benefits as this the standard for CBO analysis as stated in the link. These CBO numbers are approximations, as it is impossible to know what would have happened to the country in the absence of the ACA. But as they say, there is good reason to conclude that actual benefit has been slightly better than predicted. All the evidence implies that the ACA's effect on the overall fiscal situation is neutral to positive.

Employer Mandate

One concern about the ACA was that, with subsidized health insurance available on the individual market, fewer employers would offer health insurance to their employees. This would have been a continuation of an ongoing trend, but the passage of the ACA could be expected to accelerate it. To counteract any effect of the ACA on the employer-sponsored market, employers are required to pay penalties if they do not provide affordable health insurance to their full-time employees.

Young Adults on Parents' Insurance

In one of the law's most popular provisions, young adults gained the right to remain on their parents' health plan up to age 26.

Medicare and Other Cost Savings

During the debates about the ACA, there was a lot of talk about cost control. The ACA's cost control measures have an element of trial and error; there are a lot of experimental programs, some will succeed and some won't. The ACA did create explicit savings for Medicare. In exchange for a promise of increasing the number of people with health insurance, and thus decreasing uncompensated care, Medicare negotiated $716 billion in savings in the first decade of the ACA. These savings will not affect the services received by Medicare beneficiaries—it is the same level of care at a lower cost.

Other Insurance Regulations

On top of the three-legged stool provisions of guaranteed issue and community rating, individual mandate, and subsidies, the ACA imposes other minimum requirements on insurance policies:

- Anything sold as health insurance must cover various types of preventative care;
- Overhead and profits at insurance companies are limited to 20% of premiums;
- Annual and lifetime caps on benefits are prohibited; and

- Insurance companies can no longer cancel benefits via
  rescission.[19]

—§—

So that's what's in the Affordable Care Act, probably the most controversial piece of legislation of the last 40 years. Yet the ACA's structure is a definitional requirement of any stable health insurance system. Its core provisions should not be controversial. At one point, even Republicans agreed with the concept of an individual mandate. The Heritage Foundation, a conservative think tank, was an early proponent. In the 1990s, the official Republican health care plan was structurally similar to the ACA. And of course, the ACA is largely modelled on the health reform legislation implemented in Massachusetts in 2006, signed by its Republican governor, Mitt Romney.

Of course, the fact that Republicans used to support ACA-style reform doesn't prove that the law is effective. But, without getting into the details yet, let's look at the American health insurance ecosystem today compared to 2010.

In 2010, the uninsured rate in the United States was 16.5% and increasing by approximately 0.5% per year. By 2014, when the major provisions of the ACA began to take effect, it had reached 18%. In the first year, with the exchanges operating and Medicaid expanding, the rate of uninsured had been reduced to 11.4%. By the end of 2016 it reached 8.6%, the lowest level ever recorded.[20] We can say, unequivocally, that because of the ACA, many more people have access to medical care and a way to pay for it.

Who are the 8.6% who are still uninsured? The best description of the American population according to insurance type comes from Charles Gaba, who has created a snapshot of the current sources of

---

19. Rescission was an especially nasty trick, but it can no longer be played. It allowed insurance companies to deny care if the patient's insurance application was incorrect. In theory, this was intended to prevent people from lying about pre-existing conditions. In practice, many were denied care due to purely typographical errors.
20. At the time of publication, the uninsured rate has risen slightly from this level. It is not coincidental that the trend reversed just as the Trump Administration began to subvert the ACA via various rule changes.

insurance for everybody living in the United States. He identifies six main pools of uninsured people:

- Eligible for Medicaid, but not signed up (many people are not aware of their eligibility)
- Eligible for CHIP, but not signed up
- Ineligible for Medicaid due to living in a state that did not expand
- Undocumented immigrants
- Eligible for tax credits on the exchange
- Ineligible for tax credits on the exchange

In later chapters we'll discuss ways to extend health insurance to these populations. But none of these solutions involves repealing the Affordable Care Act.

FOUR MONTHS IN 1933
SPRINGTIME FOR HITLER

"The composition of the Cabinet leaves Herr Hitler no scope for gratification of any dictatorial ambition."
—The New York Times, January 31, 1933

The Weimar Republic has gotten a bad rap. Created following a sudden defeat, replacing the 400-year-old Hohenzollern dynasty, and attached to the devastating reparations debt of Versailles, the first representative government of the Germanic people faced obstacles that would crush any new nation. It made mistakes and had failures, but it also achieved an era of economic stability and burgeoning culture. It was no more destined to fail than any other new state.

Adolf Hitler rose to become Führer und Reichskanzler through (mostly) legal means. Most German people—at least in 1933—were not blind followers of a murderous dictator. They were frustrated by an economy facing horrendous unemployment, austerity, and deflation. They had economic anxiety. Yet despite never receiving more than 44% of the vote in a contested election, Hitler utilized the legal machinery of the Republic to poison and destroy it.

- What was the Weimar Republic?
- How did Hitler become Chancellor?
- What did he do then?

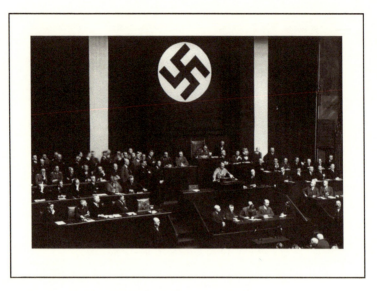

WHAT WAS THE WEIMAR REPUBLIC?

On November 11, 1918, the German people suffered a shock. Just four months earlier, in a great offensive, they had pierced the trench line at the seam between the French Army and British Expeditionary Force. They overran the defenses and stood on the doorsteps of Paris, nearing the breakthrough that had been denied to them four years prior. It nearly struck a fatal blow to the Triple Alliance. However, the German Supreme Army Command knew that their position was nowhere near as strong as it appeared. With fresh American troops arriving on the line, and the last reserves used in the attack, military leaders told the Kaiser and government that they must seek a cease fire.[1]

In October, a new prime minister was installed and tasked with negotiating with the Allies. By the end of the month, German sailors at their main naval base mutinied, refusing to leave port. This rebellion soon controlled the city of Kiel and began to spread. The government began to tumble like a line of dominos in a whirlwind: revolution spread across Germany, the Kaiser abdicated and fled, a Republic was declared, and a cease fire was signed with the Allies in the

---

1. Hence, Germany's loss in the War was entirely attributable to the military situation; there was no "stab in the back" by the politicians or other groups.

forest of Compiègne. In January, a National Assembly was elected. They met in Weimar and crafted a Constitution.

Viewed contemporaneously, the Weimar Constitution appeared well crafted. It was a liberal document, establishing the equality of citizens and rule of law.[2] The basic structure included:

- Federalism: States of the German Empire had always maintained significant autonomy, and this was preserved.
- Parliament: The Reichstag would be elected proportionally across Germany with no threshold for membership. It would select a chancellor, who would act as head of government via a cabinet of ministers.
- President: As head of state, the president was elected to a seven-year term and eligible to be re-elected once. Critically, Article 48 permitted the president to suspend portions of the Constitution. In case of such an emergency, rule would be by decree.
- Civil Liberties: The Weimar Constitution created many basic freedoms that Germans had never previously possessed. They had the right of habeas corpus, freedom of speech, privacy in their homes and communications, freedom of the press and of assembly, and a right to property. Religious and national minorities were explicitly named full citizens and received specific protection.

Given its eventual end, it is understandable that the Weimar Republic is considered a failure. But its failure is only apparent in hindsight. Before looking into its demise, it is important to consider the history of Weimar, which we will conveniently split into three eras.

1919-1923: Crisis and Inflation

The Weimar Republic generally had a centrist chancellor and cabinet, with opposition coming from both left-wing and right-wing radicals. As a new system, in a country with little democratic history, the earliest years involved several attempts to overthrow the government:

---

2. I use "liberal" in the classical sense, meaning "broad-minded."

- Spartacist Uprising: Left-wing, 1919. A splinter group of radical Communists erected barricades in Berlin. The center-left government reacted violently, deploying the army to restore order. In retaliation for the coup, moderate Communists were killed while in police custody, despite having been opposed to the uprising.
- Kapp Putsch: Right-wing, 1920. Paramilitary groups revolted against the government, which they blamed for the humiliating Versailles Treaty. Significant portions of the army, including General Erich Ludendorff,[3] were sympathetic. Without army support, the government was forced to flee Berlin. In response to this uprising, the President of the Republic called for a general strike.[4] By crippling the country, he ended the coup. Kapp himself was able to reach exile in Sweden, before returning to Germany to continue political work.[5]
- Beer Hall Putsch: Right-wing, 1923. Adolf Hitler[6] and a group of about 2,000 followers marched to the center of Munich with the goal of taking control of the Bavarian state. After provoking a clash with local troops, in which 20 people were killed, the crowd dispersed. Hitler was sent to Landsberg Prison for 264 days, but after his release he was permitted to continue political his activity. From then on, he vowed, he would attempt to gain power only via constitutional means.

Although Weimar had another ten years to live, we can already see a pattern. Left-wing groups were put down violently and excluded

---

3. Ludendorff, victor of Liège and Tannenberg, became a symbolic leader of right-wing nationalist causes in Weimar Germany. His tacit support would give other conservatives cover to radicalize and destroy the state.
4. The first Weimar President, Friedrich Ebert, is not well known today. But he is an interesting and important figure. Originally from the far left, he worked with right-wing and nationalist elements in attempting to establish a successful Republic. But he also invoked emergency powers 134 times, setting a dangerous precedent. Vilified by right-wing opponents despite a special type of patience with their violent form of politics, he died in office in 1925. He begs a fascinating question to which we will never know the answer: Would Ebert have been able to resist Hitler's rise more effectively than his successor?
5. By standing for trial for his role in the Putsch.
6. Well, look who showed up!

from the political arena. Right-wing groups were given slaps on the wrist and allowed to re-establish their organizations.

At the same time, the Republic began to face a challenge of a different type. A combination of war reparations, a shortage of raw materials, and the French occupation of the industrial Ruhr Valley caused Weimar's most famous event: hyper-inflation. It is worth quoting from Liaquat Ahamed's Pulitzer Prize-winning book, *Lords of Finance*, which features an in-depth discussion of Weimar hyperinflation:

> *"The budget deficit almost doubled, to around $1.5 billion. To finance this shortfall required the printing of ever-increasing amounts of ever more worthless paper marks...*
>
> *The task of keeping Germany adequately supplied with currency notes became a major logistical operation involving '133 printing works with 1783 machines... and more than 30 paper mills.'...*
>
> *Basic necessities were now priced in the billions—a kilo of butter cost 250 billion; a kilo of bacon 180 billion; a simple ride on a Berlin street car, which had cost 1 mark before the war, was now set at 15 billion...*
>
> *In the time that it took to drink a cup of coffee in one of Berlin's many cafes the price might have doubled... Economic existence became a rat race. Workers, once paid weekly, were now paid daily with large stacks of notes. Every morning big trucks loaded with laundry baskets full of notes rolled out of the Reichsbank printing offices and drove from factory to factory, where someone would clamber aboard to pitch great bundles to the sullen crowds of workers, who would then be given half an hour to rush out and buy something before the money became worthless."*

Image 5: Weimar children playing with banknotes.

It goes without saying, the Weimar Germans were having a tough time. Goods necessary for survival were difficult for people to obtain. Wealth, especially that which was held in any type of soft asset, was completely wiped out. Foreigners were able to buy up significant amounts of the capital stock with their francs, pounds or dollars. However, despite a trauma that is difficult for us to imagine, the leaders of the Republic were able to execute a national turnaround that deserves more credit than history has given it.

1924-1929: The Golden Age of Weimar

Somehow, they ended the inflation.[7] The German people, although shocked by the episode, began to settle into a period of normalcy. Only six years after the shocking defeat and five years after the humiliation at Versailles, Weimar was secure, prosperous, and happy. The Republic's golden era extended across society:

- Foreign Affairs: Proper behavior on the international stage allowed modifications to the Treaty of Versailles, helping the balance of payments crisis. Germany signed onto several agreements to control armaments and promote collective security in Europe.
- Political: Although most were short-lived, a pattern formed of coalition governments between center-right and center-left parties. Radicals still existed, but there were no more serious coups.
- Economic: With the currency stabilized, economic growth rebounded quickly and standards of living approached parity with other Western nations.
- Social: Weimar took advantage of the stability to create unemployment insurance, a welfare system, and worker protections. The housing stock greatly improved and there was even an attempt to achieve universal health care.
- Arts: All types of art flourished as Berlin became a center of the visual and performing arts world. Dadaism, German Expressionism, and New Objectivism were all centered in Weimar.
- Science: Albert Einstein had published his work on general relativity before the creation of Weimar, but he was working in Weimar during its golden age. Werner Heisenberg and Max Born greatly advanced particle physics during this time. Erich Fromm and Max Weber headlined the Frankfurt School of Philosophy. Göttingen maintained a top university faculty, although below its 19th-century heights.[8]

---

7. If you don't approve of my hand waving, you'll learn more by reading *Lords of Finance*. The explanation requires a significant discussion of monetary policy and isn't critical to our narrative.

1929-1933: Deflation and Suicide

A critical factor in Germany's recovery was public and private lending from the United States. After the stock market crash in 1929, American banks tightened credit to Germany. Reliance on foreign credit made Weimar uniquely susceptible to such a shock. The Great Depression hit Germany very hard, as we see in Figure 5.

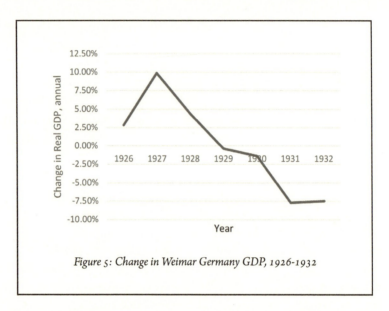

Figure 5: Change in Weimar Germany GDP, 1926-1932

Weimar responded by installing a so-called finance expert as Chancellor.[9] He responded in the classical, conservative manner: implementing austerity to eliminate budget deficits. Instead of restoring confidence, this fiscal contraction led to massive deflation, worsening the burden of Germany's debt. This decreased demand further, causing unemployment to skyrocket, as seen in Figure 6.

---

8. Everything is below Göttingen's 19th century heights. Its math department consisted of Carl Friedrich Gauss, Lejeune Dirichlet, Richard Dedekind and Bernhard Riemann.
9. Heinrich Brüning. Like Ebert, he is little known today. Unlike Ebert, he deserves the ignominy.

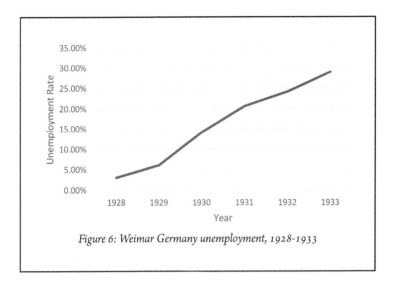

Figure 6: Weimar Germany unemployment, 1928-1933

The situation was again ripe for revolution. With his Nazi Party steadily gaining in the polls, Adolf Hitler had been waiting patiently for just such an opportunity.[10]

HOW DID HITLER BECOME CHANCELLOR?

As we've seen, Hitler and the Nazis first came to the notice of the world during the Beer Hall Putsch of 1923. During his time in Landsberg prison, he composed his treatise, describing in lurid detail the plan he wanted to implement in Germany. Even though most of his future crimes were spelled out, it would be almost 20 years before people would take his campaign promises literally. The New York Times was frequently Hitler's dupe, always willing to bend over backwards, ignoring his clearly stated plans.

"Adolph [sic] Hitler, once the demi-god of the reactionary extremists... He looked a much sadder and wiser man today... His behavior during imprisonment convinced authorities that, like his political organization, known as the Völkischer, was no longer to

10. Today's German insistence on containing inflation flows from a completely flawed understanding of history. Hitler didn't rise to power during Weimar's hyperinflation; it happened a decade later, during a period of high unemployment and *deflation*.

be feared. It is believed he will retire to private life and return to Austria, the country of his birth."

Being a master manipulator of public opinion, with a reckless disregard for the truth, Hitler set about building his organization. He fostered three constituencies and one enemy.

Constituency 1: The Junkers

During the time of the German Empire, the nation's wealth became concentrated in a small group of landed nobility, known as the *Junkers.*[11] As the Empire began to industrialize, the source of the Junkers' wealth moved from agriculture to industry, specifically armaments. The coming of the Republic took away their political power. Limits imposed on the size of Weimar's military by the Treaty of Versailles hit them in the pocketbook. Monarchists at heart, they were susceptible to an authoritarian figure who dangled future military contracts. Financing the Nazi Party was just good business sense.

Constituency 2: The Army

The fact that Germany's loss in World War I was due to military failure didn't dissuade Army leaders from promoting the myth of the "stab in the back." With the *Reichswehr* limited to 100,000 troops, there were more officers sitting around than there were troops to be led. Their prestige was ripe to be marshalled to destroy the Republic. Their acquiescence would be necessary for the success of anyone looking to take power.

Constituency 3: The People

After the hyperinflation subsided, the German people achieved great gains through the 1920s. Reforms that limited the power of the Junkers and the Army increased in turn the power of the average *landser* or *hausfrau.* Winning over the working classes would require

---

11. It's pronounced with a soft "J."

an economic shock. Nazi Party fortunes ebbed as its leaders waited for an opportunity.

But until the opportunity came, Hitler would meticulously lay groundwork. He held rallies, whipping crowds into a frenzy and promoting violence against Jews, Socialists, immigrants, and other outsiders. He started his private security force, the *Sturm Abeitlung* (SA), which would soon create terror across the country. All this anger was focused against the only thing that could stop him.

The Enemy: Institutions

In the view of Hitler, all institutions were corrupt and the enemy of the people.[12] Only he could fix them. He railed against the government, the bureaucrats, the professionals, the scientists, groups of racial and ethnic minorities, and the Western democracies of France and England. But his fiercest criticism was of the press.

Lügenpresse, or "lying press," was the word used by Hitler and the increasingly powerful Joseph Goebbels.[13] What began as words soon moved to physical violence; blacklisted reporters required security guards to report on Nazi Party activities. In place of the lying press, Hitler promoted reporting based on his set of alternative facts. With generous subsidies, these Nazi-affiliated newspapers soon became lucrative business ventures.[14]

Hitler's message was clear to anyone caring to listen; he wanted to destroy the Republic. His SA began to intimidate neutral local leaders and elections turned violent. Nazis in the Reichstag became unruly, preventing business from being conducted. Compromise with the establishment was anathema. After all, they were The Enemy.

These same institutions reacted complacently. The executive, judicial, and military leaders who had violently put down revolts from the left took little action against the Nazis. Some of Weimar's leaders were anti-Semitic, and some were anti-Republican, but most just did not take the threat seriously. They thought they could control Hitler, use his movement for their own purposes,[15] and gain back power.

---

12. Except for the Army, of course. Hitler needed the Army.
13. Hitler had his own specifically hated publications, just like Trump has CNN.
14. Hitler's personal finances, tenuous until he became chancellor, began to stabilize as he handed out printing contracts.

This came to a head after the election of November 1932, conducted during the worst of the Depression. After the votes were tallied, the Nazis became the largest party in the Reichstag, despite winning only 33% of the vote.[16] The right-wing parties were still outnumbered by the center-left. However, outgoing Chancellor Franz van Papen saw the ability for conservative elements to maintain power by creating a coalition with Hitler. President Paul von Hindenburg, an old and tired monarchist, became convinced that Hitler's extreme positions were merely campaign rhetoric. The man he had derisively called the Austrian Corporal would be installed as a figurehead Chancellor, surrounded and controlled by a cabinet of good conservatives.

WHAT DID HE DO THEN?

Like every good faux-populist demagogue-authoritarian, Hitler did not permit himself to be co-opted. He set about implementing precisely the plan that he had explained over the previous decade. His focus was on personally gathering all the power of the State. To do so, he needed a crisis.

History books may say that there are doubts as to who started the Reichstag Fire of February 27, 1933, but I think it is clear enough. A troubled Dutch Communist was certainly there, and he certainly did set a fire. But it spread too fast to be the work of one man. On the other hand, there was a tunnel from where the fire started, leading directly to offices controlled by the Nazis. The fire was not planned by three Bulgarian Comintern members, as the Nazis claimed.[17] Either way, Hitler took full advantage.

Passed on February 28, the Reichstag Fire Decree devolved power over security to the Interior Minister, who just happened to be the loyal Nazi Hanz Frick.[18] With new elections just a week away, 4,000

---

15. Such as eliminating government-sponsored health care, lowering taxes on the wealthy, eliminating government regulation of industry, and promoting growth of the military.
16. It was actually a slight decrease from their July 1932 result.
17. The so-called masterminds of the Reichstag Fire were found innocent, despite being tried in a court under complete Nazi control.
18. Who would later be executed at Nuremberg for war crimes.

opposition leaders were imprisoned, and their parties removed from the ballots. Following orders from Prussian Minister Hermann Göring,[19] Nazi brown shirts "monitored" the balloting. Violence was primarily directed against the Communist enemy, but also against the centrist parties. The resources of the Junkers were thrown behind Hitler, who promised that this would be the last election. Despite all of this, the Nazis were still only able to gain 44% of the vote. It wasn't a majority, but it was enough for Hitler to form a majority government, finally taking control of the cabinet in his own right.

After this election, there remained opposition parties in the Reichstag, preventing Hitler from gaining full legislative control. One hundred Communist members never took their seats; they were jailed or went into hiding. The Catholic Center Party was placated by the promise of a treaty with the Vatican. These missing or co-opted members gave Hitler the two-thirds majority necessary to pass the Enabling Act, moving all legislative power to the cabinet, which he controlled. Germany was now a dictatorship.

Of course, there were still threats to Hitler's absolute power, but Hitler could deal with them in due course. Trade unions survived until May. They were disbanded and replaced by the German Labor Front, run by Robert Ley, previously head of the Nazi party apparatus.[20] In July, all opposition parties were formally banned; with few other candidates on the ballot, the finally Nazis won an election outright with 92% of the vote. Opposition and neutral press offices were raided and shut down; editors who valued their personal freedom began to take orders from the Propaganda Minister. In 1934, the traditional German states were replaced with a new system of *Gaue*. The German Emperors had always respected the states' autonomy, but Hitler ensured that each *Gauleiter* answered directly to him. In June 1934, the Night of the Long Knives neutered the SA, eliminating the possibility of rebellion from within the party. After the death of Hindenburg, the offices of president were merged with those of chancellor, and Hitler became Führer of the German State. He waited until 1938 to deal with the military; a contrived scandal allowed him to push out the high command and name himself Commander

---

19. Who committed suicide the night before he was to be executed at Nuremberg, for war crimes.
20. Ley committed suicide while waiting for trial at Nuremberg

in Chief. With all power bases now under his personal control, Hitler could move forward with the next phase of his plan: expanding the Reich.

"So what?" you ask. "Are you going to be the 10,000[th] person to tell me that some modern-day person is the second coming of Hitler?" No, I don't plan to do this.[21] But I do want to scare you.

When talking about the state of the United States in the era of Trump, I'm often told that "they" won't allow it, there are "things" in place to prevent it, "it" could never happen here. When Trump said those things, it was just the campaign, he didn't mean them, don't take him so literally, give him a chance. Obviously, the United States is a more stable nation than Weimar Germany. But built within its structure is the ability to be legally transformed into an authoritarian dictatorship. There are no institutional guardrails to protect us. The only defense we have against a tyrant is to not elect one President.

The historical parallels are frankly stunning. Disparate treatment of opposition from the left (e.g., Black Lives Matter, athletes protesting racism) and the right (e.g., Tea Party, white supremacist militias, and the KKK) is common. The press, which strained to maintain false balance during the 2016 presidential campaign, is undermined any time they dare to report critical items about the administration. As a candidate, Trump made specific promises to eliminate freedoms, but we are told not to take him seriously.

We can learn something from the demise of Weimar.

---

21. In fact, I actually think a better historical comparison for Trump is Neville Chamberlain, who, in the interest of "making good deals," sold out traditional allies and handed a totalitarian dictator the means to enslave most of Europe.

HEALTH INSURANCE, PART III
OBAMACARE
THE LONG WAR

"I'm not on Obamacare. My health insurance is through the
ACA."
—*Twitter, various*

Almost seven years after its passage, the Affordable Care Act is no less controversial.

After laws are passed, even controversial laws, most settle down into an implementation mode. Even their opponents try to make them work as well as possible, for the sake of their constituents. Not so with Obamacare. From the day of its passage, its opponents have tried to dismantle the so-called disaster. Along the way, they have attempted to undermine it in any way possible. The law's proponents have refused to consider changes that they expected would result in fewer people being insured, coverage being less comprehensive, or premiums increasing.

How do we consider the effects of this complex law? This question is indelibly linked to our personal views as to how a health care system should operate. Rather than assuming one system is better than another, let's judge the ACA by the terms of its debate. What did people think would happen, and how did these predictions compare with what has come to pass?

- What did the proponents of the ACA predict?
- What did the opponents predict?
- How is each side describing the current state of the health insurance system?

WHAT DID THE PROPONENTS OF THE ACA PREDICT?

Before we dive in, let's set some ground rules. It would be easy to cherry-pick people on either side of the argument making crazy predictions and then shoot them down. We will avoid this; all quotes given here are intended to be representative of the larger debate. We'll also need a consistent set of rulings to rate how everybody did. Politifact's system—True, Mostly True, Half True, Mostly False, False, and Pants on Fire—seems to cover our bases. I'll reserve rulings of Pants on Fire for deliberate fabrications intended to mislead the public. An honestly made prediction that didn't bear out is just False. Let's dive in...

Prediction: "If you like your plan, you can keep it." – Barack Obama, June 5, 2009 (among other dates)

The President should not have made this statement. It was a promise that he lacked the power to keep. One of the goals of the ACA was to eliminate non-comprehensive policies that were sold as health insurance. An extreme case of such policies were the **mini-meds**. These plans did the opposite of what we expect from health insurance. They offered discounts and paid for some types of care but had annual benefit caps as low as $2,500. They offered little protection for those with even moderate medical needs. Because of this, they were cheap. Some lucky people who didn't need significant medical care liked them. However, they poisoned the system by siphoning off the currently healthy. The ACA prohibited such plans, and we are better off for their demise.

A fundamental purpose of the ACA was to create various criteria that an insurance plan must have in order to be considered health insurance. A significant percentage of existing plans on the individual marketplace lacked these requisites. The White House seemed genuinely surprised by the number of people whose plan was cancelled. They tried to soften the blow for those affected. Existing plans were permitted to continue operating under a grandfathering arrangement. Despite this, some providers canceled non-conforming plans for business reasons. This wasn't Obamacare's fault; private companies make their own decisions on what products to offer. Before the ACA, the market had never featured stable offerings; plans came and went frequently. What happened was not so different from how the non-group market had always operated.

In any case, people holding these policies received a notification that their plan would be cancelled. The clear majority of affected people were eligible for superior plans, in terms of cost, coverage, and patient protections. Even still, some of them were upset; people fear change. The number of people whose plans were cancelled is not known exactly, but they represented about 1% of the population.[1]

Rating: False.

Politifact rated this Pants on Fire, but I disagree. I see no evidence that the statement not was made in good faith.[2]

Prediction: The ACA will significantly reduce the number of uninsured Americans.—Congressional Budget Office, 2012

---

1. You can find estimates as low as 1.5 million and up to 4.7 million.
2. It could have been marked True with some context: "If you like your plan, you can keep it, if it provides basic minimum benefits. Otherwise, you'll have at least three years to transition to a new plan that does. This plan may be cheaper and will provide better coverage. And we don't control private companies, so if they want to cancel a plan, that's not my fault."

In 2012, the CBO predicted that 26 million additional people would be covered by health insurance due to the ACA.[3] This number included:

- 10 million additional due to Medicaid/CHIP expansion
- 23 million additional on exchanges
- 5 million fewer covered by employers
- 2 million fewer in the individual market (i.e. outside of the exchanges)

On net, the CBO predicted that the uninsured non-elderly population would be 30 million in 2016.

To see how this compares with the results, we can refer to the ACA Signups Health Care Coverage Breakout. The categories of insurance don't agree match those used by the CBO, but:

- Medicaid/CHIP expansion has added 14 million beneficiaries.
- Exchanges have added 11 million. An additional 8 million people have purchased Obamacare-compliant policies outside of the exchanges.

Many Republicans have criticized the CBO's prediction of health insurance coverage. As evidence, they point to the fact that only 11 million people enrolled through the exchanges, rather than the 23 million predicted. However, the CBO assumed that everybody buying an ACA-compliant plan would do so via the exchange. Eight million people have bought policies outside the exchanges, for various reasons. In addition, the employer-based market has fared better than expected; the number covered is roughly unchanged from 2012. The big picture is that 29 million people remained uninsured in 2016, exactly in line with the CBO's prediction.

Rating: True.

Remember this the next time you hear or read that the CBO's projections are inaccurate.

---

3. Based on their 2012 score, which came after the Supreme Court ruling in NFIB v. Sebelius. This analysis correctly predicted that some states would choose to give up the free Medicaid money, leaving their citizens uninsured.

Prediction: "I will not sign a plan that adds one dime to our deficits, either now or in the future."—Barack Obama, remarks to Congress, 2009

When considering the fiscal effects of legislation, we must always caveat that we don't know the counter-factual. It is impossible to know what would have happened if the ACA had not passed. With this proviso, the evidence is strong that deficits have been and will be smaller because of the ACA. As evidence, we can look at the 2010 CBO projection for the law; it showed a significant fiscal benefit (see Figure 7).

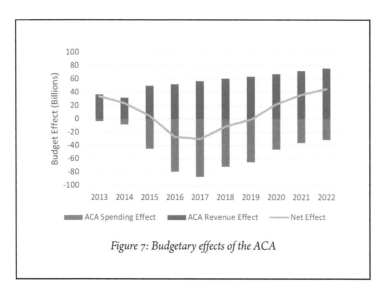

Figure 7: Budgetary effects of the ACA

With its revenue effects greater than its spending, the ACA was expected to improve the budget deficit. As the law has taken effect, the ACA's costs have been lower than projected. Some of this difference is because premiums on the exchanges are lower than expected, decreasing the amount spent on subsidies. In addition, the failure of 19 states to expand Medicaid has decreased federal spending on that program.

Rating: Mostly True.

Obamacare's fiscal effects appear better than predicted so far, but the full law has been in effect only three years. President Obama's prediction said, "in the future," so let's be cautious.

WHAT DID THE OPPONENTS PREDICT?

Prediction: "The bill's tax hikes are a job killer... individual mandate is a job killer... employer mandate is a job killer."– John Boehner, Speaker's Office

A common prediction about the ACA was that it would kill jobs.[4] There were some coherent reasons to think the ACA would hurt employment. First, some people who had previously been in the labor market primarily to obtain health insurance might willingly drop out as other sources became available.[5] Second, to avoid providing insurance to workers, some companies might reduce employment or move full-time employees to part-time status.

Since the passage of the ACA, the number of people employed nationally has increased every single month. This is a record streak for unbroken employment growth. There is no evidence of significant movement of full-time employees to part-time status.[6] The law's proponents haven't claimed that the historically strong job growth over the past seven years is specifically *because* of the ACA. The American economy is complex, and any effect of the ACA on job growth would be visible only in the long-term. However, Speaker Boehner said that the ACA would kill jobs and it has not done so.[7]

Rating: False.

There is no way to conclusively prove how the ACA has affected employment. But if it was truly a job killer the impact would have been evident by now.

Prediction: "The America I know and love is not one in which my parents or my baby with Down Syndrome will have to stand in front of Obama's 'death panel'"—Sarah Palin

---

4. In what was a greater assault on the English language than the law itself, one of the many repeal attempts was entitled the *Repealing the Job-Killing Health Care Law Act*.

5. The heavily-reported CBO report predicting this made clear that the decrease it expected in employment represented people making the choice not to work.

6. Involuntary part-time employment has decreased during the relevant period.

7. There is a lot of discussion about the effect of the ACA on employment levels. My best estimate of the data is that employment is about where it would have been without the ACA.

I promised not to cherry-pick and using the words of the former half-term Governor of Alaska may appear to break this rule. But while her words are the most quotable, the idea that the ACA would lead to government involvement in individual health care decisions is a fair representation of the arguments of the law's opponents.[8]

We can dispense with this one quickly. To the extent that there was any logic behind these complaints, Palin was probably referring to the Independent Payment Advisory Board. This is one of the cost-control mechanisms in the ACA. It was created to consider what types of treatments were effective and which were simply expensive. Or maybe she was talking about end-of-life counseling, which insurance companies were now required to pay for (and whose use is voluntary). Either way, you don't need to worry. As you may have noticed, no government bureaucrats are making life or death decisions about your family members.

Rating: Pants on fire.

Opponents were telling people that the ACA was going to kill their babies and grandmothers. By eliminating insurance provisions like pre-existing conditions and rescission, the ACA has greatly improved the ability of a baby with Down Syndrome to get necessary care. And because the ACA eliminated annual and lifetime caps on coverage, this care is far less likely to bankrupt the baby's parents.

Prediction: "The whole scheme is enlisting young adults to overpay, so other people can have subsidies."—Dean Clancy, FreedomWorks

Before the ACA, a lot of healthy, young people paid less for insurance than they do today. This was inevitable: if we want to cover lower- and middle-income people who have health problems, either wealthy people or healthy people (or both) will have to pay more. But the costlier insurance they have today guarantees essential health benefits, has no lifetime caps, precludes the denial of coverage due to pre-existing conditions, and so on. Even young invincibles will eventually become old or sick. They might get in a car accident. The ACA ensures that everyone can always get insurance.

---

8. Chuck Grassley, 35-year Iowa Senator: "[You] should not have a government-run plan to decide when to pull the plug on Grandma." Grassley has been the Senate chairman or senior Republican on committees with jurisdiction over health care.

Clancy also shows a fundamental misunderstanding of how the ACA works. The "overpayment" by the young and healthy results in lower premiums for sicker and older people. The money for subsidies comes from the ACA's taxes, mostly the surtaxes on top earners' incomes. Both of these are due to the ACA, but they are separate mechanisms.

Rating: Half true.

Without context, the statement is misleading. But it is true that benefits to the young and healthy are in the longer-term, while they often spend more out of pocket today. They gain from the law in other ways, but their complaints are understandable.

HOW IS EACH SIDE DESCRIBING THE CURRENT STATE OF THE HEALTH INSURANCE SYSTEM?

Statement: "You have to remember this law is getting much worse. It is what actuaries say, 'Entering a death spiral.'"—Paul Ryan, December 7, 2016

The increases in premiums for exchange-based policies have been a major focus of the debate on the ACA's future. However, the headline prices of policies, which are reported breathlessly by the press, affect only a small portion of the overall health insurance market. Less than 1% of the population gets health coverage unsubsidized through the exchanges.[9] Otherwise, the cost to policy buyers is fixed, with the remainder paid by the government. So, when you see premium increases quoted in the press, remember that this mostly affects the amount spent by the government. Therefore, the real question is: has the government's subsidy cost per enrollee been higher than expected? This is easy to check. Figure 8 compares the original CBO projected subsidies against what we have experienced and expect in the future.[10]

---

9. For what it's worth, I'm one of them. I am mostly happy with my experience using Obamacare. I wish the premiums were lower, but they represent how much health care costs in America. I had a lot of plans to choose from, and easily found one that has most of my doctors in its network. Remember that before the ACA, New York did not have a functioning non-group market. So, what I have is clearly far better than the alternative: nothing!

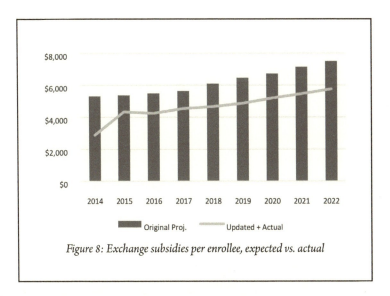

Figure 8: Exchange subsidies per enrollee, expected vs. actual

Obamacare subsidies are costing a less than we thought they would. This means that premiums have been lower than expected, directly conflicting with press reports, as well as Paul Ryan.

This conflict is due to the fact that, like most topics in health insurance, the story is more complex. At first, exchange premiums were a lot lower than expected. Perhaps insurers were trying to gain market share. They also may have mispriced the risk pool. Now that the exchanges are established, insurers are using pricing power to increase premiums. This is the normal operation of a functioning free market. And it is in line with the expectations of the law's creators.

But Paul Ryan didn't just say that premiums were increasing; he said Obamacare is in a death spiral. Death spirals have two features. Not only do premiums increase, but people start exiting the market, going without health insurance. We can take a quick trip over to ACA Signups and see that enrollment in 2017 was *higher* than in 2016. The health insurance exchanges are not in a death spiral.

Rating: Pants on fire.

The ACA isn't in a death spiral. Premiums are lower than originally projected, and enrollment remains steady.

---

10. These projections were made before the repeal of the individual mandate in late 2017. Without the mandate, premiums will increase, the only doubt is by how much. However, this increase is due to the subversion of Obamacare, rather than the law itself.

Paul Ryan is the Speaker of the House. It is his job to understand policy. Given that he has carefully curated an image as a policy expert over many years, he should be expected to know what a death spiral is. His claim was not simply a mis-statement, but rather made in bad faith.

—§—

One claim about the ACA that we did not analyze is its effect on national health spending. I avoided this question for a specific reason: I don't know the answer. The evidence is ambiguous, and we don't know what would have happened had the ACA never passed. Even if we assume that it has failed to bend the cost curve, the ACA's proponents have clearly succeeded at predicting what the law would do. We can debate whether providing more and better insurance via government regulations and mandates is a good thing for society. But this was the policy goal set by its authors, it has come to pass, and without most of the negative effects its opponents expected.

Health insurance is important, and government policy helps people get it. After the passage of the ACA, the Republican Party trotted out (and continues to trot out) supposed victims of Obamacare. Their stories seldom stand up to any scrutiny. These unfortunate people are usually just lacking knowledge about the options that are available for them, or benefitting from the ACA without realizing it.

At its core, in the ACA, everybody pays a small amount, in order to spread risks out across the entire population. That's what insurance is supposed to do. There are still people who are struggling to get care and cover its costs. The job isn't done. But anybody who claims our health system was better before Obamacare is not looking at the evidence.

ORBITAL MECHANICS AND THE MARTIAN
WITH MATH AND SPOILERS

*"I am definitely going to die up here… if I have to listen to any
more god-awful disco music,"*
—Mark Watney, from The Martian, by Andy Weir

L et's move on to something lighter, a palate cleanser of sorts. We
will take our analytic approach and apply it to fact-checking a
work of popular science fiction.

I read *The Martian* a while ago, and more recently watched the
film version. The author, Andy Weir, has been deservedly praised for
his scientific accuracy. However, there is one significant plot point in
his book that struck me as implausible. As far as I can tell, Weir made
appropriate use of orbital mechanics, describing the orbits taken by
the various craft transferring to and from Mars. But when a spacecraft is used for a purpose vastly different from its intended mission,
we need to check and make sure it had the appropriate capabilities.

Andy Weir's *The Martian* is the story of a human voyage to Mars gone wrong and the use of science to save a stranded crew member. In a sense, the strategy used to rescue this astronaut is no different from what distressed square-rigged sailing ships did in the 17th century. The mission plan was discarded, and every resource was put to maximum use, often for purposes far different than originally intended.

In *The Martian*, the original mission plan was for the Mars Ascent Vehicle (MAV) to rendezvous with the larger Hermes ship in low Mars orbit (LMO). This is similar to the mission plan from the Apollo program, when the Lunar Module met the Command Module in moon orbit. This so-called moon orbit rendezvous was critical to the success of the Apollo program; it makes sense that Weir envisioned a similar maneuver in his hypothetical Mars mission. However, when things go awry, the MAV meets up with the Hermes while it is flying by Mars, rather than orbiting. This poses a problem.

During the fly-by of a planet, a spaceship is going a lot faster than when it is in orbit. Could a ship built to rendezvous in LMO reach the speed necessary to escape Mars orbit? Spaceships are generally built for specific purposes. There is some margin of error in the design, but was Weir's plan feasible? Let's find out!

I think of **delta-v** as the currency of space travel. When a spacecraft takes off, it starts with a certain amount of delta-v, depending on the weight of the spacecraft, amount of fuel carried, and the efficiency of its engines. When a spacecraft performs any maneuver—taking off, reaching orbit, transferring to another planet's orbit, or descending to the surface—it uses up some of this delta-v. In space, there is no way to create any more. The only maneuver possible without expending delta-v is landing on a planet with an atmosphere. When you slam into the air, it slows you down without using any fuel.[1]

Because moving from one orbit to another requires a fixed amount of delta-v, we can draw a delta-v map. Think of it as a road map, but one in which distances are expressed as the amount of gasoline required to get from place to place. Unlike driving on I-94, in orbit you have nowhere to stop for more fuel. Delta-v is usually quoted in terms of meters per second, or m/s. For our discussion we only care about three segments on the map:

- Mars surface to low Mars orbit: 3,800 m/s
- Low Mars orbit to Mars intercept: 1,440 m/s
- Mars surface to Mars escape: 5,240 m/s

So our question is: could a spaceship designed with 3,800 m/s of delta-v get to 5,240 m/s?

This brings us to my third-favorite equation of all time:[2] the Tsiolkovsky rocket equation:

---

1. Come to think of it, you could land on a planet without using any delta-v, even if it doesn't have an atmosphere. But because you won't slow down before landing, I don't recommend it.
2. Bayes Theorem is number one. The Reimann zeta function comes in second.

$$\Delta v = v_e * ln\left(\frac{m_0}{m_f}\right), where$$

$$\Delta v = delta\text{-}v$$

$$v_e = exhaust\ velocity$$

$$m_0\ is\ the\ spacecraft\ mass\ without\ any\ fuel$$

$$m_f\ is\ the\ spacecraft\ mass\ fully\ fueled$$

What does this tell us? It says that for a spaceship to go far, you want to carry as much fuel as possible, and shoot it out as fast as possible. Translated back to terms relevant to *The Martian*: we take a spaceship with a given delta-v, reduce its weight, and see how much further it can go. This gives us three equations and three unknowns:

$$\Delta v(1) = v_e * ln\left(\frac{m_0(1)}{m_f(1)}\right)$$

$$\Delta v(2) = v_e * ln\left(\frac{m_0(2)}{m_f(2)}\right)$$

$$m_0(2) = m_0(1) - m_{cut}$$

You can reduce these equations to find the maximum mass of the un-altered Mars Ascent Vehicle that would permit the change to work:

$$m_f = m_{cut} * \frac{e^{\frac{\Delta v_2}{v_e}} - 1}{e^{\frac{\Delta v_2}{v_e}} - e^{\frac{\Delta v_1}{v_e}}}$$

The original MAV was probably built with some margin of error, perhaps 100 m/s, bringing it to 3,900 m/s as designed. There was also a buffer on speed it had to reach, as it fell short of the 5,240 m/s needed to complete the maneuver. Let's say that the modified MAV carried 5,200 m/s delta-v. The book said that the mass of the MAV was reduced by 5,000 kilograms. It also contained six fewer passengers than expected, saving an additional 420 kilograms. Unfortunately, I'm not able to find anybody crazy enough to publish fan fiction MAV specs, so we need to guess its v_e, or exhaust velocity.

The Apollo Lunar Module, the closest real-world analogue to the MAV, had an exhaust velocity of 3,050 m/s. The just-launched SpaceX Falcon Heavy has similar specifications. The most powerful machine man has ever built, the Saturn V, has an exhaust velocity of around 4,130 m/s. If the MAV's engines performed in this range of values, the MAV's maximum mass would be between 12,800 and 14,400 kilograms. Even if, in the future, we can build a rocket engine twice as efficient as the Lunar Module had, it would allow a MAV mass of only 16,300 kilograms. Given that the MAV was able to achieve escape velocity from Mars despite the removal of 5,000 kilograms of mass, this seems improbable.[3] Ships that cut one-third of their mass are usually left unable to fly.

And there is another issue: if the original MAV mass were 16,300 kilograms, that means the MAV mass with fuel would be around 31,000 kilograms. Using Mars' gravitational constant of 3.71 gives a total ship weight of 115kN. Taking off from Mars would require a minimum thrust-to-weight ratio of 1.75.[4] This means you would need 200kN of thrust in your hypothetical super-efficient engine. To compare, the Lunar Module ascent engine had 16kN of thrust. So, the hypothetical engine would need to be twelve times as powerful, as well as twice as efficient.

We haven't proven the plot to be literally impossible, but we were right to be skeptical.

---

3. It bears noting, however, that the Lunar Module had a dry mass of only 2,150 kg.
4. The Lunar Module was closer to 2.1.

THE RULE OF BAYES
WHY YOU CAN NEVER BE SURE OF ANYTHING

"Bet you $50 it hasn't."
—XKCD # 1132, "Frequentists vs. Bayesians"

People don't like thinking probabilistically. We crave certainty. That rock on the side of the road is definitely a rock. That apple is definitely red. It rained today, so the probability of rain was 100%. Thinking about what we know is considered part of philosophy, not mathematics.

Bayesian inference provides a mathematical framework for thinking about uncertainty and describing what we learned. In a Bayesian world, we begin by thinking some things. As we gain information, we know more. The difference from what we knew before to what we know now is our learning. Bayesian thinking can provide insight as to how much a piece of information should change what you think to be true.

Bayes Theorem has applications beyond such philosophical questions. Since its renaissance in the middle of the last century, it has been applied to business, sports, medicine, and national defense. Many who gamble for a living, or trade in the financial markets, use Bayesian thinking as an integral part of their daily framework.

- Who was Thomas Bayes? What is Bayes Theorem?
- How is Frequentist probability different from Bayesian probability? Why do Frequentists and Bayesians fight so much?
- How can I use Bayesian Statistics in my everyday life?

Image 10: Thomas Bayes, maybe

WHO WAS THOMAS BAYES? WHAT IS BAYES THEOREM?

The story of the 18th century is the story of rising British world domination. After a century of religious conflict and battles between the King and Parliament, the Glorious Revolution of 1688 installed a new royal dynasty, settling the major points of internal dispute. Britain has faced no violent revolutions in the 300 years since. The government would evolve into a constitutional monarchy, but it would happen slowly and peacefully. By avoiding the internal strife that plagued France, Germany, Spain, and other European nations, Britain could focus on building the world's first industrial economy and its finest navy. This would lead to untold wealth as Britons reaped the benefits of their global empire.

A small side benefit of this golden age was the ability of the British Empire to afford a system of country pastors. Often formed from the later sons of the lesser nobility, these parish priests were intended to spread across the country, advancing the Church of England. But for many of them, the life of a country preacher was not so arduous. Fortunately for us, many of their side pursuits were of great cultural and scientific value. Jonathan Swift and Joseph Priestly are just two examples of great contributors whose day job was working for the Church of England.

Why do I go on at length about English country parish life in the 18th century? Well, we just don't know that much about Thomas Bayes, so describing his world is the best we can do. We think he might have been born in 1701 but we aren't sure.[1] His father was a well-known preacher; we can surmise that they were part of the society described at the beginning of this discussion. Thomas spent his early years working with his father before moving to his own parish in Kent around 1735. In this seat, we can surmise that he was one of the parish priests with free time to pursue other interests.

Today, we know of only two non-posthumous publications by Bayes, and only one of those is about mathematics. We believe that he was elected to the Royal Society around 1742, so he had some stature among post-Newtonian British scientists. We don't know how he began to think about probability; it was not considered a proper branch of mathematics at that time. His interest was likely philosophical or religious, perhaps trying to understand the likelihood of miracles. What we do know is that he never published his lasting work, containing the eponymous Theorem. It came to light after his death.[2]

Now that we've talked about the man, we can get to our point; here is Bayes Theorem in all its glory:

---

1. The image shown at the start of this chapter is always used as Bayes' portrait. But there is no reason to think that it is really him, and many reasons to think otherwise. There are journal articles dedicated to proving that this image is not consistent with Bayes' time period. Unfortunately, even if the image is definitely not of him, we have no better idea what Bayes looked like. Given that (in my opinion) it's a flattering image, I choose to think of Bayes as he is shown here. He has been deceased for more than 250 years and is unlikely to mind.
2. We know that he died in 1761. A famous, but awful, math joke is that we know more about Bayes' posterior than his prior.

$$P(A|B) = \frac{P(B|A) * P(A)}{P(B)}$$

In this equation, A is our hypothesis, and B is our data. $P(A)$ means the **probability** that A is true, without any assumption as to the veracity of B. $P(A|B)$ is the **conditional probability** of A being true, knowing B is true.[3] $P(B|A)$ is the probability that we would find data point B, given that we know A is true. The letters A and B can represent almost anything, from a statement like "that man is six feet tall" to an event like "this coin flip will come up heads." Remember that probability is the likelihood of an occurrence. It is expressed as a number between zero and one (equivalently, between 0% and 100%). Let's apply Bayes Rule through a simple example.

Let's say you see a man on the street. You want to know if he has a college degree. The prevalence of college degrees among the American working population is 40%; without any more information, you would assign this unknown man the same probability. However, if you then learn that he works in a job earning more than $100,000 per year, that would be a valuable piece of information. Out of the general population, only 25% earn this much. Among college graduates, the number rises to 54%. We can plug these numbers into Bayes Theorem, with A representing "has a college degree" and B representing "earns over $100,000 per year:"

$$P(A|B) = \frac{P(B|A) * P(A)}{P(B)} = \frac{54\% * 40\%}{25\%} = 86\%$$

---

3. Conditional probability is a tricky concept. It is often best expressed with the phrase "given that." For example, what is the probability that it will be cloudy tomorrow? Perhaps 50%. What is the probability that it will be cloudy outside, given that it will snow? Close to 100%. This is a conditional probability.

With just this one additional piece of information, there is now an 86% probability that this man has a college degree. Bayes Theorem allows us to quantify how much knowledge we've gained.

On its own, Bayes Theorem is a trivial piece of mathematics; it can be proven on one side of an index card. But as the previous example shows, this simple formula can help us gain insights into the nature of learning and information. Let's look at another example, this time applying the information learned from a narcotics test.

Approximately 1% of the American population uses cocaine. Say you're in a long line at the grocery store. Knowing nothing about the man ahead of you in line, the probability that he uses cocaine is 1%. You start chatting about the long wait and he tells you that he took a drug test on the previous day and failed it. What is the probability that the person is a cocaine user?

You may be tempted to say close to 100%, but you would be wrong. Drug tests are far from perfect; people who don't use drugs sometimes test positive and users sometimes test negative. Cocaine tests have a false positive rate of 5% and a false negative rate of 2%.[4] Going back to our friend in line, there are two ways in which he could have tested positive: a correct test on a user and an incorrect test on a non-user. Together, these two scenarios have a probability of approximately 6%.[5] We can apply Bayes Theorem.

$$P\left(\text{User}|\text{Positive}\right) = \frac{P\left(\text{Positive}|\text{User}\right) * P\left(\text{User}\right)}{P\left(\text{Positive}\right)}$$

4. False positive means the test returns a positive result for a non-user; a false negative means a negative test result for a user. The values used in this example approximate the statistics for drug usage and testing in the United States.
5. In the first scenario, a 98% accuracy rate for users, who represent 1% of the population leads to 0.98% of the population testing positive. In the second scenario, a 5% chance of error on the 99% of the population that doesn't use cocaine gives 4.95% additional probability of a positive test. Added together, we would expect 5.93% of the entire population to test positive for cocaine use.

$$P\,(\text{User}|\text{Positive}) = \frac{98\% \; * \; 1\%}{5.93\%} = 16.5\%$$

This means that the probability that somebody who tests positive for cocaine is indeed a user is only about one chance in six! I won't go through the math again, you can check that if he failed a second drug test, the probability he is a user becomes 79%. A third failed test would make the probability 98.7%.[6] No matter how many tests were failed, it would never reach 100%. In Bayesian theory, unless you are already certain of something, no amount of additional information can make you completely certain.

An Aside: Bayesian thinking, no formulas allowed

Bayes was an amateur mathematician, of whose work we know little. One tiny morsel that has reached us is a thought experiment that conditioned his thinking on these topics. It reminds us of Albert Einstein, although Einstein wouldn't imagine riding on a beam of light for another 150 years.

Bayes wanted to know what we could learn about the future probability of an event when all we know is the number of times it had occurred in the past. To formulate his idea, he proposed a modified game of billiards.

Imagine you are standing with your back to a pool table, so you can't see anything happening on it. Your friend rolls a cue ball on the table; we assume that it is equally likely to stop at any spot on the surface. You then ask your friend to roll another ball, and report if it stopped to the left or the right of the cue ball. If it lands to the left, then we know the cue ball is more likely to be to the right, and vice versa. If we repeatedly roll more

---

6. I'll leave these calculations as an exercise for the reader.

balls and report on their relative location, uncertainty about the cue ball's position will decrease each time. If half the balls are on each side, it is likely that the cue ball is toward the middle. If each of 1,000 balls land to the right, we can become quite sure our cue ball is far to the left. Even though we can never know for sure, we are still gaining information with each throw.

Everything you really need to know about Bayes Rule is incorporated in this thought experiment. The initial throw of the cue ball is a random process. Your initial guess as to its location is your prior. Each additional ball is also a random process. Despite being random, they still give information, with which we can refine our guess. Our refined guess is a new prior, and we run our experiment again. Soon, these guesses start to be well-informed; with enough balls, you can greatly narrow down where the cue ball is likely to be.

But you'll never be certain—certainty is an impossibility in a Bayesian world.

HOW IS FREQUENTIST PROBABILITY DIFFERENT FROM BAYESIAN PROBABILITY? WHY DO FREQUENTISTS AND BAYESIANS FIGHT SO MUCH?

So far, this has been straightforward. We found a formula and proved that everybody you see might be using cocaine. Now it gets tricky.

Probability is not wired correctly into the human brain. After 2,000 years of study, back to the time of Aristotle, top mathematicians still don't agree on exactly what probability means or how it should be interpreted. There are three major interpretations of probability.

Classical Probability

In classical probability, there are a certain number of outcomes, each of which is equally likely. The probability of an event is the number of favorable outcomes divided by the number of possible outcomes. A fair die has six total sides, of which three are even. The probability of rolling an even number is $3/6 = 50\%$. This is a problem that is easily handled in classical probability.

While most of mathematics was developed with the classical view holding sway, it has some significant limitations. First, in our example we specified a fair die. But this is a circular definition; how do you know what a fair die is if you haven't defined probability? Classical probability also has no way to handle an infinite number of possible outcomes, which is a big limitation. Much of what we care about, such as the location of stars in the Milky Way to the results of a never-ending series of coin tosses, requires an infinite number of choices.

Frequentist Probability

Frequentist theory states that the probability of an event is its relative frequency over many trials. If I repeatedly roll a die and half of the rolls are even, Frequentism says that the probability of rolling an even number is 50%. Two major problems of classical theory are thus solved: we don't have to assume a fair die, and it works even if we imagine a theoretical infinite-sided die.[7] However, because the Frequentist interpretation of probability is based on the frequency of events, it is susceptible to misuse.

Reliance purely on frequency severely limits its use when the number of trials is very low. In Frequentist thinking, one trial is never enough to provide much information. This means that, in situations where repeated events are not possible, you are effectively prohibited from asking the question of how frequently they occur. This is a severe limitation to Frequentism; there are many probabilistic questions we'd like to answer outside of its scope.

For example, in the 1950s, air travel was growing, but there was very limited data on commercial airline accidents. How could insur-

---

7. Maybe I wouldn't throw as many 7s at the craps table with this one.

ance companies determine the probability of accidents in the future? So far as we know, a major earthquake has never hit New York City. What is the probability of a big tremor in the next 100 years? Just because events have been rare (or nonexistent) in the past does not mean that they will continue to not occur. There must be some way to gain some information about their likelihood.

Image 11 – Bayesians and Frequentists

Bayesian Probability

As we said earlier, Bayes Theorem is just a formula. However, there is an interpretation of probability that is consistent with, based on, and named after the Theorem. Bayesians say that probability means the degree of certainty, given a set of information.[8] The situation described in Image 11 provides a straightforward demonstration of the power of thinking like a Bayesian.

In this example, it is nighttime, so we have no direct evidence whether the sun has exploded. Our machine that can sense such an explosion and tell us if it has occurred. However, before it does so, it rolls two dice. If the result is a 12, an infrequent but not implausible event, the machine will lie to us, saying the opposite of what really happened. The question is, what is the probability that life on earth will end, given that the machine has told us the sun is no more.

We can apply Bayesian thinking to this question. If the sun is no more, the probability the machine says yes is 35/36, or 97.2%; the probability that it says yes, without any knowledge of what happened to the sun, is $1/36^{\text{th}}$, or about 2.8%. Now, the tough part: we need to guess the probability that the sun exploded, irrespective of the machine's answer. I have no real idea, but it is obviously a small number. Let's go with 0.000001%. We can now apply Bayes Theorem:

$$P(A|B) = \frac{P(B|A) * P(A)}{P(B)} = \frac{97.2\% * 0.00001\%}{2.8\%}$$
$$= 0.00035\%$$

This makes intuitive sense; it is far more likely that the machine lied than that the sun exploded.[9] We don't need to worry about the end of our species quite yet. Bayes has provided us an answer to a question that Frequentism wouldn't let us ask. We aren't certain about our answer; it was based on several assumptions where we

---

8. You'll see this called Bayesian analysis or Bayesian inference.
9. Citation: You are reading this.

were forced to just guess. But we deal with this type of uncertainty constantly in our lives. An imperfect answer is far better than none at all, especially if we are honest with ourselves about the uncertainty.

This example also shows a drawback of Bayesian logic: Where did we come up with the initial probability that the sun exploded? I made it up with no insight other than assuming it was unlikely. A wide range of values would be equally reasonable. Despite being completely made up, this guess greatly affected the result. Bayesian analysis always requires making such assumptions, which are called **Bayesian priors**. They are a problem with Bayesian probability, because priors will almost always involve some level of subjectivity. Aversion of mathematicians to this subjectivity is a major reason why Bayes Theorem sat, ignored and maligned, for nearly 200 years after its formulator's death.

For two groups of people who disagree only about the details of a subtle mathematical philosophy, Frequentists and Bayesians have an ongoing, contentious debate over who is right. I think that some of this is really a proxy battle between mathematicians and hard scientists. Hard scientists tend to prefer the Frequentist approach. They design an experiment and run it many times. If it comes out as expected, they write a paper and get published. If it doesn't, they go back to the drawing board. One can see how this system would look down on the notion of priors; how can you decide what's going to happen *before* you've done any experiments?

Mathematicians, on the other hand, dislike the certainty that comes from the Frequentist approach. They view it as falsely ignoring the uncertainty inherent in the universe. Our example of incorrect results in drug testing was based on pure mathematics, not Bayesian Theory. This is a real problem in real life, and the best we could do is a highly uncertain result. Science abounds with sightings of false positives which were then treated as great breakthroughs. Bayesians agree that priors are annoying, but they also find them useful. Before starting an experiment, you need to think about how the system works and consider what answer makes sense.[10]

---

10. This is a vast oversimplification and overgeneralization of the debate. Frequentists and Bayesians don't need to be from separate disciplines in order to fight.

It won't surprise you when I say that, in my opinion, both Frequentist and Bayesian Theories have uses and misuses. But I find that Bayes is far deeper and provides longer-reaching insight. At its broadest level, thinking like Bayes is an attempt to answer the question of what we know—or, more specifically, what we learn.

HOW CAN I USE BAYESIAN STATISTICS IN MY EVERYDAY LIFE?

As I discussed in the Introduction, I try to use Bayesian principles whenever I incorporate new information into my worldview. Which is to say, almost always. There are several ways that Bayesian logic is useful in this process.

Understanding degrees of certainty

A basic precept of Bayesian thinking is that it is never possible to achieve perfect certainty. New information should always affect your thinking about what is and is not true. With Bayes Theorem, probability can never reach 100% unless one of the inputs itself is 100%. Alternatively, if any prior is ever taken to be 100% certain, no new Bayesian information can change this belief. Thus, having certainty will lead you to predict certainty for things which are not true. Therefore, beliefs are especially dangerous in a Bayesian world. Certainty on a topic, in the absence of evidence, can lead to incorrect certainty on other topics.

Considering new pieces of information

How important is a piece of information? According to Bayes, information is important to the extent that we learn from it. If you are fairly certain (say 99%) that it is raining outside, and then see that everybody outside is carrying an umbrella, your posterior probability will not change significantly due to this new information. This means that you didn't learn much, so the information wasn't very

---

There is plenty of internal infighting in both groups as to the precise nature and proper applications of their preferred flavor of probability.

important. On the other hand, if you thought it was sunny, seeing umbrellas will drastically change what you know. With a different prior, the same information is now far more important.

Acting without complete information

Because we can never be truly certain, Bayesians know that they must act in the face of uncertainty. Criminal juries are asked to decide beyond a *reasonable* doubt, rather than beyond *any* doubt. This is consistent with Bayes. We have taken many measurements that show the Earth getting warmer as carbon dioxide levels increase. We are also fairly certain that this is happening because of the actions of our species. Bayes tells us that we should act now, even though we are not certain. Perhaps we can't state with certainty that the Affordable Care Act reduced the population of uninsured Americans. But the evidence for this statement is strong; we should act as if it were true, absent new, contradictory evidence.

Perhaps the best-known application of Bayesian inference is regarding gambling.[11] Let's consider a basketball game and a single wager. Say that the odds on the game imply that Team A has a 75% chance to win and Team B a 25% chance. If you bet on Team A, you risk losing $75 to win $25; if on Team B, you risk $25 to win $75. If the information you have leads to probabilities agreeing with these odds, you have no expectation to win a bet:

$$P(A\ Win) * Win(A) + P(A\ Lose) * Lose(A) =$$

$$75\% * \$25 + 25\% * (-\$75) = \$0$$

However, if you suddenly get better information, telling you that Team A has an 85% chance to win, you could now place a bet with positive expected value:

---

11. Or trading, which isn't so different.

$$P(A\ Win) * Win(A) + P(A\ Lose) * Lose(A) =$$

$$85\% * \$25 + 15\% * (-\$75) = \$10$$

What this shows us is that when gambling, you can expect to profit only if you have better information than other people. You should place a bet only if your information results in probabilities that are different from those of others. Which brings us back to Bayes: to win at sports gambling (or in the markets) we must be able to determine the difference between important and unimportant information.

Why did we go on a long digression about an obscure 18th-century Englishman? What is the relevance to a book allegedly focused on systematic methods of considering government policy and related historical topics? As I have said, it is impossible to properly understand what I've written—impossible to understand me—without knowing my mindset. That mindset is many things, but it is certainly Bayesian.

Bayesian thinking can be applied to many everyday problems. Thinking in terms of probabilities, rather than certainties. Incorporating new information, even when it doesn't fit your prior view. Realizing when information has become clear enough to lead to a conclusion or action. Then challenging that conclusion when new information points the other way!

A famous quote tells us, "if the human brain were simple enough that we could understand it, we would be so simple that we couldn't."[12] At least so far, it has proven true; at a core level we have a limited understanding of how millions of neurons, synapses, and chemicals can create logical thought via the passing of electrical charges. However, it appears that our brains are Bayesian. When you

---

12. This is one of those quotes that's been around a while, and nobody seems sure who was first to devise it.

see a new, round object, you assign a probability that it is a baseball, a dinner plate or the moon. More information causes you to revise these probabilities; the moon doesn't fit comfortably in your hand and a dinner plate doesn't feel like rawhide. Instantaneously, and with only a few pieces of information, you become mostly, but never completely, certain as to the object's nature. You act accordingly. This may be why you didn't need to actually use Bayes Theorem to know that the sun will rise tomorrow. Existing information in your possession created a prior of exceptionally high certainty.

What I continually learn from Bayes is this importance of information. Success in many endeavors is directly related to the quality of information possessed. Good information must be sought out, because it isn't always readily available. This good information will help you both to re-weight the probabilities of various hypotheses under consideration as well as guide you to further useful knowledge. You then keep updating your priors and act accordingly.

HEALTH INSURANCE, PART IV
REPEAL AND REPLACE? WITH WHAT?

*"If we're just going to replace Obamacare with Obamacare-lite,
then it begs the question, 'Were we just against Obamacare
because it was proposed by Democrats?'"*
—Congressman Raul Labrador, R-ID

Republicans do not like Obamacare.

They are quick to point out faults in the law, real or imagined. It doesn't cover enough people. It forces people to have coverage. It requires people to pay too much out of pocket. It covers unnecessary benefits. It is a vast increase in government spending. Doctors hate it. Insurance companies are fleeing. It's a giveaway to the insurance companies, or the drug companies, or the trial lawyers, or the bureaucrats.

While the ACA has had problems—serious ones—in the years since it passed, the Republican Party has not yet come up with a plausible alternative. After the 2016 election, they were no longer able to take symbolic repeal votes. The actual plans proposed failed to please their own senators, let alone the general public.

There are structural reasons why GOP attempts to "repeal and replace" are doomed to fail. Turns out, improving the health care system is more challenging than criticizing it.

- What are the different ways to repeal the ACA?
- What are the GOP proposals to replace the ACA?
- What has the Trump Administration done so far?

WHAT ARE THE DIFFERENT WAYS TO REPEAL THE ACA?

Virtually all Republicans agree on the goal of repealing the ACA. But they don't agree on exactly what repealing Obamacare means. Some Republicans admit that some portions of the ACA are working. Especially in the Senate, some hear their constituents' concerns about repealing Medicaid expansion. Some understand limitations resulting from the rules of Congress. While the details are critical, there are four basic pathways by which the ACA could theoretically be repealed.

1. Actually Repeal Obamacare

Many Republicans are on the record saying the ACA should be repealed "root and branch," and nothing should be kept.[1] We know what a full repeal means; "Health Insurance Part III" explored the effects of the ACA. Repealing it would just reverse these effects.

Around 20 million people would lose insurance, split evenly between those receiving expanded Medicaid and those buying their

---

1. For example, Mitch McConnell's said so at a debate for his most recent campaign.

own policies on- or off-exchange. The long-term federal debt level would increase. Medical bankruptcies would increase. Provider losses also would increase, as levels of uncompensated care reverted to pre-2010 levels. The Medicare trust fund would deplete sooner. On the other hand, healthy people would no longer have to pay a mandate penalty if they chose not to have insurance. However, if they later got sick, they would likely be out of luck.

Why would the GOP base its existence for a full seven years on a policy that is clearly destructive? Well, it bears noting that repealing Obamacare would give the highest earning 0.1% of households an average annual tax cut of $197,000. The 400 households in America with the highest incomes would get an average annual tax cut of $7,000,000 each.

2. Repeal Obamacare, but keep the popular parts

Republicans have had trouble when challenged about parts of the ACA that the public clearly likes. Specifically, there is strong support to maintain protections for pre-existing medical conditions and to permit dependents to remain on their parents' plans up to age 26. The GOP could repeal everything else: end individual and employer mandates, eliminate the essential health benefits, shut down the health insurance exchanges, and cut the subsidies given to those who purchase insurance.

In "Health Insurance, Part I", we talked about states which, pre-ACA, had guaranteed issue provisions without the two other legs of the health care stool. They entered death spirals. The Urban Institute conducted an analysis of the so-called partial repeal and determined that nearly 30 million additional people would be uninsured by 2019. In other words, everybody who got insurance through the ACA would lose it, as well as ten million who were covered before the Act took effect.

In my opinion, this 30 million is a conservative estimate. A system where the non-group insurance markets are experiencing nationwide death spirals will strain the entire market. People will create small businesses just to access the group insurance market. This creates a selection bias, because those that join such groups be those requiring more health care. This may cause a death spiral in the small group market, putting the insurance of 17 million more people at risk. We can go even further: consider the effect on the large-group market, which covers 100 million people. People with pre-existing conditions would seek employment with companies offering health benefits, as it would be their only way to get insurance. Adverse selection could destabilize even the large employer market.

Partial repeal has one advantage over full repeal: it could probably happen without the support of any Democrats.[2] A bill doing just this passed Congress in 2016, before being vetoed by President Obama. No Democrats voted for it, and none will vote for it without a real replacement plan that maintains coverage and premium levels. No version of Trumpcare so far has done much for those that would lose coverage.

But, this partial repeal would allow roughly the same tax cuts as a complete repeal.

3. Repeal Obamacare, but leave the Medicaid expansion

At least 11 million people have gained health coverage due to the ACA's Medicaid expansion provision. Each state decides whether or not to take part in Medicaid expansion. Despite the federal government picking up 100% of the cost until 2020 and 90% beyond that point, 19 states chose not to expand their programs.

That leaves 31 states and the District of Columbia which expanded their Medicaid program. At the time of this publication, those states have 20 Republican senators. Given 48 Democratic votes in the Senate, just three of these senators could block the repeal of Medicaid expansion. At this point, it seems very likely that at least three would.[3]

---

2. Specifically, via reconciliation, which is the only way to move legislation through the Senate with only 51 votes.

3. There are some other state-specific concerns that have reared their heads in the Senate. For example, health care costs are very high in Alaska. Among other reasons, this is due to its vast size and difficulty of transportation (ambulances are less expensive than Medevac helicopters). Obamacare is especially helpful to states with higher health costs because its subsidies are based on health plans available locally. Any replace plan that cuts the link between subsidies and local cost of care will devastate the ability of Alaskans to get health coverage.

Retaining Medicaid expansion would reduce the number of newly uninsured by 11 million, as compared to full repeal. In addition, if a repeal bill that left Medicaid expansion intact passed, some of the additional 19 GOP-led states might choose to expand their programs. Several of these states were moving toward expansion until the 2016 election changed the playing field.

Retaining Medicaid expansion could occur in tandem with either of the above repeal scenarios. Because it is a separate risk pool, retaining Medicaid expansion would have little effect on the non-group health insurance market. Therefore, the results of retaining Medicaid expansion would be similar to previous options, but with the 11 million continuing to be covered by Medicaid. However, keeping Medicaid expansion would require funding.[4] Consequently, there could be some tax cuts, but the amount would be significantly less. These scenarios are summarized in Figure 9.

	Medicaid	Non-Group (Subsidized)	Non-Group (Unsubsidized)	Under 25	Small Group	Large Group	Total
Current Policy	0	0	0	0	0	0	0
Full Repeal	11	10	5	2	0	0	28
Partial Repeal	11	10	9	0	8	15	53
Full, keep Medicaid	-1	10	5	2	0	0	16
Partial, keep Medicaid	-1	10	9	0	8	15	41

Figure 9: Uninsured by repeal scenario (millions)".

---

4. It could theoretically be unfunded, but this would require Democratic votes. Again, this is due to the complexities of Senate rules.

WHAT ARE THE PROPOSALS TO REPLACE THE ACA?

Republicans have many, many ideas to replace the ACA. That's one of their problems—there are so many ideas that they can't all be part of a single, consistent plan.

Health insurance is complex. If two changes are made to the market, they will interact, possibly in a highly destabilizing manner. Keeping this in mind, we're going to go through some of the provisions frequently proposed by Republican leaders and consider the effect each would have on the overall market for health insurance.

1. *Guaranteed issue for continuous coverage*

Just because the individual mandate is an anathema to Republicans doesn't mean that they completely ignore the concept of adverse selection. One of their ideas to address it is to say that insurance companies could not deny coverage to an applicant who had maintained insurance coverage for the previous 18 months. This provision is called **continuous coverage**. It was included in the Empowering Patients First Act (EPFA) proposed by Tom Price before he became Secretary of Health and Human Services. In theory, currently healthy people would buy insurance out of fear that they would be denied coverage when they later got sick. This improves the risk pool.

As far as I know, a continuous coverage provision has never been tried.[5] Therefore, we don't know if it would be as effective as an individual mandate. My opinion is that it is likely to be significantly less effective. In a mandate-based system, people have a clear choice: get insured or pay a penalty. A continuous coverage provision relies on individual consumers understanding a complex, long-term incentive structure. To make rational decisions in a world with continuous coverage, people must weigh the risk of future illness against the cost of buying insurance today. Buying health insurance on the individual insurance market is challenging already. Making these decisions even more challenging is cruel.

---

5. If you have an example, please let me know.

Even if individuals can understand the trade-offs and decide whether they want to buy health insurance, a successful continuous coverage-based plan must have two other components. First, there needs to be a definition of the plans that count as coverage. If skimpy plans count towards continuous coverage, healthy people would game the system, buying cheap coverage until they were sick. This would harm the risk pool for comprehensive plans. Second, because significant portions of the population cannot afford the full cost of health insurance, subsidies would still be required. If people are literally unable to afford insurance, continuous coverage won't bring them into the system. There is no reason to think that moving from an individual mandate to continuous coverage would require less subsidy money to encourage people to purchase insurance.[6]

2. Reduce/eliminate minimum benefits

Another common feature in Republican replace plans is allowing non-comprehensive plans to be sold in the health insurance market. They think that people should only have to pay for only the benefits they want. Allowing this would indeed lower the cost of health insurance. Sounds great, but as you may have guessed, it is not so simple.

Without defined minimum benefit packages, it is impossible to enforce an individual mandate.[7] If you could sell a loaf of bread and call it health insurance, then people would buy the bread, switching to real insurance only when they get sick. The mandate therefore falls apart, and with it the entire system. We can debate endlessly which benefits should be deemed essential, but the list included in the ACA seems pretty reasonable:

- Ambulatory care (i.e., hospital care where the patient isn't admitted)
- Emergency services
- Hospitalization
- Pregnancy, maternity, and newborn care
- Mental health and substance abuse services

---

6. Unless it led to significantly fewer people having health insurance.
7. Or continuous coverage.

- Prescription drugs
- Rehabilitative services
- Laboratory services
- Preventative care
- Pediatric services, including dental and vision care[8]

Do we really want to allow health insurance to be sold that doesn't cover hospitalization? It might be cheap, but a person with such insurance is not really covered.

Other GOP proposals would permit annual and lifetime benefit caps, which were common before the ACA. While this could again lower premiums, plans with caps don't protect against catastrophic medical needs.[9] That being said, helping insurance companies with a few extremely expensive policyholders would lower the cost of insurance. But the way to do this is via a reinsurance program. Alaska has established one, and it has worked well, reducing premiums without noticeable adverse effects.

3. Decrease premium subsidies

Most GOP replacement plans reduce the subsidies compared to those in the ACA. In the EPFA, for example, subsidies would be determined by age rather than income. The new subsidy amounts would be $1,200 per year for people 18 to 35 years old, increasing to $3,000 per year for people over 51. The average silver-level plan purchased today has premiums ranging from $3,700 per year (age 30) up to $8,900 per year (age 60). Clearly, with the EPFA's subsidy levels, health insurance will be completely unaffordable to many households. Figure 10 shows the change in subsidies between Obamacare and the EPFA, for varying ages and levels of income:

---

8. Adult dental and vision care are not required benefits and are generally sold separately.
9. If you don't know somebody who reached their cap in the pre-ACA era, ask around. Their story will horrify you. The CBO properly treats people with such non-comprehensive plans as not being covered at all.

Current Subsidy   FPL=*Federal Poverty Level*

Age	100% FPL	200% FPL	300% FPL	400% FPL+
25	$3,156	$1,836	$0	$0
35	$3,888	$2,580	$648	$0
45	$4,644	$3,324	$1,402	$0
55	$7,308	$5,988	$4,068	$0

EFPA Subsidy

Age	100% FPL	200% FPL	300% FPL	400% FPL+
25	$1,200	$1,200	$1,200	$1,200
35	$1,200	$1,200	$1,200	$1,200
45	$2,100	$2,100	$2,100	$2,100
55	$3,000	$3,000	$3,000	$3,000

Change in Subsidy

Age	100% FPL	200% FPL	300% FPL	400% FPL+
25	-$1,956	-$636	$1,200	$1,200
35	-$2,688	-$1,380	$552	$1,200
45	-$2,544	-$1,224	$698	$2,100
55	-$4,308	-$2,988	-$1,068	$3,000

Figure 10: Subsidy changes under the EPFA

As we can see, in this GOP plan, poor people will pay more while the wealthy get a tax cut. I'm not shocked.

4. Selling insurance across state lines

All insurance is regulated by the states. Whether they protect your auto, life, home or health, policies are sold on a by-state basis. Republicans have a theory that allowing multi-state health plans would increase competition, lowering premiums. It might, especially for smaller states which lack economy of scale.

This is the thing, though—Obamacare already includes provisions to encourage precisely this. Some states have tried, but none have succeeded because insurance companies have not been interested in participating. If your insurance company has a network of doctors based in Idaho, it is hard to sell to consumers in Florida.[10]

Currently, in order to sell policies across state lines, each state must approve the plan. The GOP idea is to go further, forcing states to allow any policies to be sold within their borders. This is an odd idea coming from a party claiming to be opposed to federal mandates. Your state would lose control, and there would be a race to the bottom in terms of policy protections.[11] Unfortunately for the GOP, I have even worse news. Georgia already passed a bill to unilaterally permit allow the sale of health insurance policies approved by any state. In five years, not a single insurance company has participated.[12]

Creating inter-state markets is unlikely to harm the insurance market. But there is also no reason to think they would help. Death spirals can happen just as easily in a larger pool. It may be a solution worth trying, but there is no reason to repeal the ACA to do so. The machinery to erase the state lines is already in there.

5. Create high-risk pools

Another frequent GOP proposal is to create high-risk pools. The concept of these pools is simple. Rules enforcing guaranteed issue would be eliminated, allowing insurance companies to screen out applicants with high health costs. Healthy people would pay less for

---

10. And expensive to create a new network in Florida.
11. Most credit cards are issued out of Delaware. This is because Delaware has weak usury laws, allowing credit cards companies to charge any interest rate they want. When states were forced to allow out-of-state cards, banks relocated to Delaware, and interest rates for consumers skyrocketed. The GOP wants to do something similar for health insurance.
12. The Georgia State Insurance Commissioner is "dumbfounded." Apparently, he knows less about health insurance than you will after reading this.

their insurance. Those who couldn't get insurance elsewhere would buy through a government-run program designed just for them.[13]

It's easy to see the problem: the people in the high-risk pool will be incredibly expensive to insure. They will need to be massively subsidized. The only source for these subsidies is the government. The result is that insurance companies make money by cherry-picking healthy clients, and tax money pays for those with chronic conditions. The latter are always at risk of politicians cutting the risk-pool subsidies, which are literally critical to their survival. There is no reason to think that splitting people into two groups will decrease costs overall.[14]

Before the ACA, 34 states had high-risk pools. They did not work well. Most had exclusion periods, forcing those who suddenly become sick to wait for their chemotherapy or brain surgery. Premiums were more than double the rates in the regular market and covered only a portion of the total cost of care. State-based subsidies for the pools were limited, meaning only a small portion of their residents could be covered. The result was waiting periods for high-risk pools that exceeded the expected lifespans of many of their applicants.

A fully funded system of high-risk pools could theoretically be stable. However, recent GOP plans have proposed funding for them of less than $2.5 billion per year. Estimates of their actual cost are around $100 billion per year. I hope you aren't relying on a high-risk pool when you get sick.

6. Medicaid block grants

Going back to "Health Insurance Part I," recall that Medicaid is a federal-state partnership. If a state agrees to provide certain medical services to poorer residents, the federal government picks up a lot of the cost. Currently, Medicaid is uncapped; if a state provides services, Washington will pick up its share of its costs, no matter how high. Many Republican plans involve changing this cost sharing to

---

13. Recall that about 27% of the adult population under 65 has a pre-existing condition.

14. I find reliance on high-risk pools to be especially odd coming from a party worrying about government takeover of the health system. Replacing the exchanges with high-risk pools would increase the number of people covered by government health plans.

be a fixed payment for each state. They could do what they wished with the money. The theory is that states would be more efficient once they are on the hook for cost overruns. The amount of the block grants would be significantly less than what states currently receive.

It is true that, in the current system, states are not incentivized to maximize Medicaid efficiency. Despite this, Medicaid insures patients for significantly less than private insurers. Given their already superior cost control, it is unlikely that states will be able to find significant additional savings. More likely, they would respond by covering fewer people or by providing fewer benefits for those that are covered. Either way, block grants would increase the ranks of the uninsured working poor.

There are many more replace ideas out there,[15] but a pattern has clearly emerged. No Republican plan will cover a significant number of those who would lose care if the ACA were repealed. Some of their plans would cause even more people to lose coverage than in a simple repeal. The upper middle class may get more subsidies and the ultra-wealthy get massive tax breaks.

WHAT HAS THE TRUMP ADMINISTRATION DONE SO FAR?

We will keep this short; despite promises to the contrary, Obamacare was not repealed on day one of the Trump administration. At the time of this publication, Republicans have failed to enact any reforms to the health insurance system. Most of their plans have centered on restructuring Medicaid, in ways that have little to do with the ACA. One could be forgiven for believing that their prime goal was to either cut taxes, or to hurt the young, old, disabled, and working poor, 75 million of whom rely on Medicaid. But after seven years of castigating Obamacare's effects on the non-group market, they have come up with precisely nothing to help this segment.

---

15. For example, I didn't get to HSAs, tax deductions vs. tax credits, malpractice reform, or various other goodies. Trust me that none of them address the core issues of how to pay for universal care.

It is very difficult to know where the debate will go from here. On alternating days, Trump and the Congressional GOP go back and forth: work to improve the system or, by destabilizing it, fulfill their campaign promises. Uncertainty was only increased when Tom Price, former secretary of Health and Human Services, got himself fired for taking private planes to travel distances that you and I would usually walk. Although, Price's departure may have had less to do with his profligate travel that his failure to repeal Obamacare.[16]

The executive branch can do a lot to weaken our health insurance system without any legislation. So far, the most concrete action on health insurance regulation was the release of two early executive orders. While both were vague, the uncertainty caused insurers to hesitate about participating in the exchanges in 2018.[17] There were also severe cuts to marketing and facilitation budgets for the ACA, just as enrollment for 2018 was about to begin. Under President Obama, there was a big, behind-the-scenes effort to encourage insurance companies to participate in the exchanges. Now, the Administration hardly hides its glee whenever an insurer decides to depart or to raise rates. They are openly rooting for our health system to collapse, and this attitude matters to insurance companies when they are making difficult business decisions. There was significant progress in the Senate on a short-term bipartisan plan to stabilize the system; but the GOP refused to allow a vote on this legislation.[18] How could they, as they have been screaming for years that Obamacare can't be fixed.

---

16. The entire Cabinet thinks little of spending taxpayer money on travel, security, and other questionable perks. To date, only Price has paid the price of dismissal.

17. After the failure of legislative Trumpcare, the administration took two further, significant actions. Both intentionally destabilize the non-group health insurance market. First, Trump instructed his departments to consider rules to allow association plans and short-term plans, either of which would worsen risk pools for comprehensive insurance. Then, he unilaterally ended cost-sharing reduction subsidies. While these may be reinstated by the courts, and states have found workarounds in case they are not, the major insurers have noted that capricious and unilateral actions discourage the kind of public-private partnership necessary for a healthy insurance market in this country. Trump's motivation here is unclear. He seems to think that destroying the health care system will give him leverage in ensuing negotiations.

18. Instead, they repealed the individual mandate. We'll soon see exactly how critical this provision was to the three-legged stool.

—§—

What does this mean for the future? Well, here's what we know:

- Republicans have promised their base a repeal of Obamacare. However, they don't have enough votes to do so.
- Republicans have not agreed internally on any plan to replace Obamacare.
- Trump has promised that nobody will lose coverage. He has also promised that everybody will be covered.
- Democrats will not vote for ACA repeal.
- Polling consistently shows the ACA is gaining popularity and that there is strong opposition to repeal.
- The GOP has done everything possible to expose their plans to as little scrutiny as possible, knowing they will be unpopular.

Based on these assumptions, my best guess is that Republicans will continue the strategy that I call "Undermine and Blame." Others call it "Repeal and Delay," but my title is more descriptive. Congress and the Administration are taking small actions to destabilize the exchanges. The markets are already shaky; it won't be very difficult to kill them by neglect. As the uninsured population increases, they will blame the ACA, rather than the GOP's intentional efforts to destabilize it. I don't know what happens then and I don't think that they know either. What I do know is that people have been and will be hurt by these actions.

If you are watching the legislative debate, focus on what happens to the ACA's taxes. Bending the health care cost curve is important, but this will take years or decades to lower premiums without degrading care. In the meantime, there is no way to get people health insurance without money. And without the ACA's tax increases, there isn't any money. As we saw, this will cause at least 20 million people will lose their coverage. But if the taxes stay, those 400 families will miss out on their $7,000,000 tax cuts.

FISCAL POLICY, PART I
TAXES
WHERE DOES IT COME FROM?

"There's one for you, nineteen for me."
—*The Beatles*

The U.S. government does everything on a massive scale. The rest of the world shares eight aircraft carriers. The U.S. has ten. Eisenhower wanted highways like the ones he saw in Germany. So we built 47,856 miles of Interstates. The federal government spends close to $1.1 trillion per year just on health care. That's more than the gross domestic product of Mexico.

But the federal government is nearly as good at collecting money as it is at spending it. To pay for all these goodies, it needs to collect $3.6 trillion in taxes every year. That's $10 billion per day, seven days a week, 365 days a year. The collection of this money greatly affects everything we do: how people work, invest, and live.

- What is the difference between the deficit and the debt?
- What are some principles of good tax policy?
- How does the U.S. federal government raise tax revenue?

"I'm taxes."

WHAT IS THE DIFFERENCE BETWEEN THE DEFICIT AND THE DEBT?

Before we dive into the weeds, we need to get our terminology straight. It is a topic that is often misunderstood, so we have to start on the same page.

The deficit is the difference between money that the government takes in and what it spends. It is usually expressed as an annual number. If a government receives $3 trillion from taxes, fees, penalties, and so forth, while spending $4 trillion on Social Security, aircraft carriers, trips to Mar-a-Lago, and the like, then the deficit for that year is $1 trillion.[1] They need to come up with that money from somewhere. The best bet is to borrow it.[2]

The federal (or, more commonly, national) debt is the total amount of all the debt backed by the U.S. government outstanding at a point in time. If the Treasury sells $50 billion of four-week Trea-

---

1. The convention is to express deficits as a positive number. If a government takes in more than it spends, this is called a surplus.
2. Or, sometimes, to print it. But that creates inflation, so governments tend to avoid it if they can.

sury bills, the debt increases by $50 billion. When they are paid back in four weeks, the debt will decrease by the same amount.

A good way to remember the difference is that the debt is a snapshot, taken at a specific time, while the deficit is the summary of activity over a period. We can compare them to a company's financial statements. The debt is equivalent to liabilities on a company's balance sheet; the deficit is similar to net income. Roughly speaking, the debt today is equal to the debt of one year ago, plus the deficit over the intervening year.[3]

To demonstrate the confusion, I've heard many times—even from reputable sources—that "President Obama increased the deficit." This is false. When he took office, the deficit was $1,413 billion. The fiscal year 2017 budget, the final one for which Obama was responsible, projected a deficit of $504 billion.[4] So he decreased the deficit by around two-thirds. However, because there were deficits during time, it is true that the debt increased under President Obama. We see this in Figure 11.

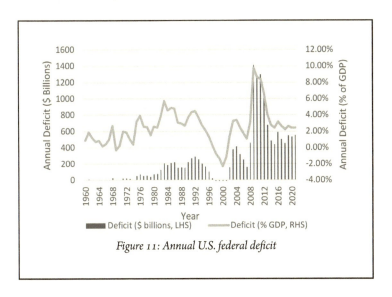

Figure 11: Annual U.S. federal deficit

---

3. There are various technical reasons why this doesn't add up exactly.
4. The amount of deficit reduction during President Obama's tenure is an oft-argued point. Some will compare the deficit at the end of his two terms to 2007, before the recession worsened the fiscal situation. Using this time frame, it did increase slightly. Of course, a global financial crisis did happen in between, and its fiscal effects outlasted our return to economic growth.

To get a little more technical, the national debt has two components:

1. **Debt held by the public:** all the debt owned by people, corporations, foreign governments, and the Federal Reserve System. This debt totals around $14.5 trillion.
2. **Intra-governmental debt:** debt held by other federal accounts. Most of this is in the trust funds for Social Security and Medicare. This debt is an additional $5 trillion.

When you talk about the debt, should you talk about the total debt or the public debt? Well, it depends on the question you are trying to answer.[5] If you view the Social Security and Medicare as being economically separate from the rest of government (which is accurate legally), then their trust funds are holders of the debt like any other entity; you should speak about the gross level. If you view them as being inextricably intertwined with the rest of the country (which is usually how we think of them), then you can more easily ignore the intra-governmental portion of the debt.

WHAT ARE SOME PRINCIPLES OF GOOD TAX POLICY?

Before getting into the details of how we *do* raise tax money, let's discuss the theory, both economic and philosophical, of how we *should* raise tax money.

There are three generally agreed principles of tax policy: efficiency, simplicity, and equity. All other principles should flow from these three. In order to get closer to direct application, it makes sense to create more specific goals. I think the following is a worthy list, given in my rough order of importance:

1. Progressivity: The wealthy should pay a higher percentage of their income in taxes. It sounds controversial, but the math makes it necessary.
2. Straightforward: All else being equal, minimizing the difficulty of tax compliance is a worthy goal.

---

5. And, all too frequently, your political views.

3. Good Incentives: People follow the incentives they are given. Citizens will attempt to pay as little tax as possible. Taxing actions that harm society and rewarding those that help is a valid use of the tax code.
4. Diversification: When different methods of taxation are used, the chances of a certain group being taxed unfairly decrease.
5. Countercyclical: We raise more tax revenue in good economic times and less in bad. This will help to counter said economic cycles, automatically stabilizing the economy.
6. Go where the money is: We can't take money from where there isn't any to be taken. The United States currently has no wealth tax, but other countries do,[6] and they are effective revenue raisers.

Others list different principles, but I think this is a good set. Of course, in practice we follow principles like these in the same way nuts are found by a blind squirrel: only dumb luck.

HOW DOES THE U.S. FEDERAL GOVERNMENT RAISE TAX REVENUE?

Now that we've been through the basics, it's time to get into the details of how the U.S. government takes all that money out of your pocket. In fiscal year 2016, the most recent completed at the time of publication, total federal tax revenue was $3.27 trillion.

Personal income taxes: $1.5 trillion

This is the biggest source of government revenues, representing 47% of federal receipts. Because of their size and prevalence, personal income taxes get the most attention in the press. There are two basic classes of personal income tax: ordinary income and capital gains.

Ordinary income is exactly what it sounds like: money received for labor you personally perform, including wages, tips, and bonus-

---

6. For example, France. The United States has an estate tax, which is similar, but it affects a tiny number of estates and can be largely avoided by planning ahead.

es. Earnings from a sole proprietorship, as well as items like royalties, interest, and rental income, are also treated as ordinary income.

Capital gains are profits realized from selling assets, like stocks or bonds. In the United States, any profits from selling an asset that was held for more than a year before being sold are treated as long-term gains and taxed at a lower rate. This is intended to encourage investing over speculating, although in practice it is used for many other purposes. Attempts to reclassify ordinary income as long-term capital gains is a significant reason why tax compliance is complex.

Ordinary income tax rates are highly progressive. The first dollar of taxable income faces a rate of 10%; above $441,000 of income, the marginal rate is 39.6%.[7] They are also countercyclical; when national income slows during in a recession, income tax receipts slow faster.

For reasons good and bad, individuals have various methods to reduce the amount of their income subject to taxation. The reason for these allowances, in theory, is to create incentives for behavior deemed societally beneficial. For example, if a society wanted to encourage individuals to save money, it could create tax-advantaged investment accounts.[8] People who invest via these vehicles will pay different (lower) tax rates for the same activity, just due to the legal structure in which they are held. Deviations like this, where some income faces lower rates of taxation than a baseline, are called tax expenditures.[9] Offering tax expenditures is expensive for the government. The most expensive categories of tax expenditures for the U.S. government are:

---

7. Figures are for those filing as head of household. Other types of filers have different brackets.

8. Which, of course, the United States has done with 401ks, IRAs, and several other vehicles. Unfortunately, having citizens save more is not necessarily good for a nation's economy. One of the reasons that Japan has had weak economic growth for two decades is its high savings rate.

9. I didn't know the difference between a deduction and a tax expenditure, so I asked Todd Wilkinson, an attorney in the Tax Practice at Jones Day. He told me: *"What is a deduction to taxpayers is a tax expenditure to the government. A deduction costs something in terms of the tax revenue that would otherwise have been collected by the government. Rather than an outright spend, the government just collects less tax. Deductions are not the only tax expenditures. Tax credits, favored tax rates, and allowing a delay in the recognition of income are also tax expenditures. A tax expenditure is easier to achieve politically than a direct spend by the government, both procedurally under the rules of Congress and usually in how it appears to voters."*

Tax Expenditure	Billions, 2016
Exclusion of employer contributions for medical insurance and medical care	216.1
Capital gains	93.0
Exclusion of net imputed rental income	82.4
Mortgage interest expense	75.3
Defined contribution employer plans	73.9
Deferral of income from foreign controlled corporations	67.8
Step-up of capital gains basis at death	66.7
Earned income tax credit	63.8
Deductibility of non-business state and local taxes	51.2
Deductibility of charitable contributions	47.4
Defined benefit employer plans	46.3
Child credit	46.3
Refundable premium assistance tax credit[10]	42.7

Table 2: Largest U.S. tax expenditures

Tax expenditures often create unintended incentives. The ability to deduct mortgage interest is intended to increase home ownership, a valid societal goal. However, it also encourages homeowners to borrow more than they otherwise would. Deductions for state and local taxes are intended to avoid double taxation and encourage states to adopt progressive tax schemes. But they can also discourage local government efficiency, as the federal government pays some of the cost. Economists tend to oppose almost all tax expenditures. There is good evidence that economic growth is maximized if a society has lower tax rates with fewer exclusions.[11] When politicians talk about

---

10. Also known as Obamacare subsidies.
11. There are myriad exceptions to economists' oppositions to tax deductions. For example, some deductions are required in order to properly measure income.

tax reform this is what they mean: lower rates and eliminate deductions. Unfortunately, most tax deductions are popular and have committed constituencies. For instance, the rationale for the charitable contribution deduction is especially dubious. Why should you pay more tax in order to support other peoples' charities? But the forces protecting this deduction are organized, strident, and committed.

Another goal you hear frequently is to "simplify the tax code." Tax compliance is not simple; if we could lessen this burden without unfortunate side effects, it would be a good thing. I hinted before at a humble suggestion. An enormous amount of the effort toward tax compliance is expended to structure income so that it is treated as capital gains rather than ordinary income. Taxing them both at the same rate would eliminate the need for this structuring. This would eliminate the time and cost of completing said structuring. I know the arguments against this: in theory it would discourage investment.[12] But I don't see any valid economic reason to discourage work (i.e., ordinary income) more than investment. If the income tax is meant to tax the accretion of wealth, one dollar of capital gain is the same as a dollar of ordinary income. As we saw in Table 2, this would raise around $93 billion per year, and make our tax code significantly more progressive.[13] If you liked, rates for the top ordinary income brackets could be reduced at the same time, make the change revenue neutral while still decreasing compliance costs.

Payroll taxes: $1.15 trillion

We covered Social Security at length in our dedicated chapter, so we won't belabor the details. Social insurance taxes are withheld from wages at given percentages. These withholdings are used to fund their related program directly: Social Security, disability insurance, Medicare, unemployment insurance, and a few smaller programs.

However, because these taxes are paid on the first dollar of income and are subject to a cap, they are regressive. Lower earners pay a higher percentage of their income in payroll taxes. There are some

---

12. Also, because investment income is generally increased by inflation, preferential capital gains rates can help to properly represent actual, as opposed to inflationary, gains in wealth.

13. The top 1%, 0.1% and 0.01% incomes earn an inordinate amount of capital gains.

good reasons why this is the case; for example, the benefits from these programs are also capped. However, when you hear on television that 40% of Americans pay no income tax, the person saying this is trying to intentionally mislead you. They are ignoring payroll taxes, which are the largest component of the tax bill for most households. Because of preferential rates on capital gains and caps on payroll taxes, federal taxes are actually not progressive at the highest levels of income. Warren Buffett was right—he likely pays a lower tax rate than his secretary.[14]

Corporate income taxes: $0.3 trillion

Corporate taxes in the United States are ridiculously complex.[15] Our fine nation has managed to create a system where we have one of the world's highest corporate tax rates without collecting very much corporate tax. We see this in Figure 12.

Country	Maximum Corporate Tax Rate	Corporate Taxes, % GDP
United States	38.9%	2.20%
France	30.9%	2.11%
Italy	29.7%	2.06%
Mexico	34.6%	3.28%
Germany	31.4%	1.74%
Canada	34.0%	3.13%
Spain	24.2%	2.42%
United Kingdom	30.0%	2.45%

14. The top 400 earners in the United States paid an average of 16.7% in income taxes in 2012. As a comparison, a married couple earning $75,000 per year with one allowance, living in New York City, with no other deductions, will pay federal taxes at a rate of around 20%. In addition, state and local taxes are usually regressive, especially sales taxes.

15. According to Manoj Viswanathan, Associate Professor of Law, University of California—Hastings: "Corporate income taxation is an exceedingly complex area of law, as evidenced by the fact that many tax lawyers charge upwards of $1,000 an hour to advise clients on the subject."

Figure 12: Corporate tax rates and collections for selected countries, 2015

Clearly, corporate taxes break a lot of our rules. They are not at all simple. They are as likely to reward bad behavior as to penalize it. The problems in our corporate tax code are so complex, and so slanted towards special interests and favored constituencies, that I can't even pretend to offer a way to improve the corporate tax system. Let's leave this one to the experts.

Ad valorem taxes: $0.17 trillion

"Ad valorem" means "according to the value." These are taxes that are charged when people use specific things. Think alcohol, tobacco, gasoline, airport usage, and customs. They are a small part of the total but help toward our goals of diversification and simplicity. They often align the cost of government-sponsored services with those that use them; only people who fly pay airport usage taxes, and this is clearly appropriate. Unfortunately, they tend to be regressive, like most consumption-based taxes.

Estate and gift taxes: $0.02 trillion

Tax money has to come from somewhere. If we don't collect it from the estates of the deceased ultra-wealthy, we'll have to collect it from somewhere else. Estates are exempted from paying any tax on the first $11.2 million of their value.[16] Above this, they are taxed up to a maximum rate of 40%. From a societal perspective, is it better to collect tax from multimillionaire deceased persons, or from middle-class families earning the national median income of $51,939 per year? The dead people literally won't miss the money.

The worst argument against the estate tax is that it is double taxation. This statement has at least two major snags. First, the estate tax is far from the only instance of double taxation. For example, sales

---

16. The amount exempt from estate taxes was roughly doubled by the recently passed Tax Cuts and Jobs Act. Note that inheritance by a spouse is tax-free, so a married couple can easily pass $22.5 million to their children without paying any tax. If some work is done in advance, the estate tax can be avoided on a much larger amount.

taxes are paid out of after-tax income. Second, just because an asset is in an estate does not mean that it has already been taxed. Capital gains taxes are paid only when an asset is sold. If an asset appreciates in value, is never sold, and ends up in the estate, then the estate tax would be the first tax applied. If the estate tax didn't exist, then these assets would never be taxed. And there are a lot of assets fitting this description in the largest estates.[17]

Federal Reserve deposits: $0.11 trillion

The nature of the Federal Reserve is a topic beyond the scope of this chapter. For now, let's just say that it is a series of banks that, among other activities, holds U.S. Treasury and mortgage-backed securities. When it earns income on these assets, it sends such income to the Treasury. It is a circular process—the Treasury pays interest to the Federal Reserve, who pays back the profits. But with a cool $4.5 trillion on the Fed's balance sheet, the income produced is nothing to sneeze at.

One point of note is that, at the federal level, there is no general tax on consumption. Of course, most states have sales taxes. While I'm not necessarily opposed to consumption taxes, they tend to be regressive. If we were going to move to a system that included more of them, we would need to engineer a system that would ensure that such taxes were not unduly punitive to paid to those of below-median income. Of course, doing so would limit the simplicity of a so-called value added tax, which is one of the benefits espoused by its proponents in the first place.

Let's make an unrealistic assumption: we are able to come to a basic agreement as to what the government should spend money on. Fixing roads? Yes. National Institutes of Health? Yes. NASA? Yes, but not as much as they want. A new superhighway, tunneling beneath Manhattan? No, too expensive.[18] After friendly debate, we agree to

---

17. For example, stock received by an executive or founder of a company. Or, an heir who inherited from their parent and lived off the income while the underlying assets increased in value.

disagree on a few things, but we need a plan, we make one, and we move forward.

That money to implement this plan must come from somewhere. We can borrow some. If your economy is growing, a little bit of government borrowing won't hurt. But after that, the rest must be raised through taxes.

You don't like paying taxes. I don't like paying taxes. Nobody likes paying taxes. You think the government should be more efficient, so that you don't have to pay so much tax. I do too. However, I also know that only a very small amount of government spending goes to that famous trio of "waste, fraud, and abuse." We'll get into the spending side in a later chapter, but you can trust me that most federal spending is on things you care about.

Since we largely agree on how much tax to collect, the only question is: how should we collect it? This brings me to my favorite way to think about societal "shoulds"—the Veil of Ignorance.

Created by philosopher John Rawls in his landmark book *A Theory of Justice*, the idea is that the people who make decisions like these for society should do so from a position of equality and ignorance. In other words, they know about their society, but not their personal situation within. They don't know their personal wealth, intelligence, talents, race, gender, religion, or anything else. They make decisions as if they are a member of the society chosen at random. According to Rawls, this is the best way to ensure that the rules of society are set up in a just manner.

The Veil of Ignorance argument applies clearly to tax policy. A tax policy may be good for you, but is it good for society? We can't expect people to be altruistic, but by using this approach we can try to understand our biases. Looking at what makes sense for a random member of the society—or every member of society—is an important step toward achieving fairness in a tax system.

Creating a better tax system is a worthy goal for any society. Speaking for the United States in 2017, the tax code is riddled with inefficiencies that promote behavior detrimental to society. It encourages complex structuring of income to take advantage of com-

---

18. A wall on the Mexican border? Obviously, this is nonsense; we wouldn't want one even if somebody else paid.

plex loopholes. You can complain about the general unfairness of taxes, if you must—it's a time-honored tradition. But it's a better use of your energy to recognize the importance of tax policy and work to improve the system.

TAXES AND GROWTH RATES AND PLENTY OF CHARTS
KILLING A MISGUIDED THEORY THAT REFUSES TO DIE

"Are you living in a fantasy world?",
Savannah Guthrie to Paul Ryan

What's the most famous thing ever invented on a dinner napkin? If you guessed the Laffer Curve, you'd be right.

While the idea had long existed that increasing tax rates reduces economic output, it was at a dinner with Donald Rumsfeld, Dick Cheney, and Jude Wanniski when Arthur Laffer pioneered his belief that lowering tax rates can actually increase the amount of tax collected. As you might expect of an economic theory birthed on a table linen, the theory of the Laffer Curve has seldom been supported by real-world events.

Even if few believe that they pay for themselves, the idea that tax cuts create economic growth is widely accepted in our political sphere. The question usually considered is not whether tax cuts create growth, but how much.

Clearly, confiscatory tax rates stifle an economy. I'm not aware of anybody who claims otherwise. But this tells us little about how tax policy affects societies like ours. Predicting the future is, of course, difficult. It is far easier to look at past changes in tax policy and see how the economy has reacted. Have lower taxes historically created higher economic growth?

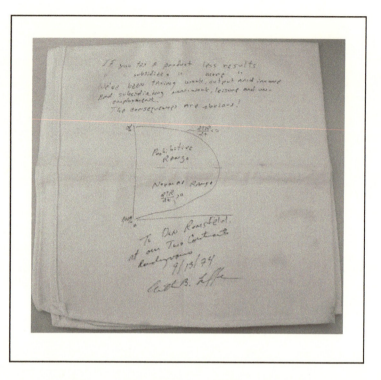

The concept of the **Laffer Curve** sounds simple: as tax rates decrease, people have more incentive to work. Therefore, they work more. As they work more, the economy grows, and the government takes in more tax revenue. According to Arthur Laffer, in many economic conditions, cutting taxes will lead to enough growth where tax revenues will actually increase. Everybody wins when we cut taxes!

Laffer's lexicon has entered our politics. When somebody says that tax cuts pay for themselves, the statement directly descended from Laffer's theory. Unfortunately, the problems with the Laffer Curve are readily apparent. The federal government collects around 25% of our gross domestic product in taxes. This means that, to pay for themselves, each dollar of tax cuts would have to create approximately four dollars of new gross domestic product (GDP). It doesn't take a degree in economics to know that this seems too good to be true. Even if paying for themselves is unlikely, it is usually assumed that tax cuts lead to at least some economic growth. Do they?

A regression is a mathematical tool used to see if one thing is caused by another thing.[1] If we regressed rainfall against clouds in the sky, we would see that the relationship is strong. We can then infer that that rain is likely caused by clouds. Regressions can also give spurious results, telling us causation exists where it does not. For example, you might find a strong relationship between people carrying umbrellas and people wearing rubber boots. But umbrella use doesn't *cause* people to put on their galoshes. Both are caused by a third factor: rain.

There are a lot of fancy techniques and terminologies in regression analysis; the only one you need to know for our purposes is **R-squared**. R-squared is a measure that tells you how well a model fits a set of data. It is expressed as a number between zero and one. If the R-squared for a regression is one, then the model fits the data perfectly. If it is zero, then the model has no predictive value at all. In other words, an R-squared of zero tells us that the variables in question have no relationship.

Let's have some fun with some basic regression analysis.[2] Fortunately, we have good data sets for all the relevant tax and economic data. We will use 1961-2015 as the period for our study.[3] We can start by asking a simple question: is there a relationship between top marginal tax rates and GDP growth.[4] If Arthur Laffer was right, we should see a strong *negative* relationship between them. Figure 13 is a scatter plot, with each point representing a given year's top personal income tax rate against the GDP growth for said year.

---

1. If you are reading this, there is a good chance that you know the basics of regression analysis. If so, please feel free to skip ahead two paragraphs. In fact, it's best if you do—I'm going to be using some bad math here.
2. I'll assume this is what you also do in your spare time.
3. We'll look at data only for the United States; other countries could have different results, but one country will already give us enough charts.
4. All of our GDP figures are real GDP meaning that they exclude the effects of inflation.

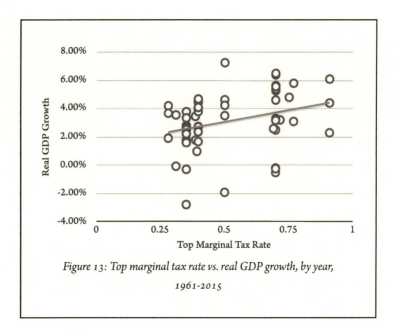

Figure 13: Top marginal tax rate vs. real GDP growth, by year,
1961-2015

Well...that's not good for Laffer.

The relationship between taxes and growth is weak, with an R-squared of 9%. Even worse, to the extent there is any relationship, *higher* tax rates are associated with *higher* growth. I know what you are thinking—the complex incentive effects of tax policy take time to work their way into the economy. We can address this by "lagging" our GDP measure, comparing tax rates for a given year against economic growth in the next year:

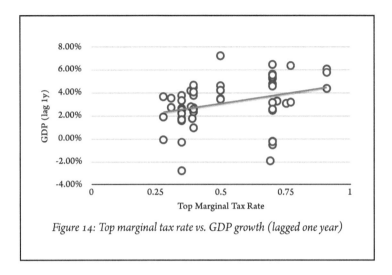

Figure 14: Top marginal tax rate vs. GDP growth (lagged one year)

We get the same answer, a weak relationship in the direction opposite of that predicted by Laffer. Maybe one year is too short a time on which to perform such an analysis. What if we compare tax rates to the average GDP growth for the next five years?

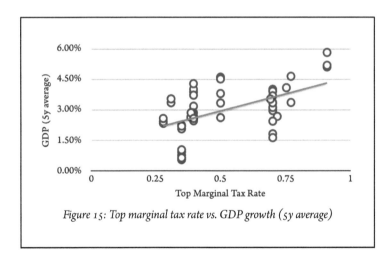

Figure 15: Top marginal tax rate vs. GDP growth (5y average)

This is getting worse for Mr. Laffer. An R-squared of 30% is still a weak relationship, but it has some significance. In other words, there is at least some evidence that economic growth is stronger during periods of higher tax rates.

GDP is a metric with many flaws. The average American cares more about whether they have a job. Let's regress marginal tax rates against unemployment:[5]

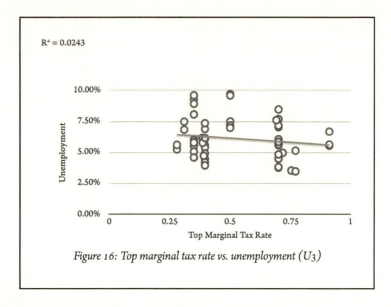

Figure 16: Top marginal tax rate vs. unemployment (U3)

Well, at least it isn't going the wrong way anymore. But an R-squared of 2% means there is virtually no relationship at all. We can introduce our lag and try again:

---

5. I'm using the U-3 as my measure of unemployment. The broader definition of unemployment, U-6, gives similar results.

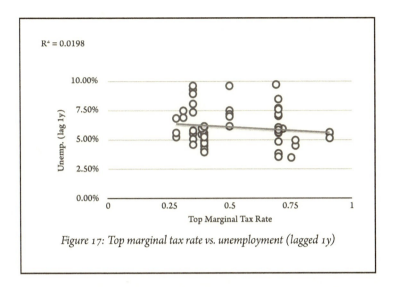

Figure 17: Top marginal tax rate vs. unemployment (lagged 1y)

Again, nothing there. I won't belabor the point but moving to a five-year average doesn't help. If you think about it, comparing unemployment to top marginal rates doesn't make a lot of sense. One applies to top earners, the other to those people on the edge of the labor force. Perhaps it is the total tax collected, rather than marginal rates, that put a drag on the economy.[6] Let's look at whether total taxes collected (as a percentage of GDP) show a stronger relationship. First, we regress against GDP growth:

---

6. For what it's worth, Laffer has said many times that, he was talking specifically about top marginal rates, not the amount of tax collected. I'm searching for any evidence that might help him out.

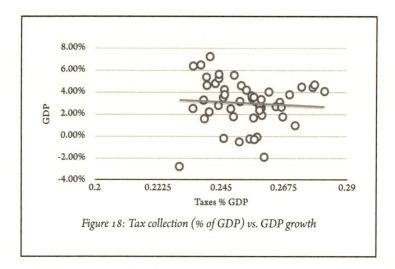

Figure 18: Tax collection (% of GDP) vs. GDP growth

An R-squared of zero—no relation. The same holds if we lag GDP or use a five-year average. Let's try unemployment regressed against total tax collection:

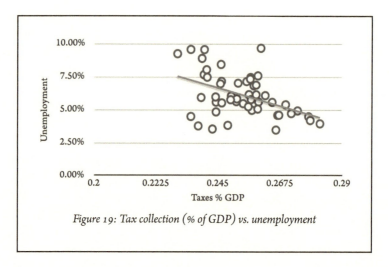

Figure 19: Tax collection (% of GDP) vs. unemployment

Finally, we've found one economic variable that correlates with the tax burden in the direction predicted by Laffer. It's not a strong relationship, but it's something. Unfortunately, there's a problem when we bring in the lag:

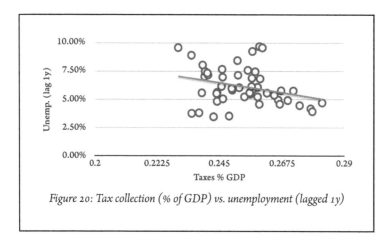

Figure 20: Tax collection (% of GDP) vs. unemployment (lagged 1y)

If the positive effects on the economy of lower taxes were real, then the effect should persist. This regression shows the opposite; by the time they have actually filtered through the economy, lower taxes no longer reduce unemployment. It gets worse. When we use the lag in the other direction, looking at the relationship between last year's unemployment with this year's taxes, we get an interesting result:

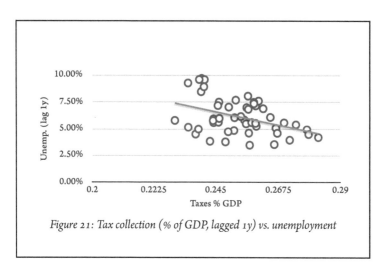

Figure 21: Tax collection (% of GDP, lagged 1y) vs. unemployment

All of the relationships between these variables are weak, almost insignificant statistically. However, if anything, the data tells us that unemployment causes lower tax collections, rather than the other way around. And this, of course, makes sense. When unemployment is higher, there will be a smaller personal income base to collect taxes from. In addition, the government often responds to increased unemployment with targeted tax cuts.

Where did Art Laffer go so wrong? Basic economics tell us that when you tax something less of it will be produced. When referencing labor, economists call this relationship the **substitution effect**.[7] Why is it not showing up in the data? The regression analyses themselves do not explain why. But my best guess is that Laffer missed a factor called the **income effect**.

Say that you need one thousand dollars each month, in after-tax money, to maintain your lifestyle. If tax rates increase, the same amount of work will no longer produce your desired income. In Laffer's world, based only on the substitution effect, increased taxes will cause you to work less, because your reward for working is lower. But in my hypothetical, you are likely to do the opposite: work more, in order to maintain your after-tax income. This extra work leads to extra output for the economy, increasing GDP. The income effect seems to roughly offset the substitution effect. Other studies return similar results. This explains the data we've seen here: little relationship between tax rates and economic conditions.

To clarify: I'm not saying that higher taxes are a good thing, or that they lead to higher economic output. Rather, taxes affect the supply of labor in a complex way, as the income effect and substitution effect interact. The quantitative evidence confirms this understanding; changes in tax law don't have an obvious, one-directional effect on the economy. Good economists recognize this.[8]

This finding is not just relevant to macroeconomic theory but is also an important statement in politics. When a politician says that tax cuts will grow the economy, be skeptical. The evidence, both theoretical and practical, for that politician's position is weak. At best, any effect would be small. Knowing this, we can easily dispense with trickle-down economics. If cutting tax rates does not significantly increase the size of the economy, then the benefits of tax cuts to the wealthy go only to the wealthy. Tax cuts increase future deficits and must eventually be dealt with, by either increasing fu-

---

7. So named because if compensation is low enough, people will substitute our working time with leisure time.
8. In other words, Arthur Laffer is not a good economist.

ture taxes or cutting future services. When the bill comes due, it will most likely fall on everybody. Tax policy has no free lunch.

CONGRESS
THE WORLD'S LARGEST DYSFUNCTIONAL FAMILY

"With all this money coming in from both sides, how does anything ever get done?"

"It doesn't. That's the genius of the system."
—*The Distinguished Gentleman, 1992*

When your approval ratings have been hovering between 10 and 20 percent for nearly a decade, you might want to change things up a bit.

Congress does its best to look bad. They constantly fail to make tough but important decisions. Important pieces of legislation are consistently left undone or rushed through. Everything happens via arcane processes that the public knows better than to understand. Most of the work appears to consist of blaming the other side for everything from the failure of the health care system to the weather. When they do manage to pass legislation, it is usually convoluted and frequently hated. Screaming and fearmongering during the debate makes sure of that.

How we got here is a good question, and one that we'll try to answer. But first, we need to understand what Congress is and what it does.

- How do these people get elected in the first place?
- Once they get there, how do they organize?
- What does Congress actually do?
- How does Congress exercise its power?

HOW DO THESE PEOPLE GET ELECTED IN THE FIRST PLACE?

Let's start with the basics. There are two chambers in the United States Congress: The House of Representatives (lower chamber) and the Senate (upper chamber). They are the first thing defined in our Constitution, in Article I.

The 435 members of the House of Representatives are elected every two years. Senators serve six-year terms, staggered so that equal portions of the chamber face the voters every two years. Representatives are divided among the states proportionally, based on population. This division is recalculated every ten years, via a process called **apportionment**. Each state has two Senators, no matter its population. This results in states having vastly different representation per capita, especially the Senate. We see this in Figure 22.

State	Population	Representatives	Ratio
Montana	1,005,141	1	1,005,141:1
Rhode Island	1,055,173	2	527,587:1

State	Population	Senators	Ratio
California	38,802,500	2	19,401,250:1
Wyoming	576,412	2	288,206:1

Figure 22: Disparities in Congressional representation

Giving each state two Senators was a compromise made in 1787 to ensure that smaller states would ratify the Constitution.[1] But it causes today's Congress to represent a consistency that looks little like the actual population of the country. Rural voters, who mostly live in states with smaller populations, have massively disproportionate power in Congress.

Even though Congress makes laws of national applicability, each state decides how to choose its own members. Our elections are conducted locally, with only minimal federal control. For the House of Representatives, each state decides how to divide its members within its borders; this is called **redistricting**. In most states, redistricting is done through a partisan process, so a political party in control of the state government can give itself a significant electoral advantage, no matter who wins the most votes.

ONCE THEY GET THERE, HOW DO THEY ORGANIZE?

There are two political parties in this country.[2] When a new Congress comes in, one party will have more seats in each chamber. That party is the **majority party**, the other is the **minority party**. In the House, the majority party chooses a Speaker, who is the head of the

---

1. They did, so I guess it worked.
2. The Senate currently has two independents, Angus King of Maine and Bernie Sanders of Vermont. Both King and Sanders reliably vote with the Democrats. Therefore, for our purposes, we group them with the Democrats.

House. The Vice President, who might not be a member of the majority party, serves as President of the Senate. This role is mostly ceremonial, although the Vice President does vote in the case of any tie. In both chambers, each party chooses a leader, who heads his or her party delegation. Each party in each chamber also has a whip, who assists the leader in rounding up votes and other duties.[3] There are various other officers that differ by chamber and party.

It is traditional to refer to each biannual session of Congress as a distinct, numbered entity. For example, we could say that "the 115th Congress is in session until January 2019." Each chamber makes the rules to govern its procedures. Many of these rules are codified in an **organizing resolution**. Usually, passing the organizing resolution is the first thing a new Congress does.[4] In the House, the majority party can include nearly whatever it wants in this document. In the Senate, the game is trickier because the organizing resolution is subject to **unanimous consent**.

Since its founding, most of the Senate's business has been conducted via unanimous consent. This is just what it sounds like: every single Senator must agree to something to let business go forward. There are two types of unanimous consent. Simple unanimous consent is used for all sorts of mundane procedures, such as waiving reading of the minutes and naming post offices. But because Senate rules are so arcane, when they want to get something done, they must change their rules via a **unanimous consent agreement**. These agreements specify details such as the number and type of amendments that can be offered on a bill and how debate will proceed. But again, they require unanimity. Any Senator—or, more likely, a small group of them—can throw a monkey wrench into the process by blocking unanimous consent. In today's partisan environment, we can envision a determined minority preventing all unanimous consent agreements, potentially halting all Senate business.

---

3. The only "her" leader so far is Nancy Pelosi, D-California. She is also the only "her" Speaker and only "her" whip.
4. Because most of its members carry over from the previous Congress, the Senate technically doesn't need to reorganize with new rules every two years. But it still does. The Senate also has a lot of long-standing traditions. Despite not being part of the official rules, they are often enforceable as if they were. The Senate is weird.

One of the major items included in the organizing resolution is the makeup of each chamber's committees. Each majority party will have a majority of the seats on all of its chamber's committees, as well as all of the committee chairmanships.[5] Although their power waxes and wanes over the years, committees are critical to the operation of both chambers. It is difficult to move legislation to a final vote without first passing through its relevant committee.[6] Most bills are written by committee staff, and the provisions are advanced by the **committee markup** process. Because of their power, members of Congress fight to get onto their preferred committees. Committee chairpersons can wield enormous authority to shape legislation.[7] Both chambers and both parties have different procedures to determine committee memberships and chairs, but seniority is a key factor. Figure 23 shows the list of Congressional committees in existence at the time of publication.

---

5. Except Ethics, which is always split evenly, but with the majority party still holding the chairmanship.
6. One way to avoid the need to go through committee is via a discharge petition. But these are rare. The last time one was successfully used was to pass the Bipartisan Campaign Reform Act, better known as McCain-Feingold, in 2002. Before that, the previous instance of a bill becoming law via a discharge petition was (no joke) the Discharge Petition Disclosure Bill, which required signers of discharge petitions to do so publicly.
7. Frequently, the first version of a bill is published by the chairperson of the committee with the relevant jurisdiction. This is called the Chairman's Mark.

House Committees	Senate Committees
Agriculture	Agriculture, Nutrition and Forestry
Appropriations	Appropriations
Armed Services	Armed Services
Budget	Banking, Housing and Urban Affairs
Education and the Workforce	Budget
Energy and Commerce	Commerce, Science and Technology
Ethics	Energy and Natural Resources
Financial Services	Environment and Public Works
Foreign Affairs	Finance
Homeland Security	Foreign Relations
House Administration	Health, Education, Labor and Pensions
Judiciary	Homeland Security and Governmental Affairs
Natural Resources	Judiciary
Oversight and Government Reform	Rules and Administration
Rules	Small Business and Entrepreneurship
Science, Space and Technology	Veterans Affairs
Small Business	
Transportation and Infrastructure	
Veterans' Affairs	
Ways and Means	
Special / Select Committees	
Intelligence	Aging
	Ethics
	Indian Affairs
	Intelligence
Joint Committees	
Joint Economic	
Joint Library	
Joint Printing	
Joint Taxation	

Figure 23: Extant congressional committees

Historically, there have been several organization resolutions involving high drama.[8] My favorite is the story of the Senate's 2001-2003 session.

Before the 2000 election, Republicans held 54 Senate seats to the Democrats' 46. In the 2000 election, Republicans lost four Senate seats (along with the popular vote for President). Therefore, when the Senate began its new session on January 3, 2001, it consisted of 50 Democrats and 50 Republicans. A quirk in our system is that new Presidents (and Vice Presidents) do not take office until nearly three weeks after the new Congress opens for business. Therefore, Democratic Vice President Al Gore still held the tie-breaking vote in the Senate at the opening of its session. Via Gore's tiebreaking vote, Democrats would control the chamber until January 20th, when the new Vice President was inaugurated, and control would change. The Senate would therefore need to be organized and then reorganized under new leadership, which could happen only with the consent of both parties. What emerged was a historic power-sharing arrangement: the two parties would have equal representation on all committees, *unless the partisan makeup of the Senate were to change further.*

Well, that's a provision just asking for trouble. In the summer of 2001, Senator Jim Jeffords of Vermont left the Republican Party, becoming the 51st Democratic senator.[9] Under its own terms, the power-sharing agreement in the organizing resolution ceased to exist. But the 51 Democrats also couldn't unilaterally pass a new resolution, which requires 60 votes. The result was another compromise: Democrats were acknowledged as the majority party in the chamber and on committees, while Republicans received guarantees for greater than usual minority party rights. This was a simpler time; I can't picture either party being willing to share power today.

Two tragedies involving its members made the 107th Senate organization even stranger. Missouri's Democratic Governor and Senate candidate Mel Carnahan was killed in a plane crash one month before the 2000 election. It was too late to remove his name from the ballot, but he won the election anyway. Missouri law said that the new Governor, who was previously Mel Carnahan's Deputy, got to

---

8. My definition of high drama may be different from yours.
9. Technically, he was an independent who voted with the Democrats.

choose an interim Senator who would serve until November 2002. He appointed Mel Carnahan's widow, Jean Carnahan. In the 2002 election, Jean Carnahan lost to Republican Jim Talent, who took office immediately. The Senate was therefore back to 50-50, with the Republican Vice President as tie-breaker. No, they did not re-re-re-organize; maybe they were just worn out. Senator Paul Wellstone (D-Minnesota) was also killed in a plane crash during that session, along with his wife, daughter, two pilots and two members of his staff.[10]

WHAT DOES CONGRESS ACTUALLY DO?

After fundraising, getting themselves elected, organizing themselves, and doing some more fundraising, Congress sometimes does things.

Congress is the legislative branch of the federal government. That means that it writes bills and determines which bills become law. The areas in which Congress has power to legislate are specified in Article I of the Constitution:[11]

The Congress shall have Power To lay and collect Taxes, Duties, Imposts and Excises, to pay the Debts and provide for the common defense and general Welfare of the United States...

To borrow Money on the credit of the United States;

To regulate Commerce with foreign Nations, and among the several States, and with the Indian Tribes...

To establish Post Offices and post Roads...

To constitute Tribunals inferior to the Supreme Court...

To declare War, grant Letters of Marque and Reprisal, and make Rules concerning Captures on Land and Water;

---

10. This was such a tragic end to an already troubling time for our nation. During this same Congress, the September 11 attacks occurred, and we began blundering our way into the Iraq War.
11. Edited by me, for length.

To raise and support Armies, but no Appropriation of Money to that Use shall be for a longer Term than two Years;

To provide and maintain a Navy...

To exercise exclusive Legislation in all Cases whatsoever, over such District (not exceeding ten Miles square) as may, by Cession of particular States, and the Acceptance of Congress, become the Seat of the Government of the United States...

To make all Laws which shall be necessary and proper for carrying into Execution the foregoing Powers, and all other Powers vested by this Constitution in the Government of the United States, or in any Department or Officer thereof.

The specifically named items in this list are called Congress's **enumerated powers**. Congress's power to legislate in these areas is spelled out clearly. However, note the last line: "make all Laws which shall be necessary and proper..." This is known as the **elastic clause**[12] because it gives Congress the ability to stretch its own power based on only a vague guideline. Fights over exactly what is within Congress's power have been going on for 200 years and I doubt we will have a definitive answer soon.

In order to remain on the right side of the Constitutional line, Congress prefers to link legislation to its enumerated powers rather than relying on the elastic clause. For example, the Supreme Court validated the Constitutionality of the Affordable Care Act's individual mandate based on Congress's enumerated power to collect taxes. Congress often tries to find safe harbor in its enumerated power to regulate commerce, which can potentially justify a lot of actions. Nearly any Congressional action imaginable has at least a minimal effect on interstate commerce.[13]

For a bill to become a law, identical legislative language needs to be passed by majorities of both chambers of Congress. A bill can be

---

12. More formally, the Necessary and Proper clause.
13. The Commerce Clause trick is well known, and courts are on the lookout for its misuse. For example, when Congress claimed expansive power over gun control due to its relationship to economic activity, the Supreme Court rejected the argument. See United States v. Lopez and Printz v. United States (specifically, Clarence Thomas in concurrence).

introduced in either chamber.[14] It will be referred to one or more committees, where it will be amended. Then it goes to the chamber as a whole, where it can be amended again. If passed by the first chamber, it is sent to the other chamber and assigned to committee there—where it can be amended again. Then it might face changes on the floor of the second chamber. All of these chances for amendments make it likely that the bills passed by the two chambers will have differences. There are two ways to handle differing House and Senate versions of a bill.

The classical way to resolve differences between the chambers is in a **conference committee**. When differing versions of a bill are passed, a conference happens if majorities of both chambers vote to have one. A conference committee is a group of members from both chambers that exists solely to negotiate between different versions of a single bill. Each chamber can instruct its conferees as to what changes to the bill they are willing to accept in such a compromise, but these instructions are not binding. If a majority of the conference committee members of each chamber agree on a final version of the bill, then a **conference report** is issued. Theoretically, a conference report needs to be a compromise between the versions of the bill passed by the two chambers. For example, if the House wants to spend $100 on a new aircraft carrier and the Senate $200, then a conference committee can't decide to spend $300. When the disagreement isn't quantitative, however, it is difficult to enforce this rule. If and when a report is issued by a conference, the compromise bill must still be passed by both chambers. A conference report cannot be amended, but neither chamber is required to hold a vote on it.

If they don't want to go through the formality of a conference, they can play **Congressional ping-pong**.[15] We can explain this process best with an example. Let's say that the House passes a bill and sends it to the Senate. The Senate amends the bill and passes the amended version. Rather than hold a conference, they could "ping-pong" the bill back to the House. The House can either:

---

14. In theory, all bills affecting money need to start in the House. In practice, it's easy to get around this requirement. For example, the Senate could amend any House bill, crossing out the entire text and replacing it with a money-related bill.
15. Officially called "amendment exchange."

1. Agree to the Senate's amendments, passing the bill,
2. Disagree, killing the bill (at least temporarily), or,
3. Amend the Senate bill and pass the new version.

If the latter occurs, the House could amend it again and ping-pong the bill right back to the Senate. Fortunately, there is a limit: three ping-pongs. But there are, of course, ways to get around this limit, letting the game continue for as long as both sides are enjoying it.[16]

We could say much more about Congressional procedure, but this is a good foundation. However, it doesn't answer the big question.

HOW DOES CONGRESS EXERCISE ITS POWER?

From the outside, much of Congress's work appears trivial. They rename post offices and celebrate sports teams winning their championship. It seems like the Executive and Judicial branches get to have all the fun: conduct war, appoint Cabinet officers, interpret the law, and put people in jail. Congress has two key ways to really make sure its voice is heard: money and executive oversight.[17]

Whatever other branches want to do, they can't do it without money and Congress controls the money. On the way in, Congress writes the tax code. On the way out, Congress controls the **budget** and **appropriations** processes that determine how the money gets spent. In its budget, Congress creates an overview of tax and spending priorities for each fiscal year. Then, twelve annual appropriations bills must be passed, each one funding its specific area of the government. Appropriations bills can direct spending down to a very granular level. They can require that money be spent in some areas and proscribe it from being spent in others. The committees involved in taxation and spending—Budget, Ways and Means, Finance and Appropriations—are some of the most desirable assign-

---

16. For instance, either chamber could take a different bill, cross out all of its language, and replace it with what they want. Or, even easier, since Congress made the three-ping-pong rule, they could waive it.
17. It also controls the Judiciary in the sense that it determines the size and makeup of the Federal courts. In practice, this is almost never used to set policy.

ments in both chambers. Members can wait a decade or more to get seats on these committees.[18]

A lot of day-to-day Congressional activity is oversight, usually of the executive branch. Interestingly, Congress's oversight power is not mentioned in the Constitution; it is an implied power. The first formal recognition of Congress's oversight role was the Legislative Reorganization Act of 1946, almost 175 years after Congress first sat in session. The Watergate Committee, Truman Committee, and House Un-American Activities Committee all conducted activity of an oversight, rather than legislative, nature.[19]

Congress's oversight power is expansive. It can subpoena documents and demand witness testimony, both from private citizens and the executive branch. Ignoring Congressional subpoenas is a bad idea, as contempt of Congress is a crime and gets referred to the Department of Justice. When Congress asks, you need to show up and to tell the truth. Oversight power is usually vested in the committees, where the majority party always has the most seats. This means that only the majority party in each chamber of Congress has the real power to investigate. A committee chairperson's signature is always required to issue a subpoena. Congress's oversight power is also related to the ultimate penalty: impeachment. Congress has the power to remove nearly anyone from their federal office. Including, of course, the President.

The Senate has two other significant powers that bear mentioning. First, all agreements with foreign nations must be approved by two-thirds of the Senate. This includes peace treaties and trade agreements.[20] Second, the Senate must advise on and consent to many executive branch appointments, as well as federal judgeships. As the executive and judicial branches have grown over the last 200

---

18. The chairmanships of the Appropriations sub-committees, each of which manages one of the appropriations bills, are also plum assignments. They are more desirable than the chairmanships of some full committees.

19. As well as the Benghazi Committee, which amazingly required several years to investigate. While tragic, it was quickly determined that there were no significant outstanding questions about what happened.

20. There are some exceptions to the two-thirds rule for trade agreements through what is called fast-tracking. Specifically, fast track trade bills sent to the Senate cannot be amended or filibustered, although they still need to be approved.

years, the number of positions requiring Senate confirmation has increased far beyond what the Framers likely envisioned.[21]

We've only begun to scratch the surface of how Congress works. The list of Congressional topics we have not mentioned is as distinguished as its members. We haven't discussed cloture, regular order, or motions to recommit. These and other rules are endless and full of exceptions. And they can be changed or suspended at almost any time. May we all exist in organizations that are allowed to make their own rules.

Mainstream reporting on the day-to-day details of Congressional activity is incredibly weak. I won't quote the common statistics about how few Americans can name their member of Congress, but they are depressing. If we all knew a bit more about what members did, Americans would be more likely to care who they are. Instead, all they see is endless bickering, dueling press releases, or grandstanding in front of an empty chamber on C-SPAN.

Understanding Congress is critical to the ability to comprehend what our government does. When we hear talk about gerrymandering, or campaign finance, or the appropriations process, it must be understood in the context of the legislative operations behind it. Congress was mentioned first in the Constitution for a reason; our founders intended it to be the real locus of power in our government. Years of shooting themselves (and each other) in the foot have allowed the other branches to gain authority at their expense. If, however, we were to reach a time where an imperial executive attempted to overreach—stymie the press, suppress voting, or use the Justice Department to pursue political opponents—it would be up to Congress to rein in such a potential autocrat. In this case, they would be our only hope.

---

21. The official document naming Senate-confirmable positions is 50 pages long. The Senate spends an enormous amount of its time on nominations. We should find a way to make this more efficient.

THE POINCARÉ CONJECTURE
A TALE OF RUBBER BANDS AND THE SHAPE OF THE UNIVERSE

"There is a theory which states that if ever anybody discovers exactly what the Universe is for and why it is here, it will instantly disappear and be replaced by something even more bizarre and inexplicable. There is another theory which states that this has already happened."
—Douglas Adams, *The Restaurant at the End of the Universe*

What is the shape of the universe? Does it even have one? Over the past 500 years, we have learned a lot about our universe. Through painstaking work we've learned much about what's in it, how it began, how it is changing and even how it might end. A century of study on the vastest scales and the smallest scales has given us a glimpse of what's out there. So much of what we've learned was highly unexpected. We have more questions today than ever before.

Our story doesn't begin in the present. It begins in France at the end of the 19th century. It begins with Henri Poincaré, considered the last universal mathematician. It begins with a piece of pure mathematics from the discipline of topology.

- What is topology?
- What is the Poincaré Conjecture?
- What is the shape of the universe?

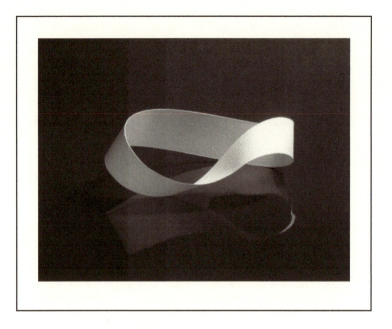

WHAT IS TOPOLOGY?

Over the last 150 years, mathematicians have focused on making their topic more general—or to use the mathematical term, abstract. Number theory is the abstract version of arithmetic. Analysis is the abstract version of calculus. Abstract algebra is the abstract version of algebra.[1]

Topology is the abstract version of geometry. It is geometry on steroids.[2] You remember geometry: 9th grade, compass, straight-edge, step-by-step proofs. In geometry, you were concerned with sizes, shapes, and distances. A circle is the collection of all points equidistant from its center. An equilateral triangle has three sides of equal length. Exactly one parallel line can be drawn through a point not on said line.[3] Topology is concerned with similar objects, but properties in topology are of a more general nature.

Unhelpfully, topology is usually defined as "the study of topological spaces." It's more helpful to think of topology as geometry, but

---

1. That degree in theoretical mathematics is hard at work here.
2. Or maybe something stronger.
3. Or no lines. Or an infinite number of lines, depending on your assumptions.

with rules that allow any object to be bent or stretched, as long as you never tear it or use glue to attach parts of it together.[4] In topology, if you can mold one object into another object within these rules, the two objects are considered the same thing. A square can be smoothed to make a circle; so they are equivalent.[5] But a circle is different from a figure 8, which you can only get by pinching together and gluing the center of the circle. Similarly, a donut and a drinking straw are equivalent to each other, but different from a sphere or a cube.

A good example to describe topological equivalence is the alphabet. In Figure 24, the alphabet is split into classes of letter. Each class consists of letters equivalent to all the members of its class, and different from the members of all other classes.[6]

Class	Members	Holes	Tails
1	A, R	1	2
2	B	2	0
3	C, G, I, J, L, M, N, S, U, V, W, Z	0	0
4	D, O	1	0
5	E, F, T, Y	0	3
6	H, K	0	4
7	P, Q	1	1
8	X	0	4

4. A good analogy for topology is Play-Doh. Generally, what you can do with Play-Doh is allowed in topology. If you take a random blob and roll it between your hands, you'll end up with a nice smooth sphere. If you roll it on a table, you get a fun little snake. These actions are allowed in topology. If you tear your Play-Doh in half, you end up with ugly, rough edges where the halves used to meet. Similarly, if you squeeze together the head and tail of a snake, your ring will have an ugly seam that seems like it will never smooth away. Topology forbids these actions.
5. Technically, you would say they are "homeomorphic" but we'll use that word as little as possible because it's scary and this isn't a math class.
6. Depending on the font, classes of letters will be different. Also, lowercase letters will be different from uppercase; we're talking about the shape of the letters, not the sounds they represent.

Figure 24: The alphabet, by topological class

Each class can be described by the number of holes and tails of its members. Within a class, all letters must have the same number of holes and tails. However, it is possible to have two classes to be different, despite matching in these criteria. For example, consider K and X. In the latter, the four tails meet at a central point, whereas in the former, there is a tiny connector. Equivalence in topology is transitive. In other words, if C is equivalent to J and J to L, then C must also be equivalent to L.

Topologists love to think and talk about properties of objects, which they call **invariants**. In topology, we care only about properties that are preserved among objects that are equivalent. We saw some examples of invariants above—the number of holes and tails are topological properties. However, having corners is not an invariant. We know this because L and C are equivalent, but only one has corners. Because it is not conserved between these equivalent shapes, it is not a property in topology.

We are going to work with some of these properties, so it makes sense to define them and describe some examples. These definitions are non-technical. Feel free to look them up if you want their formal meanings.[7]

Manifold

If an object looks flat when you zoom in on any small portion, it is a manifold. The surface of the Earth is a two-dimensional manifold. When you stand on the street it appears flat, as the curvature is too far away to see. The letter X is not a manifold; there is no way to make the intersection look flat. A manifold with *n* dimensions is called an **n-Manifold**.

Boundary

The points you can get to both from inside and outside of an object are its boundary. In Figure 25, the dark line is the boundary of the object.

---

7. For example, I'm using the word "object" a lot. This word doesn't mean anything in topology, but it gets the point across better than the correct terminology.

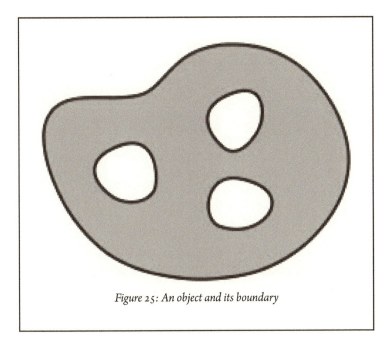

Figure 25: An object and its boundary

Not all objects have boundaries. For example, the surface of the Earth has none. No matter how far you walk (or swim), you will never reach an edge. The boundary of an object can be itself part of the object, or not.

Compact

An object is compact if it includes its boundary and is of finite size. The object in Figure 25 is compact, if the boundary were part of it. The surface of a donut is compact. A line, extending forever in both directions, is not of finite size. Therefore, it is not compact.

Closed

If an object is compact and has no boundary, it is closed. The skin of a balloon, which is two-dimensional, is closed. Figure 25 is not closed because it has a boundary.

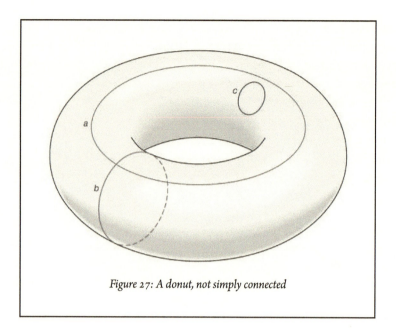

Figure 27: A donut, not simply connected

Simply Connected

This one is a bit trickier, so we'll define it with an example. Pretend you have a rubber band. A huge rubber band, very strong. If you wrap the rubber band around the Earth, it can constrict down to a single point and "snap off."[8] Because this happens no matter how you wrap the rubber band, the Earth is simply connected.

On the other hand, if we put our rubber band around the handle of a coffee mug, it has no way to constrict completely. The same is true for a rubber band going through the hole of a donut. These objects are not simple connected.

WHAT IS THE POINCARÉ CONJECTURE?

When Fermat's Last Theorem was proven by Andrew Wiles in 1994, it was heavily reported, and Wiles became a minor celebrity. When Grigori Perelman proved the Poincaré Conjecture in 2002,[9] the pop-

---

8. In topology, we ignore skyscrapers, mountains and similar features.
9. Not fully verified until 2006.

ular response was more muted. This happened despite a consensus among virtually all mathematicians that the Poincaré Conjecture is the more important piece of mathematics.[10] Why was Perelman's proof given short shrift?

There are a few reasons. First, Fermat's Theorem is much older. More than 350 years passed from Fermat's proposal until Wiles' proof, compared to 100 years from Poincaré to Perelman. Second, while Wiles does not actively seek publicity, Perelman worked in near obscurity at the Steklov Institute in Saint Petersburg.[11]

Figure 28: The Earth, whose surface is a 2-sphere

More than anything else, the hesitancy to report on Perelman's breakthrough is probably because the Poincaré Conjecture is diffi-

---

10. The unproven Riemann Hypothesis is more important than either. Our progress in its proof is excruciatingly slow. But it's from a different branch of mathematics, and thus a different story.

11. If any Steklovians are reading this, no offense intended.

cult to visualize. It involves three-dimensional objects that exist only in four-dimensional space. You have never existed in four dimensions of visible space and have no good way to picture it in your mind. But to understand Poincaré, we must at least try.

Consider two disks—circles on a piece of paper with the insides colored in. Recalling our definitions above, these disks are compact, but not closed—each is finite, but has a boundary. On the boundary of each disk, draw the Earth's equator. These borders are identical, starting off the coast of Nigeria, passing east through Africa, the Indian Ocean, Indonesia, the Pacific, South America, across the Atlantic and back to where we started. Now, sew together the two disks so they align—Indonesia to Indonesia, Peru to Peru, and so forth.[12] Pull the result apart at the poles; it will be a hollow sphere, the two-dimensional surface of the Earth. In topology, we call this a **2-sphere**. It is compact, closed, and simply connected; therefore, all 2-spheres must have these properties. In theory, it is possible that objects that are not 2-spheres also have these properties. However, it has long since been proven that such objects don't exist: all 2-dimensional manifolds that are compact, closed and simply connected are equivalent to the 2-sphere.

Now, consider two globes that are solid on the inside, like the Earth is. These globes have three dimensions, unlike our 2-sphere. Like the discs from which we built the 2-sphere, they have boundaries and are not closed. Stitch the globes together, just like you did with the disks: Brooklyn to Brooklyn, Iceland to Iceland, Sydney to Sydney. You might think it's impossible to do this, and it is, unless you use a fourth dimension.[13] The resulting object is a **3-sphere**. I know you can't picture it. I can't picture it either; nobody really can. But we can think about what it's like to live on this world.

Start in Detroit, on Globe A. Travel toward this globe's core. You pass through the center of Globe A and continue out to the surface of the Indian Ocean on what was the boundary of Globe A. Instantaneously, you pass to the Indian Ocean on the boundary of Globe

---

12. This wouldn't be allowed in topology, because of the rules against gluing pieces together.
13. The 4th dimension isn't necessarily Einstein's time. It isn't necessarily anything. Topology is general, so we talk about the number of dimensions without caring what they represent.

B; after all, they are stitched together. You keep going, through the core of Globe B, and back to the surface, at Detroit on Globe B. But this is stitched to Detroit on Globe A; you are right back where you started.

This sounds weird but is no different from travelling around our current planet. If you start at any point and travel in any direction, you'll eventually get back to where you started. Just because you can't picture it in higher dimensions doesn't mean it is fundamentally different. With the 3-sphere in mind, we can finally state our Conjecture:

The Poincaré Conjecture:

Every simply connected, closed 3-manifold is homeomorphic to the 3-sphere.

A bit scary, but I'm here to help. Homeomorphic is just topology-speak for "the same as." As we discussed, an object is homeomorphic to the 3-sphere if you can change it into the 3-sphere by bending and stretching, without tearing or gluing. Simply connected, closed, and 3-manifold—these are the topological properties that we discussed. If the Conjecture is true, then any object that meets these properties is the same thing as a 3-sphere, our stitched-together globes. This is equivalent to how all 2-dimentional objects with these properties are the same as the 2-sphere. Adding a third dimension, however, makes it fiendishly difficult to prove.

An Aside: The Strange Existence of Grigori Perelman

The start of Grigori "Grisha" Perelman's life was typical enough. Born in Leningrad to a mathematics professor, Perelman excelled from an early age, taking advantage of late-Soviet programs to develop top scientific talent. The fall of Communism was timed precipitously for him. He took advantage of the post-doctoral circuit to study in the U.S. and other places that were previously hard to reach for Russian scientists. His 1994 proof of the Soul Conjecture established him as one of the world's leading topologists. But he turned down offers to work at several top universities, returning home to St. Petersburg.

At the same time, global efforts toward solving Poincaré were advancing quickly. Perelman was a prominent name in the field, and that he would prove the Conjecture was not shocking. But rather than appearing in a prestigious journal, the math world watched Perelman's steady assault on Poincaré via the public repository arXiv, over a tantalizing eight months. The result was elegant; the final act a svelte seven pages. The plaudits begin to roll in.

He turned down the Fields Medal, saying that he didn't "want to be on display like an animal in the zoo." The Conjecture was one of seven "Millennium Problems" chosen by the Clay Mathematics Institute for their difficulty and importance. Perelman, presumably not a rich man, turned down the $1 million prize, saying his contributions were no greater than those of Richard Hamilton. Hamilton's work was certainly important to the solution. But Perelman didn't take the last step in a 100-yard dash. He ran the last fifteen miles of the marathon.

In the aftermath of his proof, there were questions as to whether Perelman deserved full credit. Despite a complete lack of desire for personal recognition, the controversy clearly bothered him. This may be the reason he left the Steklov Institute in 2005. He hasn't published since; he may have stopped working in mathematics entirely. His life since then is shrouded in rumor. His current whereabouts are unknown.

WHAT IS THE SHAPE OF THE UNIVERSE?

Before we talk about the universe, let's talk about the Earth. There was a time when people thought the Earth had a boundary, an edge that you could fall off. It doesn't, but they weren't crazy to imagine one. To them, the Earth looked flat. They guessed it had a finite area. Flat things with finite size usually have an edge, like the top of a table.

Then, there was a period where we knew the Earth had no boundary but couldn't be sure of its shape. How could we know for sure that we lived on a sphere, rather than an enormous donut? Mathematics tells us one way to tell a sphere from a donut. We put our theoretical rubber band around every possible loop. If it always contracts to a point, then our world is simply connected and therefore a 2-sphere.[14]

As we leave our home planet, it may be useful to define what the universe is. This is not as simple as it may sound. Was whatever existed before our universe began part of our universe? What about what will exist after it ends (if it ends)? My favorite definition is that the universe is everything that we can possibly, in theory, interact with. On a practical level, faraway stars are unreachable, but we can see their light and feel their gravitational pull. They are part of our universe. Spooky virtual particles affect us, even if they exist only for tiny fractions of a second. They are an integral part of the universe.

---

14. Of course, this involves an infinite number of rubber band checks, so it isn't a practical solution.

If there were something in another dimension that couldn't ever affect us, that would be outside our universe.[15]

We know a lot about the universe. We can see light emitted just after the universe began, over 13 billion years ago. Because the universe is expanding, the stars that emitted this light are now unimaginably far away, more than 1 septillion miles.[16] The scale is so massive that it is nearly impossible to translate into everyday terms. For example, if you traveled fast enough to go from the Earth to the sun and back *every second*,[17] it would still take you 47,000,000 years to get to the farthest points of the universe that we can see.

So the universe huge—but what can we say about it topologically?

Let's start with the easy one: as far as we can tell, on a small scale the universe is flat. There are a lot of experiments that tell us this, but the BOOMERanG experiment is the most intuitive.[18] In this project, we sent a balloon telescope up to an altitude of forty kilometers to measure huge triangles in space. The angles of these triangles always totaled 180°. This would be true only if we exist in a flat space. It's not a proof that our universe is flat. We tested only a few triangles, in areas of space relatively close to our planet. On the other hand, there is virtually no evidence contradicting the BOOMERanG results. Therefore, our best evidence is that the local geometry of the universe is flat, meaning it is a 3-manifold.

Is the universe simply connected? In other words, will the rubber band test always work? Our problem here is even worse than that of our ancestors who wanted to know if the Earth was a sphere. There is obviously no way to test every possible loop in the universe to ensure it collapses to a point.[19] But everything that we've seen—our

---

15. We don't know for sure, of course, but there are good reasons to think that our universe is not special, but rather one of many universes. Together, these make up the so-called multi-verse.
16. This is a number with 24 digits.
17. Which is impossible. You would be traveling 1,000 times faster than the speed of light.
18. The highly engineered acronym for this project was chosen because the balloon traveled around the South Pole, eventually returning to the spot where its journey had begun.
19. Recall that we're working in topology, so it's not a problem if our proverbial rubber band gets caught on a small object like a donut, a planet, or even a donut-shaped planet.

day-to-day experiences, and every observation we've taken—makes me think the universe is simply connected. It is just the most plausible explanation.

We don't know whether the universe is finite or infinite; speaking for myself, I think it is finite. To start with, we know that all the matter and energy in the universe began at a single point. You can draw a 3-sphere, finite in size, around this initial point. The universe started expanding after the Big Bang. This expansion was very fast, but it was finite.[20] Therefore, you can always draw a 3-sphere of finite size that includes all of the stuff that was once in the Big Bang. As long as the universe hasn't been around for an infinite amount of time (and it hasn't), the 3-sphere surrounding today's universe will necessarily also be finite. Convincing argument, perhaps, but again not a proof. There could be an infinite reach of spacetime in our universe, even if it is empty.

But an infinite universe has other problems. For instance, "empty space" isn't empty; it is filled with strange dark matter and dark energy. An infinite universe would therefore have an infinite amount of either mass or energy or both. If this is the case, does that mean that there are an infinite number of stars? If so, shouldn't the sky be much brighter? This is Olbers' Paradox—one of many simplistic, yet powerful arguments against an infinite universe.[21] Like a flat universe and a simply connected universe, a finite universe just makes the most sense.

When a person hears that the universe is expanding, they often ask the same question: If the universe is expanding, then what is outside of the universe? They picture the universe like the interior of a balloon as it is being blown up. But this because we lack the ability to visualize in four dimensions. The surface of our planet is a finite, two-dimensional shape, but it doesn't have an edge. Similarly, the universe almost certainly has no boundary. If it is also of finite size, this means that the universe is closed.

---

20. Probably. Object traveling through space are limited by the speed of light, but space itself doesn't face this limitation.

21. Among those who spent their life pondering Olbers' Paradox was Edgar Allen Poe, the writer and poet. He is credited with stating a possible solution, namely that while the universe may have an infinite number of stars, we may be able to see only a finite number due to the great distances. His insight was far ahead of its time, nearly a century before Einstein stated that the speed of light is constant.

Simply connected, closed, 3-manifold. If we make these assumptions and mix in the Poincaré Conjecture, we reach our result: the universe is a simple 3-sphere.

—§—

So what? The universe is a 3-sphere?[22] Why should you care?

As a theoretical mathematician (or somebody who once studied the topic), I was always asked "how you can use that?" The purpose of pure mathematics is to extend the boundaries of what we know, the immediate practical value being secondary. It is easy to find many of history's great mathematicians saying that they are not at all concerned with the applications of their work. But don't let yourself be fooled. When you look at the world 100 years after some mathematician disdains all applications, you'll often find their topic critical to everyday life.

The topological shape of the planet was clearly important to early explorers, even if the idea of an "edge" had disappeared long before Columbus. For the shape of the universe to matter, you'll have to wait a while. If you look ahead a bit—perhaps a decillion years[23]—the universe will almost certainly reach an end state. What this end state will be depends on weird things, like how much dark energy there is, as well as more trivial ideas like the shape of the universe. Depending on the exact value of a few properties, we could be headed toward a few possible ultimate ends:

- The Big Freeze, where everything is swallowed by black holes, which themselves disappear over time.
- The Big Rip, where the accelerating speed of expansion eventually tears apart all matter.
- The Big Crunch, where gravity reverses the current expansion, pulling everything back to a single point.
- The Big Slurp, where space itself is unstable, just waiting for a singularity to "gulp" up the universe, destroying everything.

---

22. Maybe. Remember we did a lot of guessing.
23. That number has 33 zeros in it.

I'm not a cosmologist. I'm not even a topologist. This isn't a peer-reviewed journal or a serious work of scholarship. It is not a proof that the universe is a 3-sphere. It's just my musings about the Poincaré Conjecture.

But, if we could prove the universe's shape, it would tell us a lot about where we will end up. If the universe is a 3-sphere, the Big Crunch is not possible. It also means that a Big Freeze is more likely than a Big Rip.[24] In other words, a 3-sphere universe will probably continue expanding forever, but never exceed the cosmic speed limit.

Too many people fear mathematics. Terms like topological space, homeomorphism, and 3-manifold aren't relatable. You might have hesitated before tackling this chapter. I've done the best I can to make the topic understandable, but complex topics cannot be made simple. You should be happy with yourself for trying something new and for making it to the end. Even if you didn't understand every word.

---

24. The Big Slurp is a newly discovered possibility, resulting from our discovery of the Higgs Boson. It is by far the weirdest scenario and involves the entire universe disintegrating. This would start from a single "vacuum metastability event" and propagate out at the speed of light.

FISCAL POLICY, PART II
SPENDING
WHERE DOES IT ALL GO?

"Don't tell me what you value. Show me your budget, and I'll tell you what you value."
—*Joseph Biden*

All of that sweet, sweet federal tax revenue—and proceeds from borrowing—is going somewhere. Given how much of it there is, a lot of somewheres.

The nearly four trillion dollars of annual federal spending represents 21% of total U.S. economic output. Federal money is everywhere, yet most people have a difficult time seeing it. In a famous example, surveys show that the average American thinks 31% of all federal spending goes to foreign aid. The real number represents less than 1%.

The majority of federal money is spent on things its citizens get back directly—Social Security, Medicare, and Medicaid. Most of the rest is spent on either defense or interest on the national debt. Fiscally speaking, our government is a big insurance company with an army. When talking about spending cuts, politicians imply—or state outright—that they plan to cut only things you don't use. Cadres of bureaucrats, bridges to nowhere, and the like. Certainly, there is waste, and, possibly, some programs that should be cut entirely. But these amount to a pittance with respect to the overall budget. Significant cuts to significant programs will affect you, your friends, and your community.

- How is federal government spending policy determined?

- Where does all that money go?
- What if the process doesn't work?

HOW IS FEDERAL GOVERNMENT SPENDING POLICY DETERMINED?

It shouldn't shock you that the federal government spends money based on a series of complex, interminable, and arcane parliamentary maneuvers, which serve largely as a front for opaque discussions which have previously occurred between members of Congress and the federal agencies. It also contains a heavy sprinkling of input from industry lobbyists and special interest groups. Considering its haphazard nature, the system works fairly well.

Federal spending comes in two flavors: **mandatory** and **discretionary**. Each follows processes that are almost entirely distinct. Let's tackle mandatory spending first. It's the bigger piece, but also simpler from a process perspective.

Mandatory spending happens without specific, annual, Congressional action. This is where the name comes from: mandatory spending runs on autopilot based on direction given previously. To change mandatory spending, Congress must actually do something, like pass a new law. When they do so, the new spending levels set in such a law will then be mandatory for future years.[1] Most of today's federal spending is mandatory. Virtually all future growth in spending is in the mandatory portion.

Most mandatory spending goes to entitlement programs like Social Security, Medicare, and Medicaid. We've covered these programs in depth in previous chapters. But another significant portion is spent on means-adjusted programs intended to provide basic necessities to those who can't afford them. The largest of these programs are unemployment insurance and the Supplemental Nutrition Assistance Program (SNAP, previously known as food stamps).

Although different legally, interest on the national debt is effectively part of mandatory spending. From a process perspective, it also runs on autopilot; interest is paid without specific Congressional action. The key difference, of course, is that Congress can pass a new law that changes spending on mandatory programs. Changing the interest rate paid on federal debt instruments is a bad idea, as it would be an event of default by the U.S. government.

All other spending by the federal government is discretionary. Levels of discretionary spending are subject to an annual, multi-step process. Congressional supremacy in setting federal spending levels is enshrined in the Constitution. However, the Constitution helpfully omits guidelines as to how the process of setting these levels should occur. This omission has led to significant changes in the process over time.[2]

Until recently, the federal spending process was informal, and Congress's specific power was squishy. Despite being nominally in control, the legislative branch had little ability to enforce its will. The process became more formal when a President specifically challenged Congressional prerogatives in this area. Richard Nixon, claiming that the federal deficit was causing inflation, refused to spend all the money that Congress had told him to. To take back control of the process, the Congressional Budget Act (CBA) of 1974 was passed. It created **Budget Committees** in both chambers as well as the **Congressional Budget Office** (CBO), which is the arbiter of

---

1. Tax law is also mandatory in the sense that last year's tax code will be applied to this year unless Congress takes specific action.
2. The 2011 Budget Control Act (aka "Sequestration") and Bipartisan Budget Act of 2013 are the two most recent examples of such changes.

the cost of legislation. This formalization increased Congress's fiscal power, at the expense of the President's.

As set forth by the CBA, the first step in the discretionary spending process is when the **President's budget** is sent to Congress. This document is created by the White House's **Office of Management and Budget** (OMB) and is due on the first Monday in February.[3] Generally, when preparing the budget, the OMB will work closely with the federal departments to get their detailed requests for funds. The President's budget, however, has no legal standing; it is a symbolic document, a statement of principles.[4] Once received by Congress, the CBO will **score** the President's budget to see how much it costs. It will also get referred to the Budget Committees, who, if not members of the President's party, generally place it directly in the circular file.[5]

The next step is the **Congressional budget**. In theory, each of the chambers is supposed to consider and review the President's budget and pass their own budget resolution before April 1st. Each chamber then can amend the other's resolution, hopefully passing identical versions through each chamber by April 15th. But, of course, there is no way to force Congress to agree, and this deadline is frequently missed.[6]

Congress's budget is also mostly symbolic. It is a **concurrent resolution**, which means that while the two chambers have agreed, it is not sent to the President for a signature and therefore does not

---

3. The federal fiscal year starts on October 1st. So, the 2018 fiscal year will run from October 1, 2017 to September 30, 2018. The President's budget for this fiscal year was due on February 5, 2017.

4. President Obama asked for $7.4 billion to fund clean energy investments, $12.9 billion to modernize the IRS, as well as funding to make more community colleges free in his 2015 budget. If you listen carefully, you can still hear the echoes of laughter from GOP Congressional leadership.

5. It's good fun to laugh at the President's Budget, but it should be an important communication tool for the executive branch. The first draft in a complex process is always going to be heavily revised before becoming final; the President is just unlucky that the law says he has to go first.

6. As far as I can tell, the only recent budget resolution that was completed on time was for fiscal year 2014, which passed on March 23, 2013. This was the year the "No Budget, No Pay" Act withheld Congressional salaries if a budget wasn't passed on time. It was also a weird year because President Obama's budget wasn't sent to Congress until mid-April, after Congress had already passed theirs. There was no Congressional budget passed at all for the years 2011, 2012, or 2013.

become law. If the President's budget is a blueprint, Congress's is a working drawing. It's getting closer, but still not a physical structure.[7]

For discretionary spending to actually leave the government's hands, it must be included in the **appropriations process**. Each year, twelve appropriations bills must be signed into law to fund government expenditures. This is no longer a drill; these are real dollar amounts that will really be spent. Most of the work for appropriations occurs in each chamber's **Appropriations Committee**. Each of the committees has twelve sub-committees, one for each of the twelve appropriations bills.[8]

Sometimes, multiple (or even all twelve) appropriations bills are passed as a single piece of legislation; these are called **omnibus spending bills**. To proponents of the omnibus method, these bills are an efficient way to get through the tedious appropriations process. To its detractors, omnibus bills are massive tomes, usually passed at the last possible moment with few members having read them.[9]

Once the appropriations bills have gone through committee, they must be passed by their respective chambers. If there are differences between the chambers' bills, these must be reconciled before going to the President. Because appropriations bills are real laws, they must be signed by the President to take effect. If they are vetoed, they go back to Congress, which can either override the veto or pass different bills. But they must be passed before the new fiscal year starts on September 30th. Unlike the budget, there are real problems if this deadline is missed.

In recent years, Congress has frequently passed **continuing resolutions** (CRs), rather than appropriations bills. Theoretically, these

---

7. The Congressional budget is also important to certain procedural points, such as reconciliation.
8. This common-sense structure came into place in 2007, a mere 33 years after the CBA created the modern budgeting process.
9. Omnibus spending bills are famous for extraneous provisions that could not possibly have been seen by many members. For example, the 2017 omnibus included provisions requiring the EPA to treat the burning of wood pellets as carbon-neutral and forced it to allow flexibility in ozone standards. Maybe these are good things; I have no idea. But neither did Congress, as the 1,665-page bill was released less than 48 hours before being voted on.

bills continue the appropriations from the previous fiscal year, hence the name. They are usually written in language linking spending levels to the previous year's, increased or decreased by a percentage. The big difference is that CRs have flexibility of duration. For example, if the deadline for passing appropriations is approaching, Congress could pass a CR covering just a few days while they finish the appropriations bills. For several reasons, CRs have become more common in recent decades. Some fiscal years have been funded entirely by a series of short-term CRs.[10] They do the job, at least for a bit, but they are not very effective ways to implement policy change and don't allow agencies to make long-term plans. Continuing resolutions are not a sign of good governance.

WHERE DOES ALL THAT MONEY GO?

Now that we know how the decisions are made, we can get into the details: where the federal government spends its money. The government does a lot of things, some of which you probably think are wonderful and some terrible. For the next few pages, we are going to ignore what the government does, looking only at where it spends its money.

It is difficult to find a simple, clear explanation of exactly where this money is going. One reason for this is because of the process described above: each stage has its own set of numbers. There is the President's budget, Congress's budget, and appropriations bills. Even the appropriations bills don't exactly match what is eventually spent. Understanding federal spending down to the last penny is an incredibly difficult exercise. If you spend a day searching around for definitive figures, you'll just end up with a big spreadsheet of numbers never quite tie out. But at least you'll know what a federal subfunction code is.[11]

---

10. An especially difficult appropriations season was 2001, which required 21 continuing resolutions.

11. In order to make some sense of how it spends its money, the government creates a hierarchy, and subfunction is one level of the hierarchy. Federal subfunction codes are more frequently referenced by a number than a name (for example, you would say "959" rather than "Other undistributed offsetting receipts").

This is a long-winded way of saying that the figures below are an amalgam of several sources, and not entirely consistent with any one of them.

There are two basic ways to look at spending: by function (e.g., health) or by department (e.g., Treasury). We are going to focus on government functions, because they give a clearer picture of what is actually being done. If money for air transportation comes from programs in several different departments, it's still being used for the same purpose, and that's what is most relevant.

Health: $1,106 billion, 29% of total spending

This is the biggest area of spending, and the one growing the fastest. All but $35 billion is disbursed via mandatory spending. The largest single health expenditure is for Medicare at $594 billion. The rest is spent on Medicaid, the Children's Health Insurance Program, exchange subsidies for the ACA, and a few smaller programs. There is also $31 billion for health research, almost all of which goes to the National Institutes of Health.[12] Veterans' health care is not included here.

We spend enough on health to fill the Empire State Building with $1 bills, with a few singles to spare.

Pensions: $984 billion (26%)

This one is simple: it's all Social Security. Of this total, $832 billion goes to the Old Age and Survivors program, the rest to Disability. Again, veterans' benefits aren't included; they are still to follow.

If you convert it into $20 bills, $984 billion would weigh as much as 20 Olympic-sized swimming pools filled with water.

Defense: $595 billion (15%)

As you've probably heard, the United States spends as much on its defense as the next six largest other countries combined. The break-

---

12. Which, in turn, awards about 80% of this to external researchers via a competitive grant process.

down of this spending is interesting; the salaries (personnel) portion is smaller than you would likely expect, as we see in Figure 30.[13]

Function	Spending ($ Billion)	Percent of Total
Operation and Maintenance	248	41%
Personnel	148	24%
Procurement	103	17%
R&D	65	11%
Nuclear	19	3%
Construction	11	2%
Other non-DoD	9	1%

Figure 30: Breakdown of defense spending

Again, this doesn't include spending on veterans' benefits.[14] It also doesn't include foreign military aid.

We spend more on defense than the gross domestic product of Iran, Syria and North Korea combined.

Welfare: $368 billion (10%)

This category is a catch-all for means-tested programs other than Medicaid. SNAP costs $105 billion. Unemployment insurance costs $35 billion, and housing assistance $48 billion. Disability insurance is another $44 billion. What you think of as welfare—formally called Temporary Assistance for Needy Families—costs only $18 billion.[15] The rest is made up of various tax rebates, with the earned income tax credit and the child credit being the largest.

---

13. These numbers don't quite add up to the $595 billion shown above. Figure 30 is from President Obama's OMB, while the total is from appropriations bills. Note that the nuclear arsenal is largely managed by the Department of Energy.
14. I promise I'm not ignoring the vets; they will be coming up soon.
15. In other words, cash payments to lower-income people are a tiny portion of our spending.

You could build your own International Space Station with this much money. And a spare, just in case.

Interest: $240 billion (6%)

No real way to get around this one. In longer-term projections showing high deficits in the future, increased interest spending is a large portion of the problem. The CBO and OMB (and others) expect U.S. government borrowing costs to rise significantly in coming decades.

Apple has about this much cash on its balance sheet. If they wanted to, they could use it to buy an iPhone 7 for every man, woman, and child in the U.S.A.[16]

Veterans: $174 billion (5%)

We spend more on our veterans than on salaries and benefits for our active-duty personnel.[17] This makes sense because the Department of Defense employs 2,800,000 people (1,300,000 active-duty military, 800,000 reservists, and 700,000 civilian employees) while there are around 22,000,000 veterans. Veterans' benefit spending is split down the middle between pensions and health care.

With this money, you could buy an inexpensive cellular plan for everybody in the world.

Education: $120 billion (3%)

This sounds like a lot, but the federal input to U.S. education spending is only 11% of the national total. Education in our country is mostly a state and local issue. Federal spending on education is split roughly into thirds. Primary and secondary education spending is on the Head Start program and on various grants. Tertiary education spending goes mostly toward Pell Grants, need-based funds to

---

16. The iPhone X was released just prior to publication. Unfortunately, Apple doesn't have quite enough cash sitting around to buy one of the latest model for each of us.
17. See? Just like I promised.

pay for college education. The remaining $44 billion goes toward job training, vocational schools, and many smaller programs.

In total, it's enough money to build around 7,000 new elementary schools each year.

Transportation: $92 billion (2%)

The majority ($68 billion) of this spending goes to ground transportation, meaning roads and a bit of rail. Air transport costs $21 billion and water transport the remainder.

With this budget, we could build 4,500 miles of new Interstate highways every year.[18]

Foreign Relations: $61 billion (1.5%)

About $15 billion each go towards foreign military aid and to running the State Department. The balance ($33 billion) goes to non-military foreign aid. As we said above, this represents less than 1% of the federal budget.

We spend about as much on foreign relations as we spent annually on the Iraq War.

Government Operations: $43 billion (1%)

The federal court system cost us $24 billion last year, and the legislative and executive branches added on $13 billion each.

It's enough money to buy a membership at Mar-a-Lago for every resident of Boise. At the new, higher price.

Protection: $33 billion (1%)

The FBI, ATF, and other federal law enforcement services cost $27 billion per year. Federal prisons cost us $6 billion per year.

---

18. If you are wondering why your roads are still so bad, despite all this money, experts think U.S. spending on infrastructure is only around half of what is needed just to maintain our transportation system. On a related topic, the average tax on U.S. gasoline is $0.53 per gallon, compared to an average of $2.62 per gallon for the rest of the developed world.

If you had $33 billion, each of the Walton siblings would still be slightly richer than you.

Other: $52 billion (1%)

The budget has a long tail of smaller items. Farm subsidies cost $19 billion, slightly more than we spend on NASA. Land management and other environmental programs cost $20 billion, and an additional $7 billion goes to the water supply.[19] Community development takes up $21 billion and the National Park System $3 billion. This spending is offset by around $50 billion of revenues from government programs to insure mortgages (FHA) and bank deposits (FDIC).

There it is. $3,853,000,000,000 goes a long way.

WHAT IF THE PROCESS DOESN'T WORK?

Going back to our process for determining government spending, there are several stages at which it could go off the rails. They range in severity from "Pundits Clutch Their Pearls" to "This Is Pretty Annoying" to "We Might Be Living in the 18th Century Again."

Congress fails to pass a budget: "Pundits Clutch Their Pearls"

As we said, the budget is important but mostly symbolic. As Washington has become more partisan and more dysfunctional over the last two decades, the cerebral budget process has become harder to complete. Practically, this hasn't mattered to the everyday American. Do you even know if a budget was passed in 2017?[20]

The budget should be an important planning document; it should set out priorities for our government for longer periods than possible through the annual appropriations bills. The process should help departments to think about their longer-term funding needs, which are then prioritized by the administration and codified in Congress. But, the de facto process has clearly evolved, with appro-

---

19. Seems like a steal at $20 per person per year.
20. One was, but only as a vehicle to repeal the ACA via the reconciliation process. Before 2015, there were five consecutive years without a budget.

priations becoming more important at the expense of the budget. We should recognize reality by amending the 1974 CBA to account for how things actually work. But in today's world, too much concern about the lack of a symbolic document seems quaint.

Appropriations bills aren't signed into law in a timely manner: "This Is Pretty Annoying"

As you now know, appropriations bills[21] are where the rubber meets the road and the decisions are made. If they are not passed by Congress and signed by the President before the hard deadline, the government is not funded. This is a **government shutdown**.

The possibility of government shutdowns exists because of the separation of powers between our executive and legislative branches. According to the Constitution, the legislative branch must approve all government spending. If they are unable (or refuse) to do so, then the executive branch (in theory) can't spend any money. In practice, until about thirty-five years ago, Congress had little actual power to force the President to spend money it hadn't allocated. It's hard to enforce rules against the President, who has a literal army behind him. Amendments to what is called the Antideficiency Act put some teeth behind Congress's power of the purse.[22]

Under current law, if the government is not funded, all departments must stop non-essential work. Employees are furloughed, and agency activities halted. In theory, a shutdown should affect only programs funded by discretionary spending. In practice, mandatory spending can also be affected. For example, if the employees of the Social Security Administration are not considered essential (and they aren't) then the mandatory Social Security checks won't go out.

Government shutdowns are unhealthier than unpassed budgets. Government employees are especially affected; they may not get re-

---

21. Or, alternatively, continuing resolutions.
22. The workings of the Antideficiency Act are tricky, but the idea is that federal employees can't spend money that Congress didn't authorize. Government employees can be individually prevented from doing so by the courts. This avoids direct confrontation between Congress and the President. The Antideficiency Act has numerous exceptions, and the interpretation of what portions of the government must close during a shutdown is based on legal advice ultimately emanating from the White House.

paid the salaries lost during their furlough.[23] Television news during a shutdown focuses on high-profile topics like the National Parks being closed. But critical portions of the government that you never see are also halted, such as processing NIH grants and infrastructure work. Even the court system will grind to a halt, if the shutdown lasts long enough.

In other words, a brief shutdown, lasting a couple days, is mostly a high-level nuisance. However, we have never faced a lengthy shutdown of several months; at that point, the effects would become more pronounced and visible.

We breach the debt ceiling: "We Might be Living in the 18th Century Again"

We've never breached the debt ceiling, so we don't know what would happen if we did. Without claiming the ability to predict the future, count me as a debt ceiling alarmist.

The debt ceiling is a piece of legislation that sets a cap on the total amount of debt that can be issued by the U.S. Treasury. On its face, this seems like a reasonable way to constrain the debt, but there is a big problem. The cap in the debt ceiling is set without considering the obligations that are taken on through mandatory spending and the appropriations bills. This sets up a potentially major conflict.[24]

The first version of what evolved into today's debt ceiling was passed in 1917. Since then, it has been raised about 100 times, in various forms. Many debt ceiling raises have been simple and clean, especially when one party controlled the entire government. However, on several occasions, both parties have taken the debt ceiling hostage to achieve a policy goal. Most critically, in 2011, Republi-

---

23. Yes, they usually get them back after it is settled, but no, that doesn't mean it's not a problem. Government employees are a big part of the economy, which suffers due to government shutdowns, hurting us all.

24. The House of Representatives tried to solve this problem from 1980 until 2010, when the Gephardt Rule was in effect. This parliamentary rule caused the debt ceiling to be raised automatically when spending was approved in the House; it could therefore never be breached, as a practical matter. Rules like this in both chambers would defuse the debt ceiling time bomb. Of course, Congress makes its own rules, and it could re-arm the bomb at any time. If fact, the original Gephardt Rule was waived for 11 of the 30 years it existed. And it has now been completely removed from the House rule book.

cans in Congress took the game of chicken too far, rattling financial markets and causing the federal debt to be downgraded by Standard & Poors.

What would happen if we breached the debt ceiling? Again, we don't know, but here is what I think.

With total debt at the level of the ceiling, the government would necessarily be unable to pay some of its bills. Federal cash accounts vary throughout the year, so this is true even if the government is running an overall surplus. If the debt ceiling breach lasted only a very short period, maybe it wouldn't be such a big deal. Maybe the federal government could act in a manner similar to a government shutdown: pay the critical bills and delay others until the crisis is averted. Federal district judges will be upset to have their paychecks delayed, but disaster would be averted. Unfortunately, the government itself says that this strategy won't work.

In the lead-up to the 2011 debt ceiling crisis, President Obama's Treasury Department made it clear that they did not have the ability to prioritize payments, for two reasons. Legally, Treasury is required to pay bills as they come due. They can't pick and choose. Technically, Treasury systems just don't allow for prioritization of outflows. Some senior politicians thought these warnings were a bluff, and that Treasury would find a way to avoid the worst. I disagree; I think that even a brief debt ceiling breach will cause a default on at least some pieces of U.S. government debt.

Banks depend on U.S. government debt as default-proof, or risk-free. This assumption is part of the bedrock of how they stay in business. A default on the debt—even if just a technical default, even if only on some of the debt, and even if just for a day—would cause, at a minimum, a breakdown in the mechanisms that fund our economy in the short-term. Commercial paper markets, repo markets, short-term asset financing—these would cease operation very quickly.

Do you know who relies on these types of funding? The power plant that generates your electricity and the utility that provides your running water. So does the company that owns the trucks bringing food to your grocery store. The city and state that you live in, and the public services they operate like fire and police departments, also have funding needs. Same with hospitals, doctors' offices, airlines, and seaports. Without cash, none of these would be able to operate for very long.

Maybe I'm wrong and a short-term, minor debt ceiling breach wouldn't cause our entire country to stop in its tracks. Do you want to find out?

The debt ceiling is a pointless instrument. It allows politicians to grandstand against government borrowing without doing anything about it. To grandstand with an economic suicide vest strapped on.

If politicians are worried about the long-term fiscal picture, then they should take action. They should convince the public that they don't need those new roads or that new health care or that we should tax billionaires' investment income at the same rate the rest of us pay. Then they should write amendments to the tax code or appropriations bills. And pass them into law. This would improve the fiscal outlook for our country in a way that the debt ceiling never has.

More generally, both politicians and civilians talk about cutting government spending. They talk about the perils of debt and ask why we spend money on this or that. You can make arguments that we should tax and spend less; you can also make arguments that we should spend more, and tax enough to pay for it. This is a decision we need to make as a society.

But as we have seen, fully 85% of federal spending is on health, pensions, military, or interest on the national debt. When a politician says that they want to cut spending, but imply that it won't affect you, they are not being honest. Government should be more efficient, and we should find ways to make it so. But, if we want to make cuts that are meaningful to the big picture, people will get hurt. Either seniors will be forced into poverty (by cutting Social Security or Medicare), or the working poor and children prevented from getting food and medical care (cutting Medicaid, CHIP or SNAP), or the military downsized significantly. All other spending combined is peanuts.

Or we could just not pay the interest on the national debt. But as we saw, that might not work out so well.

GAME THEORY AND THE NUCLEAR AGE, PART I
THE DESTROYER OF WORLDS

"It is a harnessing of the basic power of the universe. The force from which the sun draws its power has been loosed against those who brought war to the Far East."
—Harry S. Truman

Imagine wanting to know what is on the inside of a baseball. But you aren't allowed to cut into it or peel off the skin. You can't look for interactions with chemicals, heat, or fire. You can only stand a mile away, shoot at it with a rifle, and see what flies off. That is nuclear physics.

As late as the year 1895, there was little evidence of any particles smaller than the atom. A mere 50 years later, the power of such sub-atomic particles had been harnessed in the most dramatic fashion possible. The unleashing of the nuclear age changed the rules of war: mankind now had the power to destroy itself. Two superpowers soon would face off in a five-decade struggle, the likes of which had never been seen. To survive, our greatest minds had to develop a new way of thinking about the very nature of cooperation and competition. They created a new branch of mathematics, whose results have been critical in our survival through the early years of the Nuclear Age.

- How do nuclear bombs work? How were they built?
- How did nuclear weapons proliferate?
- What is game theory?

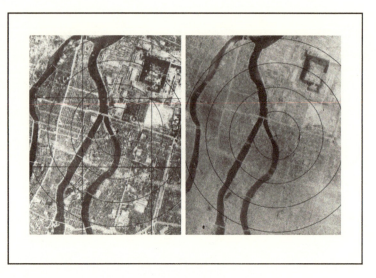

A WORD OF CAUTION FROM THE AUTHOR

Nuclear weapons are terrible things. This is true in all the meanings of the word. Terrible: extremely bad, as in "a terrible movie." Terrible: formidable in nature, as in "a terrible responsibility." Terrible: extreme or great, as in "a terrible disappointment." Nuclear weapons are not to be trifled with, joked about, or handled, except with extreme care.

Which is all to say—you will soon be reading about death, destruction, fallout, nuclear winters, and the end of humanity. We will repeatedly cause the gruesome theoretical deaths of millions. We will explicitly do this through the lens of a game, winning and losing, keeping score of the destruction, and ignoring any human effect. We will not modify our usual style of writing or the ongoing attempts at mild humor. We are not focused on the morality of these weapons, their development, or their use. Except in this short introduction.

The past 500 years have been a period of nearly uninterrupted human advancement. As our knowledge of chemistry and physics progressed, it was inevitable that we would learn about the power of the atom. Every man, woman, and child is innately aware of this power. It stares you in the face every day, from sunrise to sunset. We could not avoid thinking about the great power of the sun and eventually making attempts to harness that power. Some would want to use this power purely for peaceful means. I claim that it is inevitable that we would eventually open the Pandora's Box of nuclear weapons. It was unavoidable after five centuries of discoveries about the universe we live in.

Only by accepting the certainty of their development can we address the morality of nuclear weapons. How can these weapons be controlled to prevent their use? The decades following the first atomic bombs were not just a scramble to build bigger bombs, but also to develop these controls. Game theory is the most effective control we've found. And we can only learn the game theory of nuclear weapons by repeatedly simulating the destruction of the world.

Only by understanding these weapons can we prevent their use.

—NC

HOW DO NUCLEAR BOMBS WORK? HOW WERE THEY BUILT?

The three primary subatomic particles were discovered by three citizens of the British Empire over a period of thirty-five years around the turn of the last century. All three were associated with the famed Cavendish Laboratory at Cambridge University.[1]

In 1897, J.J. Thompson was working with cathode rays. At the time, nobody knew what these rays were made of. Thompson measured the speed at which they traveled; they moved too fast to be as large as an atom. He therefore deduced particles smaller than an atom must exist. He also found that these rays interact with an electrical field; the particle he discovered had an electric charge. It was the **electron**.

By 1908, Ernest Rutherford had already achieved results that made him immortal in the world of physics. He had won a Nobel Prize for formalizing the nature of radioactivity. But he was far from finished. One day, he decided to shoot alpha particles at a sheet of gold foil. Amazingly, some of the particles bounced back. As Rutherford himself said, "It was almost as incredible as if you fired a 15-inch shell at a piece of tissue paper and it came back and hit you." Clear-

---

1. Rutherford found the proton at Manchester, but then he moved to the Cavendish.

ly, there were some tiny, dense spots in the atoms that made up the gold foil. Because they repelled the positively charged alpha particles, they must themselves have positive charge. Rutherford named these particles **protons.**

Scientists knew that there was something still missing, because atoms were heavier than could be explained by just protons and electrons. They also knew that these theoretical particles had no charge, making them difficult to find. James Chadwick, a protégé of Rutherford's, worked tirelessly, irradiating various substances and developing new detection techniques. He found the elusive **neutrons.** The basic model of the atom was complete: a nucleus of tightly bound protons and neutrons with tiny electrons orbiting it.[2]

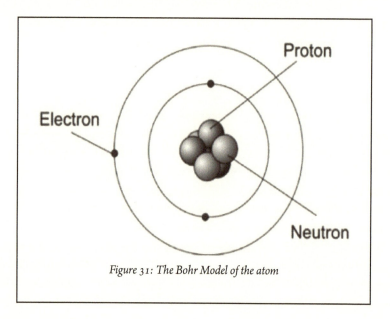

Figure 31: The Bohr Model of the atom

---

2. The Bohr Model of the atom shown in Figure 31 has been entirely refuted based on further discoveries but it works for our purposes. Recall that elements are defined as containing a specific number of protons, which is called their **atomic number.** For each element, the nucleus also contains various numbers of neutrons; the number of neutrons determines the **isotope** of the element. The sum of the number of protons and neutrons is the **atomic weight.** For example, all carbon atoms have six protons. Carbon-12 is an isotope of carbon with six neutrons, making a total atomic weight of 12. Similarly, carbon-14 has eight neutrons and an atomic weight of 14.

High school chemistry is the study of electrons; chemical reactions involve exchanging or sharing them. Radioactivity is a process of the nucleus: protons and neutrons. For instance, if you bombard an atom with neutrons, some of these will be captured by the nucleus. Do this enough, the nucleus grows enough to become unstable. It might then undergo **beta decay**, where a neutron turns into proton and an electron.[3] Your atom is now a different element, but the nucleus contains the same number of total particles. Another type of radioactivity is **alpha decay**, where an atom gets too big and spits out a particle containing two protons and two neutrons. This, again, will change our atom into a different element.

Unlike protons, the uncharged neutron is not repelled by the nucleus. They can therefore be more easily shot at nuclei in order to cause nuclear reactions. With Chadwick's discovery, scientists could start to have some real fun.[4]

In 1934, Enrico Fermi used neutrons to bombard the heaviest naturally occurring element, uranium. He hoped to create heavier elements, never before seen by man. Soon he had created two elements that were definitely not uranium; he believed these were the heavy elements that we now know as neptunium and plutonium. But Otto Hahn, Lise Meitner, Otto Frisch, and Fritz Strassman, conducting similar experiments, soon identified one of them as barium, a much smaller element. Rather than undergoing reactions like alpha or beta decay, the uranium nuclei had been cleaved in two. They had discovered **nuclear fission.**

They also found an odd property of fission reactions; they create a large amount of energy with no obvious source. We know from Albert Einstein that $E = mc^2$, where E is energy, m is mass and c is the speed of light. This suddenly appearing energy could come from only one place: the masses of the products of the fission reaction were less than those of the input. Because the speed of light is a very large number, even the tiny decrease in mass caused by fission created an enormous amount of energy.

---

3. Beta decay also spits out something called a neutrino and there are virtual particles involved too. These don't do much, so we can safely ignore them.
4. Of course, they didn't really know the risks of doing so. Marie Curie died of cancer caused by prolonged exposure to radiation.

Leo Szilard, a Hungarian-born physicist living in the United States, began to think about the possibility of **nuclear chain reactions**. In the newly discovered fission reaction, along with energy, each atom releases three neutrons when it splits.[5] If these neutrons hit other uranium atoms and cause more fission, each of these reactions would in turn release three neutrons. Each of these hit three more atoms, releasing three more. The number of fission reactions could increase at an exponential rate. Each of these reactions releases an enormous amount of energy. Szilard, explained the possibility to Einstein, who immediately saw the implication: you could make an incredibly powerful bomb out of this reaction. With Einstein's introduction, Szilard sent a letter to President Roosevelt explaining the significance of nuclear chain reactions. There were hints that Nazi Germany might be developing nuclear technology, so there was no time to lose. The United States soon committed its enormous industrial capacity to the development of a nuclear weapon.

---

5. Or two neutrons. Or sometimes another number.

An Aside: Calculating the Energy of Fission

It sounds boring, but I assure you, it's quite explosive.

In your world, when you take two things that weigh one pound each and glue them together, the product weighs two pounds. This does not hold true at the atomic level. When protons and neutrons are "glued" together, the whole weighs less than the sum of the parts. What happens to the rest of the mass?

In his famous equation, Einstein told us that mass and energy are related. Recall that the nucleus of an atom is made up of positively charged protons and uncharged neutrons. Rather than repel, as we would expect of like-charged particles, protons bunch together in the tiny nucleus. They are bound together by the so-called strong force, which is created by the energy equivalent to the missing mass. Both fission and fusion occur when products of a nuclear reaction have less mass than their inputs. The missing mass is converted to energy. Calculating the energy of fission is straightforward. We'll use a common example of the fission reaction that occurs when a uranium (U) atom is hit by a neutron (n). One common reaction is for the uranium to split into one rubidium (Rb) and one cesium (Cs) atom, while releasing two neutrons:

$$U + n \rightarrow Rb + Cs + 2n$$

By totaling the masses on each side of the equation, we see that for each uranium atom undergoing fission, $0.323 * 10^{-27}$ kilograms of mass is lost. We can convert this to energy: $E = mc^2$. Each reaction creates $2.9 * 10^{-11}$ joules of energy. This is a tiny amount of energy—too small to have an effect on a human scale. But we have a lot of atoms we can split. A chemist can tell you that $6.022 * 10^{23}$ atoms of uranium-235 have a mass of 235.04 grams, or about half a pound. Uranium is very dense; these atoms would fit in a tablespoon. If this spoonful of uranium reacted fully via fission, it would release $1.75 * 10^{13}$ joules of energy. To put it into every-day terms, you can fit enough uranium in the palm of your hand to provide the energy used by an American family in one year.

At this point, the nuclear chain reaction was only theoretical. The first step toward building The Bomb was to demonstrate one. Working on a squash court under the stands of the University of Chicago football stadium, a team led by Enrico Fermi built the first nuclear reactor on December 2, 1942.[6] Having demonstrated chain reactions were possible, the biggest challenge in building a bomb was the timely production of their fuel, uranium-235 and plutonium. The Army acquired enormous sites at Oak Ridge, Tennessee, and Hanford, Washington to do this.

In general, to create a nuclear bomb, two small pieces of nuclear fuel must be combined to make a **critical mass.** But this combination has to happen very quickly, or it will fizzle. To solve this and other problems involved in building The Bomb, a group of top scientists moved to Los Alamos, high in the New Mexico Desert. The scientific work was placed under the control of Robert Oppenheimer, the Father of the Bomb. This was the Manhattan Project.[7]

While work was proceeding on a fission bomb, scientists also recognized the possibility of creating a bomb by joining atoms together, a process called **fusion.** Fusion is what the sun does: hydrogen atoms combine to form helium. This reaction causes a much greater loss of mass than uranium fission. Therefore, it releases much more energy.[8] But to cause a fusion reaction your fuel must be at an incredibly

---

6. It weighed around 400 tons and produced ½ watt of energy. In other words, it would have taken around 100 of these reactors to power a single 50-watt lightbulb.

7. Many other sites were also part of the Project, including Oak Ridge and Hanford.

8. We can demonstrate the power of fusion. Put your hand out in the sunlight. It gets warm quickly; it is taking in a lot of energy every second. That energy is all coming from the sun's fusion reactions. Imagine a sphere around the sun as large as

high temperature. The best way to heat it up? Set off a fission bomb first. At the time, the fusion bomb was called the "Super"; today, we usually say H-Bomb, after hydrogen's chemical symbol.

HOW DID NUCLEAR WEAPONS PROLIFERATE?

All of the scientists who worked on the first nuclear weapons understood that these weapons would change the world. They saw, long before the politicians, exactly what it meant to unleash the power of uncontrolled nuclear chain reactions. Winston Churchill, for all his greatness, thought the bomb was just another weapon. Given that he had lived through The Blitz, it was reasonable for him to desire a bigger bomb with which to strike back. And humankind had been improving on weapons for millennia; to him, this looked like the logical next step. It took the scientists, with their formulas and their slide rules, to understand that the nature of war would never be the same.

During the period of the Manhattan Project, we were in a war for survival. Many fine physicists remained in Germany (and some in Japan). Fission had been known before the war; Reich scientists could easily have made the next step, discovering chain reactions. Given the enormous investment required to produce the first bombs, it was unlikely that the Axis would have one in time to affect the war's result, but there was no way to be sure. Espionage showed that at least some work continued in Germany; a heavy-water production facility in occupied Norway was especially concerning.[9] Even a small possibility of a Nazi bomb was unacceptable, especially to the many scientist-refugees who had fled Nazi terror. The scientists working on the Manhattan Project built these weapons of mass destruction despite—or, maybe, because of—a strong understanding of its implications.[10]

Earth's orbit, a diameter of 180 million miles. Think of how many hands it would take to cover that sphere. Every second of every day, the sun produces enough energy to heat them all.

9. The destruction of the Vemork, Norway heavy-water plant was one of the most spectacular Allied actions of the entire War. It is a fascinating story, but unfortunately beyond our scope.

The first real attempt by world leaders to manage the nuclear age was the Quebec Agreement, signed by Winston Churchill and Franklin Roosevelt in August 1943. It stated that the U.K. and U.S. would share resources "to bring the Tube Alloys [Manhattan] project to fruition at the earliest moment." It also included the world's first nuclear arms control agreement:

"We will never use this agency against each other.

We will not use it against third parties without each other's consent.

We will not either of us communicate any information about Tube Alloys to third parties except by mutual consent."

At this stage of the war, the immediate question was whether information on the bomb should be shared with the Soviet Union. Niels Bohr brought the topic to Roosevelt, suggesting that Stalin be brought in on the secret. Bohr did not trust the Soviet leader but knew that a Russian Bomb was inevitable. Building a bomb was just not that difficult. After the war, Russia would have the means, motive, and opportunity to do so. If they were going to get one anyway, why not try to create some type of control now? Roosevelt designated Bohr a semi-official envoy to bring this message to the British Prime Minister. Churchill, an anti-Communist of the old school and still not understanding the bomb's implications, thought Bohr mad.

After the war, Russia built a bomb. Like the American Manhattan Project, it took the Soviet Union about four years of concerted effort. We haven't mentioned any Russian physicists by name, but there were many of world-class quality. Captured German scientists augmented their program, but the half century of theoretical and experimental work had long since been complete. The bomb's feasibility was visible in two mushroom clouds over Japan. Stalin's totalitarian regime had no trouble assigning the appropriate resources; the

---

10. Many of the scientists remaining in Nazi Germany were clearly conflicted about creating a bomb for Hitler. The most prominent nuclear scientist remaining in Germany was Werner Heisenberg, head of Germany's nuclear project. His internal conflict in building a bomb for Hitler is known from contemporaneous sources. We don't know for sure if he tried and failed to build a bomb, if he thought it impossible, or if he intentionally stalled the research.

trickiest part was finding uranium.[11] The first Russian nuclear test was in 1949.

This, of course, forced a response from the U.S. During the war, development of the hydrogen bomb was not a top priority. This was due not to lack of belief in its feasibility, but rather how long its development would take. The fact that the fusion bomb would require a fission bomb meant that the latter would, a priori, be the first ready for use. The main proponent of developing H-bombs, both during and after the war, was the Hungarian-born physicist Edward Teller. President Truman responded to the Russian nuclear test by accelerating this development; Teller returned to Los Alamos. The Super was tested successfully in 1952, just three years later.

The hydrogen bomb caused another fundamental change in geopolitics. Fission bombs were terrible weapons. The Fat Man bomb dropped on Nagasaki had a yield equivalent to 21,000 tons of TNT and destroyed everything within a blast radius of one mile. Around 40,000 people were killed immediately; radiation poisoning killed many more. But the first H-bomb, code named Ivy Mike, had a yield of 10,400,000 tons of TNT. A fission bomb levels part of a city; a fusion bomb would destroy a small state. Again, the Russians weren't far behind, detonating their first H-bomb in 1953. To make matters worse, while fission weapons have technical limitations on their maximum size, fusion bombs can be built to nearly any magnitude. By 1961, the Soviets had developed the largest weapon in human history, Tsar Bomba, with a potential yield of 100 million tons of TNT.[12]

With Pandora's Box wide open, other countries wanted to join the nuclear club. When the Quebec Agreement was cancelled at the end of the war, the U.K. felt the need for an independent nuclear deterrent. Their first nuclear test was in 1952, and by 1957 they were the third state armed with fusion bombs. France, alienated from both the U.S. and U.S.S.R. after the Suez Crisis, became the fourth nuclear nation in 1960 and soon had her own Supers. China began

---

11. Yes, they also got some useful intelligence from the Manhattan Project, most famously from the Rosenbergs and Klaus Fuchs. Those who gave the Russians our nuclear secrets were awful traitors, without question. But, in the big picture, they were irrelevant. Russia was going to get the bomb.
12. The version tested had a yield of "only" 50 million tons.

to trade with the Soviet Union, giving up nuclear raw materials in exchange for nuclear know-how. This piece of the complex, multi-decade Sino-Soviet relationship helped China become the last member of the "big five" nuclear states. Today, India, Pakistan, and North Korea also acknowledge their nuclear capabilities; Israel's government is strategically vague, but few doubt the capacity is there. South Africa claims to have produced nuclear weapons but has since eliminated its program.

WHAT IS GAME THEORY?

For centuries, we have attempted to understand and systematize the way people interact in competitive situations. Diplomacy, warfare, trade—even love and marriage. The best practitioners of each are those who understand other players' choices and motivations. Henry V slew all the French prisoners at Agincourt, in full view of their commanders. His soldiers therefore knew there would be no quarter given if they surrendered. Cortez burned his ships after landing in Mexico. His soldiers knew there was no turning back, while the Aztecs feared his confidence. Nobody knew it at the time, but these were primitive applications of game theory to warfare.

It was not until 1944 that a mathematical framework for games began to develop. This was the year John von Neumann and Oskar Morgenstern published *Theory of Games and Economic Behavior*. It launched a new discipline of mathematics.[13] While many applications of game theory were still years or decades away, the basic structure and language had been created.

Game theory is the mathematics describing the way we cooperate and compete. It is concerned with situations where your best action depends on the expected behavior of your opponent. Its complexity

---

13. If you don't know him, von Neumann is one of the most brilliant and fascinating people of the 20th century. He contributed to pure and applied mathematics, statistics, computer science, and economics. He wasn't a full-time member of the Manhattan Project team, but on one of his drop-ins to Los Alamos, he invented key components of the plutonium bomb. Later, he worked with Teller on the H-Bomb. He was also an infamous eater and drinker, and a center of the Princeton social life in his impeccable three-piece suits. Like too many great mathematicians, he died before his time, in 1957 at the age of 53.

comes from the fact that the world of game theory is not a passive one. In game theory, all the players are thinking, rational beings. Strategies in game theory are dynamic, constantly responding to changes in expectations.

An important concept in game theory is **utility**. Utility is a measure of how useful something is or how much you want it.[14] In real life, determining utility can be tricky. I don't surf and have no utility for a surfboard. Others might get a lot of use out of it. I'd love to have one apple, but 1,000 apples wouldn't be 1,000 times better; most would spoil before I could eat them. How do we think about utility in a modified game of Russian Roulette where you receive a prize of $1,000,000 for playing, but risk the ultimate loss?

In game theory, we don't worry about these questions and utility is abstracted to a number. The goal of each player is to maximize this number. There is no extra credit for being nice and no penalty for causing conflict.[15] A utility of +2 is better than +1, which is itself better than 0 or -1. For simple games, utilities are usually displayed in a matrix; in each cell, the first number is the utility for Player 1, the second is for Player 2. Here is our first example:

Where will we go tonight?		Player 2	
		Party	Home
Player 1	Party	10,10	0,0
	Home	0,0	5,5

Figure 32: Pure Coordination Game

In this game, both players have a choice between going to a Party or staying Home. Both players want to be sure they are at the same place and both prefer if that place is the Party. Remembering that

---

14. For once, we've found a word that has the same meaning in mathematics as in real life.
15. Or, if you like, these credits and penalties are incorporated into the utility number.

each player is rational *and knows the other is rational*, this is a trivial game. Both will always choose to go to the Party and utility for both will be maximized. We can make the game more complex by imagining one British player and one American player, and putting them behind the steering wheels of two cars:

What side shall we drive on?		Player 2	
		Left Side	Right Side
Player 1	Left Side	10,10	0,0
	Right Side	0,0	10,10

Figure 33: Choosing Sides

Here, we have a problem. If the players have no way to communicate, they can only guess what the other will do and try to match it. There is no winning strategy; it's just luck. However, if we give them the ability to communicate, the game is again easily solved. The players don't care which side of the road they use, as long as they don't crash. They should be able to agree easily if given a chance. But it gets even more complex when my wife and I decide what to have for dinner:

What shall we have for dinner?		Wife	
		Fish	Steak
Husband	Fish	5, 10	0,0
	Steak	0,0	10, 5

Figure 34: Battle of the Sexes

Because the players now have different utilities for each result, there is potential for conflict.[16] In theory, we should be able to talk and agree on a meal; after all, if we are unable to, then neither gets anything to eat. However, we are now both incentivized to choose our preferred meal. There is a chance that neither of us is willing to compromise, leaving everybody hungry and bitter. Without any communication, the chance of this happening is even greater.[17]

The Battle of the Sexes game gives us an opportunity to define a new term, the **Nash equilibrium**.[18] A Nash equilibrium is an outcome of a game where neither player would change their decision, even with the knowledge of the other player's final decision. A game can have more than one Nash equilibrium—or none at all. In Battle of the Sexes, {Fish, Fish} and {Steak, Steak} are both Nash equilibriums. You can easily check that both players would be worse off if, starting from one of these outcomes, they unilaterally changed their strategy. In a sense, Nash equilibriums are the stable outcomes for a game.

The most famous example of game theory is the Prisoner's Dilemma. In a Prisoner's Dilemma, two criminals have been arrested after a burglary. If the criminals Cooperate (with each other) by remaining silent, the police have enough evidence to convict both on a lesser charge.[19]. If either prisoner Betrays (their partner), he will be allowed to go free, but his partner will receive a long sentence. If *both* prisoners confess, then they will both be found guilty and face a harsh penalty. We can define utility as the number of years in jail; the best-case scenario is a utility of 0, because jail is bad:

---

16. Yes, that is the real name in mathematics for this example.
17. Obviously, in my household, this would never happen. Being knowledgeable of game theory, I quickly choose whichever option will result in the greatest utility for my wife. Being a rational player, she also expects this.
18. Yes, this is what John Nash from *A Beautiful Mind* won his Nobel Prize for.
19. Say, trespassing.

Will I betray my partner?		Prisoner 2	
		Cooperate	Betray
Prisoner 1	Cooperate	-1,-1	-3,0
	Betray	0,-3	-2,-2

Figure 35: The Prisoner's Dilemma

From the perspective of the group *as a whole*, the best outcome is for both prisoners to Cooperate; they will spend only two years in jail combined. The worst outcome for the group is for both to Betray: four years combined. Despite this, no matter what the other prisoner does, you are always better off Betraying. Whether your opponent Cooperates or Betrays, your jail time is reduced one year by selling him out. Therefore, the only Nash equilibrium in this game is {Betray, Betray}— the worst outcome for the group.[20]

Our final game, and the one that will tie back to nuclear war, is Chicken. It's just like famous scene in the movie *Rebel Without a Cause*. Two drivers are headed toward a cliff, and each must decide to Swerve First or Swerve Last. If both Swerve First, the game is a draw. If exactly one Swerves First, he is the Chicken and is embarrassed in front of his friends. If both Swerve Last, they drive off the cliff and lose:

---

20. The Prisoner's Dilemma has been extensively studied, both theoretically and in real-life. Despite Betray being the optimal strategy, many real-life participants choose to Cooperate. The Prisoner's Dilemma has several interesting variations. What if the players can communicate before making their decisions? What if the game is played multiple times, allowing players to build trust?

When will I swerve?		Player 2	
		First	Last
Player 1	First	0, 0	-1, 1
	Last	1, -1	-10, -10

Figure 36: Chicken

If you look closely, you can also see two countries holding nuclear weapons, deciding whether to use them.

—§—

Writing this, I was struck by the global confluence of great scientists working during the interwar period. This great, global salon was not our first; the period from 1850 until 1880 featured the best work of Maxwell, Riemann, Faraday, Mendeleev, and Darwin, among many others.

For every great mind I included in this section, three were left out. A discussion of nuclear physics is incomplete without Marie and Pierre Curie, who developed radioactivity. The great theoretical physicists behind quantum mechanics, including Paul Dirac and Erwin Schrödinger, are also absent. I even skipped many of those directly involved in the Manhattan Project: Ernest Lawrence, Hans Bethe, Rudolf Peierls, Emilio Segrè, George Kistiakowsky, Luis Alvarez—the more I name, the wider the circle I've drawn, and the more I've left out.

I suppose it isn't my responsibility to give them what's due; they racked up shelves of Nobel Prizes for their efforts.[21] Yet, it seems relevant to note that Alfred Nobel created the Prizes as a penance, to atone for his creation of dynamite. It gained him immense wealth,

---

21. Others were snubbed. Otto Hahn won a Nobel for the discovery of fission, but history provides no clue why the prize wasn't shared with Lise Meitner and Otto Frisch.

partially by causing great death and destruction. In a great irony, the early laureates in physics and chemistry are littered with the key players in the creation of an even larger explosive.

But these scientists, almost to a person, understood the power of the forces with which they played. Before the politicians, they recognized that a new framework would be necessary in order to prevent our destruction as a species. Relying on morality, or altruism, would be a weak reed. They created instead a new mathematical discipline, describing how players compete, always trying to maximize their personal utilities. Only be creating frameworks by which people were personally incentivized against using them could a world with nuclear weapons be safe. Those who created the weapons were also been most responsible for limiting their use.

GERRYMANDERING
THE PRAYING MANTIS AND UPSIDE-DOWN ELEPHANT

"It is the duty of every man, though he may have but one day to live, to devote that day to the good of his country"
—*Elbridge Gerry*

Gerrymandering has been around a long time. Controlling election maps has long been a source of power. But in recent decades, partisan line-drawing has become more acute in U.S. elections. What once was an art form is now a science—with profound implications for how our government is run.

It is easy to go blissfully through life, never thinking about the shape of the Congressional district you live in. But that shape determines your Representative, who makes all those critical decisions about your life. Even worse, you care about the shape of other people's districts: Congressmen from other states each get one vote, same as the one you voted for or against. Who drew the lines for their districts?

When politicians get to decide their own voters, the possibility for conflict is obvious. Politics is a game of power; those who have it and those who want it. But we can hope that this power is used, at least occasionally, to fulfill the wishes of the people and improve their lives. Manipulating maps prevents citizens from having real input in the way they are governed.

- What is gerrymandering?
- How has it changed in the last twenty years?
- How is this possibly legal?

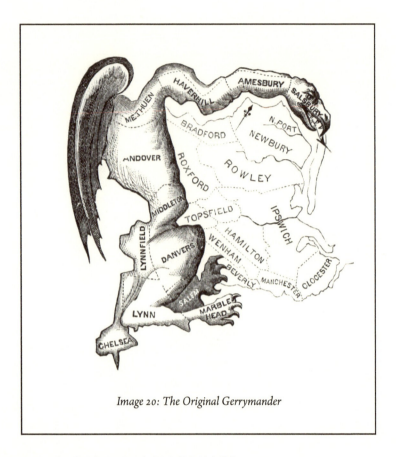

Image 20: The Original Gerrymander

WHAT IS GERRYMANDERING?

Gerrymandering is the process of drawing district lines for representatives in government via any non-algorithmic process.[1] A gerrymander is the result of such a process. It takes just two ingredients to ensure gerrymandering: district-based representation and discretion in creating said districts. Any jurisdiction which has these two features will have people involved in the drawing of lines. Humans will impart their preferences when they do this drawing.[2]

---

1. This is my personal definition. I like it because it doesn't consider the intent of those drawing the lines. "Redistricting" has a more neutral tone, but I fully admit to having non-neutral feelings about gerrymandering.
2. Gerrymandering is more powerful when the number of viable candidates in each jurisdiction is fewer. A system where the single leading vote-getter is elected regardless of vote share, known as "first past the post," is especially susceptible to

Let's go through a few examples, to see what is and is not gerrymandering:

- In the United Kingdom, the House of Commons consists of 650 seats, each held by a single member who represents a specific geographic area. This is gerrymandering, even though the districts are drawn by a non-partisan Boundary Commission.
- The French legislature has the virtually unlimited ability to draw its own maps for single-representative districts. This is gerrymandering.
- The United States Senate consists of two members from each state, whose boundaries are fixed.[3] This is not gerrymandering.
- Israel elects 120 members to its parliament, the Knesset, based on the proportion of votes received nationally. In other words, if a party receives 25% of all the votes, it will receive 30 seats. This is not gerrymandering.

There is no one best way to draw district lines. For example, consider a state with 100 total voters, 60 belonging to the Orange party and 40 to the Purple party. The area in question must be split into ten districts. We could put six Orange and four Purple people in every district, making each mirror the overall population. But then, the Orange Party would win all ten seats, which is clearly a problem. Alternatively, there could be six districts of all Orange voters to go with four districts of all Purple. The elected officials will look like the voters, but not a single seat will be remotely competitive, again far from ideal. You can split the people up geographically, but how? Put yourself in the seat of the decision maker and it is not at all simple.

When writing about gerrymandering, it is obligatory to mention where the word comes from. Elbridge Gerry was the Governor of Massachusetts in 1812 when his party, the Republicans, took control of the statehouse.[4] They took this chance to draw statehouse dis-

---

gerrymandering. Almost all U.S. Congressional and state legislative elections fit both criteria.

3. There are a few crazy proposals out there, like the fragmentation of California or Texas, to change state boundaries. These could be considered Senate gerrymandering in the unlikely event of their occurrence.

4. To confuse you a bit: Gerry's Republicans are the ancestors of today's Democrats.

tricts to maximize their electoral advantage. To do this, one seat had a particularly odd shape. A local political cartoonist thought the district looked a bit like a salamander, and the portmanteau is still active 200 years later.[5]

Image 21: Maryland's 3rd Congressional District

While other countries have their own fascinating line-drawing problems, our focus will be on the U.S. House of Representatives. As a quick refresher: every ten years the U.S. conducts a census. Based on its results, 435 House seats are divided between the states. States

---

5. Gerry is another of those fascinating persons who we are forced to deal with briefly in a footnote. He was on the Massachusetts Committee of Public Safety in 1775, and thus (in part) responsible for storing gunpowder at Concord, which the British fatefully decided to seize. He signed the Declaration of Independence and was a delegate to the Constitutional Convention but refused to sign the Constitution. Nevertheless, he was elected to the 1st Congress, where he was instrumental in passing the Bill of Rights. He got caught up in the ugly XYZ Affair, nearly leading to war with France and permanently tarnishing his reputation. Soon after creating the gerrymander, he lost his re-election for governor. James Madison then chose him as his Vice-Presidential candidate to replace George Clinton, who had died in office. Gerry himself died in office two years later. Today, there is a revisionist attempt to improve Gerry's historical image. Specifically, there are claims (that I am not able to substantiate) that he was reluctant to approve that original gerrymander. Oh, and you say his name with a hard "G", unlike his eponymous map-drawing technique.

that gain or lose a seat obviously must create new maps, but other states are required to react to internal changes in population density. As we mentioned in a previous chapter, the U.S. Constitution tells states almost nothing about how to conduct Congressional elections; it is silent as to how they should draw Congressional districts.[6] In pursuit of political goals, or their own self-interest, the paragons of virtue who inhabit our nation's 50 statehouses have been quite creative creating rules for gerrymandering.[7]

Ohio is a good example of many states' redistricting processes. Like 36 other states, Ohio's Congressional map is created by its state legislature, the Ohio General Assembly. Both houses of the Assembly must agree on a map, which can be vetoed by the governor.[8] Therefore, a party controlling both Assembly houses and the Ohio governor's mansion can draw almost any map it desires. Republicans held this so-called **trifecta** in 2012. The map they created has 12 safe Republican seats of 16 total, despite the GOP winning just 51% of the total 2012 Congressional vote.[9] If a state is unable to agree on a map, either because of split control of the state government or dysfunction within a single party, a court usually imposes its own map. This gives an incentive for the various stakeholders to compromise.

There are six states that draw Congressional maps outside of their legislatures.[10] In these states, a commission of some sort decides the lines. The goal of these redistricting commissions is to make the process less partisan; they have been largely successful. Most of these commissions were created via a citizen referendum process. Legislators seldom give up their map-drawing power voluntarily.

---

6. It took until 1963 just to clarify that the districts must have the same population.
7. A few states have only one Representative, hence no ability to gerrymander at the Federal level. But these states still do an admirable job of gerrymandering their state houses.
8. About half of the states using legislature-based redistricting allow for gubernatorial veto.
9. Total Congressional vote is an incomplete metric for determining fairness of maps because (among other reasons) not every House seat is contested by both parties. When thinking about partisan gerrymandering advantages, it's important to also look at senatorial and presidential races as well. Doing so makes the Ohio gerrymander look even worse, as the GOP lost both races in 2012, winning 44% and 47% of the vote, respectively.
10. Arizona, California, Hawaii, Idaho, New Jersey, and Washington.

There is one more wrinkle in redistricting, but it's a big one: The **Voting Rights Act** (VRA). Prior to its passage by Lyndon Johnson in 1965, equal protection of voting rights, while theoretically guaranteed by the 14th Amendment to the Constitution, had no way to be enforced by Congress. The VRA tried to remedy this in several ways, but we will focus on its Section 2. Section 2 of the VRA says that election maps are not permitted to dilute the voting power of minorities. This deceptively simple provision remains a subject of great debate, as the courts chase a formula to protect minority representation. One way that states attempt to avoid challenges of racial dilution is by creating **majority-minority districts**. Unfortunately, having such districts does not necessarily work to the advantage of said minorities. A district with an overwhelming minority population will allow them to be represented, but the same racial group split between several districts may be able to affect elections in all of them. Districts created for VRA compliance can thus result in wasted votes, with one minority candidate winning election by huge margins, but opponents winning all the surrounding seats.

An Aside: The 2003 Texas Re-Redistricting

We don't think of it today, but for over a century Texas was a Democratic bastion. It wasn't until 2003 that Republicans won a majority in the state legislature.

The Texas Congressional map drawn in 2002 was already GOP-friendly, having been created by a GOP-majority committee. But, with proper encouragement from national Republicans, they wanted to take their new-found legislative majority out for a spin. Despite the paint not yet being dry on the existing map, they conducted an unusual mid-decade gerrymander.

Things got weird when Texas Democrats attempted to prevent this by not showing up to the statehouse. Doing so would deny a quorum, preventing any business from being conducted. The GOP responded by sending the Texas Rangers to physically bring them to the Capitol. Fifty-two Texas House Democrats and then 11 Senate Democrats fled across state lines, outside the Rangers' jurisdiction.

This game couldn't continue indefinitely; the new map eventually passed, and the GOP gained several new seats. Since then, Texas maps have been challenged in court almost continually. They have been defeated several times as illegal racial gerrymanders.

But these cases take years to get through the court system. While they undergo this process, elections are conducted using a racially discriminatory map.

HOW HAS IT CHANGED IN THE LAST TWENTY YEARS?

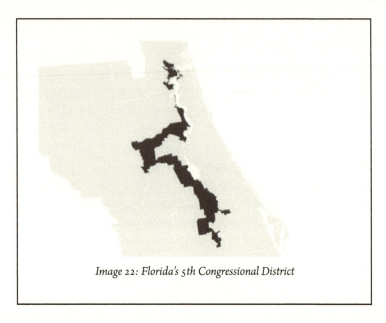

Image 22: Florida's 5th Congressional District

Before we look at the recent history of gerrymandering, let's talk a bit about its strategy. The core concept of partisan redistricting is called **packing and cracking**. To maximize the number of seats favorable to your political party, you first "pack" the other party's likely voters into as few districts as possible. The remainder are then "cracked" in equal portions between the remaining districts. If you are maximally efficient, they will be a significant, but electorally ineffective, minority in each. By packing and cracking, you can win a majority of seats without winning a majority of votes.

Sometimes, population geography can itself advantage one party. Packing and cracking is easier when your political opponents live in concentrated areas. New York's 15th Congressional District is an example of packing; José Serrano won a smooth 95.2% of the vote in his 2016 re-election. His district does not fit the traditional definition of gerrymandering, with a natural shape and a specific community of interest (South Bronx). But Serrano's 90% margin of victory meant that a lot of votes were wasted there.

Another fun redistricting trick is to play with the personal homes of the opposing candidates. Maybe the district lines shift, placing their abode in a neighboring district that your party safely controls. Maybe two Representatives of the other party are moved into the same district, guaranteeing that only one can be elected. Maybe the poor fool's home stays in the same district, but their base of support is moved next door. Politics ain't beanbag.

This leads to the start of our historical tale. In the olden days,[11] gerrymandering was usually intended to protect incumbents. Not that the world was less partisan, because it wasn't, but parties didn't attempt to absolutely maximize their legislative seats. Both sides agreed to a bit of back scratching, a "you can keep your seat if I can keep mine" kind of thing. These men[12] chatted together in the House Cloak Room, were shaved together at the Capitol Barber, and enjoyed bourbon in each other's offices at the end of a long legislative day.[13] They were friendly co-workers, who didn't push too hard to kick each other out of a job. Mutual non-aggression made sense for everybody.

Incumbent protection wasn't the best kind of government, but it had some redeeming features. Because the seats were usually less partisan, competitive races were more likely to pop up. By the time the 2002 map-drawing cycle was completed, however, many legislators were nakedly attempting to maximize their party's power by creating as many safe districts as possible. Without any type of check, partisan redistricting had taken over the system completely by 2012.

There are many reasons why redistricting has become more aggressively partisan in the last twenty years. Greater polarization in Congress created a motive. As more issues (and votes) involved splits along strict party lines, those with policy goals care more about maximizing blue or red seats. Also, as we described earlier, the battle for gerrymandering is really a battle in the statehouses; since 2000, races for state legislatures have become more nationalized. This is just a fancy way to say that more money has poured in. PACs, super PACs, issue advocacy groups, and spooky dark money have all made their presence clearly felt in previously obscure lo-

---

11. Meaning the 1990s.
12. Yes, men. As recently as 1993, men made up 93% of the House.
13. Although even the Cloak Rooms in Congress are partisan, as it turns out.

cal races. The parties themselves have also become more organized about gerrymandering. The GOP especially yearned for the power available to those controlling the lines. Their REDistricting MAjority Project (REDMAP) raised previously unheard-of sums to specifically target the redistricting process for the 2010 cycle.[14]

This came together in a perfect storm of the 2010 Congressional and gubernatorial elections. The President's political party usually loses seats in midterm elections. The passage of the Affordable Care Act gave the Republicans a message (if not a policy) to run on. Big money, freed from most constraints after the odious Citizens United decision earlier that year, made its presence felt across the political landscape as never before. The Republicans were focused on the redistricting prize and organized to take advantage. The results were stunning, as you can see in Table 3.[15]

---

14. Democrats also take advantage of redistricting when they are able. However, given their losses in the 2010 election, they didn't have many chances and didn't do so very effectively.
15. States not listed had either a) split control, b) a bi-partisan commission or c) a single district. Control of redistricting can be a gray area. For example, Missouri's map was passed by the GOP-controlled legislature over the Democratic governor's veto. However, they had to provide concessions; I did not list it as GOP-controlled. Washington redistricts via a commission, but in 2012 the commission had a clear GOP lean; again, I didn't include it here.

State	House Seats	Democratic Control	Republican Control
Alabama	7		X
Arkansas	4	X	
Connecticut	5	X	
Florida	27		X
Georgia	14		X
Illinois	18	X	
Indiana	9		X
Kansas	4		X
Maine	2		X
Maryland	8	X	
Massachusetts	9	X	
Michigan	14		X
Ohio	16		X
Oklahoma	5		X
Pennsylvania	18		X
South Carolina	7		X
Tennessee	9		X
Texas	36		X
Utah	4		X
West Virginia	3	X	
Wisconsin	8		X
TOTAL		47	180

Table 3: Partisan control of redistricting, 2012 cycle

As you can see, the GOP controlled redistricting for more than three times as many House seats as Democrats in this cycle.[16] How many

---

16. It's actually more lopsided than this chart shows. As of 2017, Massachusetts and Connecticut have only Democrats in Congress, meaning there is little potential for partisan gerrymandering. Maps created by Democrats in Arkansas and West Virginia resulted in those two states having precisely zero Democratic Representatives. Such maps are sometimes called "dummymanders." Only in Illinois and Maryland did the Democrats likely gain seats due to their maps. Against a theoretical neutral map, they probably gained one House seat in each.

seats did the GOP win compared to what would be expected in a neutral map? Well, there have been a lot of studies, and they involve a lot of assumptions. Generally, if a given party wins 55% of the Congressional vote in a state, you would expect it to win more than 55% of the seats. How many more depends on how the partisan populations are clustered.[17] A review of these studies shows that most experts think the GOP holds about 20 extra Congressional seats due to partisan redistricting.

By looking at the results of Congressional elections, we get a similar result. In 2012, Democrats won 50.6% of the total Congressional vote, but only 46.2% of the seats. This disparity of 4% remained consistent for the 2014 and 2016 elections. Similarly, the median Congressional seat in terms of partisanship leans about 3% toward the GOP compared to the national average.[18] This means that Democrats would need to win the national House vote by around 6% to be favored to win a House majority. Not all of this is necessarily due to gerrymandering; clustering of Democrats in cities is not an effective strategy to maximize their House seats. However, these assumption-free figures are consistent with the statistical methods: 4% of 435 nearly matches studies showing the GOP with 20 "extra" seats. In other words, control of the House of Representative in two of the three most recent Congressional sessions has been decided by the line-drawers rather than the voters.[19]

HOW IS THIS POSSIBLY LEGAL?

Let's review the process. State legislatures, operating below the radar and susceptible to out-of-state money, are the primary force in redistricting. The party that controls each statehouse can draw lines to

---

17. To take an extreme example, if 80% of a state voted for Party A, you would expect them to win nearly 100% the seats. Unless the opposition had a massive Party B cluster in a specific location, they won't have enough voters to win an outright majority in any individual district.
18. Meaning that if the national vote was equally split between the parties, we would expect the GOP to win at least 53% of the votes in half of the Congressional seats.
19. In the 114th Congress (2015-2017), the Republican Party finally won a majority of Congressional votes to go with their majority of Congressional seats.

benefit their side, irrespective of the will of the voters. This is considered okay.

Well, not quite. There are guidelines and limits on the drawing of maps. Unfortunately, the case law involved is very complex and, in many cases, not settled as of this writing.

Redistricting jurisprudence began in earnest in 1962, with the case of Baker v. Carr. At issue in Baker was the fact that Tennessee hadn't redrawn state legislature districts in sixty years. Population movement in the interim meant that the aged districts contained vastly different numbers of citizens. Some districts had ten times as many voters as others. The plaintiff claimed that the situation ran afoul of the 14th Amendment's guarantee of "equal protection of the law." Tennessee argued that district lines were a political issue, outside of the Court's purview.

Baker was one of the most challenging cases the Supreme Court ever faced. An inability to form any majority caused the case to be reargued in the following session. After a full year, Justice Brennan was able to cobble together a majority opinion to create a test to decide what types of issues are in fact purely political. Redistricting fell outside of the definition, meaning they were willing to consider its legality. The door to the courtroom was open for those wanting to challenge the maps.[20] Baker was followed by Reynolds v. Sims, which firmly established the concept of "one person, one vote." With the right to challenge redistricting in court established, and a general basis on which to make claims, courts began to grapple with district-specific lines. There quickly formed two separate but intertwined types of claims: illegal racial gerrymandering and illegal political gerrymandering.

---

20. Chief Justice Earl Warren called Baker the most important case of his Supreme Court career. He was on the court for Brown v. Board of Education, Gideon v. Wainwright, Griswold v. Connecticut, and Miranda v. Arizona.

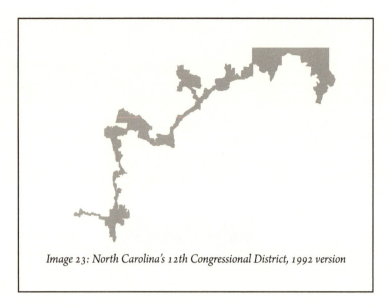

Image 23: North Carolina's 12th Congressional District, 1992 version

Racial challenges to gerrymandering were helped, but also complicated, by the Voting Rights Act. Recall that, among other goals, the VRA made it illegal to dilute the voting rights of minorities. To avoid challenges under the VRA, states could usually inoculate themselves by creating the number of majority-minority districts deemed necessary by the Justice Department.[21] There have been many cases involving allegedly illegal racial gerrymanders, but we are going to focus on those related to a single district: North Carolina's 12th.

The Supreme Court first looked at the 12th in 1993, in the case Shaw v. Reno.[22] North Carolina faced a difficult problem when conducting its 1990 redistricting process. The Justice Department required two African-American-majority Congressional districts. However, because this population was spread widely within the state, it was honestly difficult to stitch them into normal-shaped districts. So the 12th had its first iteration, connecting several small urban areas along Interstate Highway 85. At many points, the district was no wider than the highway itself. In Shaw, the Supreme Court

---

21. Due to lengthy histories of racist election policies, many of the states trying to dilute minority political power were required to obtain approval from the Justice Department for all changes to their conduct of elections, a process called **preclearance**.

22. There was even an earlier case about this district, but it is not relevant to this narrative.

set down a not-exactly-easy-to-follow guideline for the use of race in redistricting:

- Usage of race in redistricting will be reviewed on a basis of **strict scrutiny**;
- However, satisfying the requirements of the VRA can create a compelling reason for state action.

In other words, states were required to use race in redistricting, but not in the wrong way. Three years later, the Supreme Court had the 12th back on their docket, now under the name of Shaw v. Hunt. North Carolina was now claiming that, while it used race to create the district, it was forced to do so in order to comply with the VRA. The Court ruled that the 12th District wasn't "narrowly tailored" to meet VRA compliance.[23] The Court demanded that new districts be drawn in time for the next election.

The district was redrawn again; still oddly shaped, but not to the previous extent. And it was soon back in Court. Challengers claimed that the new map was still an impermissible racial gerrymander, and a lower court agreed. But this case had a fundamental difference from the Shaw era: North Carolina now explicitly said that the district was created with a partisan, rather than racial, intent. The Supreme Court, with Justice O'Connor shifting from the previous majority, agreed with this line of reasoning and upheld the new 12th District. The message was clear: the Court would be more likely to accept political than racial redistricting motivation.[24]

This begs the obvious question: are there any rules limiting partisan gerrymanders, or do the mapmakers have carte blanche?

---

23. Strict scrutiny is applied in cases involving the explicit use of race by the government. To survive a strict scrutiny review, there must be a compelling public interest and the action must be narrowly tailored to meet that interest. This is a very high standard. When the Court applies strict scrutiny, the underlying government action is usually ruled illegal.
24. Justice Thomas wrote the opinion, and his frustration at having to deal with this district is not well hidden. It begins, "This is the third time in six years that litigation over North Carolina's Twelfth Congressional District has come before this Court." Oh, and North Carolina again had to defend the same district again in 2017. It was again struck down as an illegal racial gerrymander.

Just as with questions of racial gerrymandering, the Court first had to decide if accusations of partisan gerrymandering were something they were even allowed to decide. In Davis v. Bandemer, the Court said it was willing to consider the question. There was, however, one big problem. Remember that tricky guideline the Court uses for deciding if a racial gerrymander is legal? In Davis, the Court was unable to agree on *any standard* to decide if partisan gerrymander was permissible. In other words, they were against partisan gerrymandering, but didn't know what it was.[25]

The last case in our list will be Vieth v. Jubelirer. Reaching the Court in 2003, this was a partisan challenge to the Republican-drawn Pennsylvania Congressional map. The logic of Davis was repeated in the Court's decision. Without a clear standard for partisan gerrymandering, the Court refused to do anything. But Justice Anthony Kennedy threw in a wrinkle.

In Vieth, four Supreme Court justices thought the case was nondecidable due to the lack of a standard.[26] Four other justices each presented a standard by which the dispute could be resolved. Justice Kennedy did not like any of these proposed standards and provided the decisive fifth vote, concurring that the Court could do nothing in Vieth. However, he added a critical section to a fascinating concurring opinion:

> *"The plurality thinks I resolve this case with no standard, but that is wrong... If a subsidiary standard could show how an otherwise permissible classification, as applied, burdens representational rights, we could conclude that appellants' evidence states a provable claim under the Fourteenth Amendment standard."*

Justice Kennedy is still on the Court. With four other justices willing to place limits on partisan gerrymandering, he would form a majority. By his own words, all he needs is a workable standard.

---

25. In a strange twist, this was a challenge to a gerrymander created by the Democratic-controlled Indiana State Legislature. Indiana's Democrats were supported in briefs by the Republican National Committee and opposed by the Democratic Party of California.

26. As a reminder, the Supreme Court has nine members; in usual conditions, it takes five justices to create a decision of binding precedent.

—§—

Excessive partisan gerrymandering is bad. There may be no such thing as a perfect map; there will always be bias. But an inability to achieve perfection does not mean that we should allow parties to do as they please. In our current, nearly lawless state of political gerrymandering, a political party with temporary control can enshrine majorities that will last indefinitely, no matter the results of voting.

I keep picking on the Tar Heel State, but to see how gerrymandering overrules the will of the voters, we only need to look again at North Carolina. In the 2016 election, North Carolina had a nearly equal partisan split. At the Presidential level, the Republican candidate won by 3%, while Democrats were elected to the two highest state offices, Governor and Attorney General. However, Republicans drew the maps for electing the North Carolina State Legislature. With the partisan breakdown roughly even, you might expect a small majority for either side. Instead, the GOP has a supermajority, large enough to override the Governor's veto and enact any legislation it wants.

The legislature's first action after the election was to attack the conduct of elections. Previously, each county of North Carolina had an election board consisting of one Democrat, one Republican, and one member appointed by the governor. This was bad: a highly Republican county might have a Democrat-controlled election board, which could suppress the vote there, hurting Republicans statewide.[27] At first glance, the new method appeared fairer: the parties would alternate years in which they would county boards. The only problem is that elections occur only in even-numbered years; guess which party the Republican-controlled legislature put in control of the boards in these years.

The legislature went further, attacking the power of the governor. For the first time, state cabinet appointments would be subject to the Legislature's approval. The number of jobs available for the governor to appoint dropped from 1,500 to 425. Whatever you think about patronage, the remaining 1,100 positions wouldn't go to the

---

27. The Republicans controlled the governorship for the 2016 election. They cut the number of voting precincts and early voting opportunities in Democratic-leaning counties. Republican counties did not see such cuts.

most qualified applicant, but rather continue to be held by appointees of the previous governor, a Republican. The partisan purposes of these changes are no secret. Legislators stated openly that they wouldn't have happened had their gubernatorial candidate been elected.

Changing the rules based on who wins an election is, on its face, an immoral and undemocratic practice. But it is especially egregious when the changes are clearly against the will of the voting public.[28] This is what happened in North Carolina, and it happened because of gerrymandering.

Politics exist, and, in the pursuit of power, people will try to maximize the number of seats they control in any legislature. Our defense against this is to put rules in place, limiting the abuse possible by any political party. We have discussed some best practices that would prevent these abuses. Non-partisan redistricting commissions, like those existing currently in several states, better reflect the people's will. We should push to create more of them. If you care about your voice being heard, vote for intelligently designed redistricting commissions, and encourage your friends to do the same.

However, to curb the worst abuses, the Supreme Court must get involved. For the first time in a long while, we can hope that partisan gerrymandering may soon have some limits enforced.

After the 2010 election, Republicans controlled the redistricting process in Wisconsin and put in place a clear partisan gerrymander. It was challenged by twelve Wisconsin citizens. Critically, these plaintiffs proposed a clear and simple standard to determine what constitutes a partisan gerrymander. In theory, such a standard is the only element lacking for partisan gerrymandering to receive a proper Supreme Court treatment. In Gill v. Whitford, the District Court for Western Wisconsin ruled that the 2010 map was illegally partisan, based on this standard. Will Justice Anthony Kennedy follow his own logic and finally permit some controls around partisan gerrymandering?

The stakes of the case are enormous. If the Court rules that even this map is permissible, it is unclear that any map could ever be ruled otherwise. The would give legislators—and their parties—carte

---

28. After all, the GOP governor in question had just been rejected for re-election.

blanche to maximize gains in any way possible. The next redistricting cycle is nearly upon us. If Gill is decided the wrong way, current maps will be a pleasant memory. Imagine Wisconsin with one Democratic Congressional seat, despite an even partisan split. Imagine Illinois and New York with zero Republican seats, with districts radiating outstate from heavily-Democratic Chicago or New York City, like spokes of a wheel. I'll be watching the outcome closely; if you care about your future, you should too.

GAME THEORY AND THE
NUCLEAR AGE, PART II
HOW ABOUT A NICE GAME OF CHESS?

"Gentlemen, you can't fight in here! This is the War Room!"
—Dr. Strangelove, or: How I Learned to Stop Worrying and Love
the Bomb, Stanley Kubrick, 1964

The 1960s were perhaps the most dangerous period in our species' history. At the height of the Cold War, the United States and the Soviet Union fought an unconventional war for influence on five continents. The Berlin Crisis, Bay of Pigs, and Cuban Missile Crisis flowed to escalation in Vietnam and the bellicose leaderships of Richard Nixon and Leonid Brezhnev.

The world of The Sixties existed every day in the shadow of nuclear weapons. Increasingly powerful and reliable, ready to launch from airplanes, missile silos, and submarines, the threat of nuclear war was central to geopolitics. It was the time of Duck and Cover, home nuclear shelters, and the Daisy campaign. By the end of the decade, the superpowers had nearly 40,000 bombs between them, enough to destroy the world many times over.

Somehow, we managed to avoid a nuclear holocaust. Seventy years have now passed without further use of nuclear weapons in war. This is the story of how we survived and of whether we'll be able to in the future.

- What is mutually assured destruction (MAD)?
- What are the problems with MAD?
- Will this game work in the modern nuclear paradigm?

WHAT IS MUTUALLY ASSURED DESTRUCTION (MAD)?

Recall that game theory is the study of multi-lateral strategic decision-making. It is concerned with how the expectations about what your opponents will do affect your action. A key assumption of game theory is that players always act rationally, attempting to maximize their utility, a generic measure of value. In some games, players can communicate before making decision. This often enhances their ability to predict what others will do.

Game theory has a close analogue to the nuclear arms race, the game of Chicken. We mentioned it game briefly in Part I, but will now dive in, as well as discuss some variants.

Recall that, in Chicken, two drivers are headed toward a cliff; each must decide to Swerve First or Swerve Last. If both Swerve First, the game is a draw. If only one Swerves First, he is the "chicken" and is embarrassed. If both Swerve Last, however, they drive off the cliff and are killed. Figure 37 shows the outcomes for our first iteration of Chicken:

When will I swerve?		Player 2	
		First	Last
Player 1	First	0, 0	-1, 1
	Last	1, -1	-10, -10

Figure 37: Chicken, redux

The critical feature of Chicken is that the "crash" outcome is much worse than the "lose" outcome. In other words, the embarrassment from swerving first is much less bad than being killed by driving off the cliff. Therefore, if you are certain that your opponent will Swerve Last, you must Swerve First. Even if you aren't certain what he will do, even a significant likelihood of his choosing Swerve Last should make you cautious. Using the game theory terminology, the Nash equilibriums of Chicken are where exactly one player swerves.[1] Although the math behind game theory has been developed only recently, world leaders have applied the lessons of Chicken for centuries, via the doctrine of **strategic deterrence.**

The idea of strategic deterrence is simple: you tell your opponents that if you are attacked, you will respond disproportionally. By threatening this massive retaliation, their cost of attacking you increases significantly. If they are rational, an attack therefore becomes less likely. If you can threaten a response that is deadly enough, you can render any opponent's attack irrational. Strategic deterrence has been an element of warfare long before it had a name.

Strategic deterrence only works if the threat is credible. Napoleon couldn't keep England from meddling in affairs on the European continent because he couldn't credibly threaten a crossing of the English Channel. Imperial Japan was forced to open its borders in the 1850s because of the threat posed by Matthew Perry's Black

---

1. Recall that a Nash equilibrium is an outcome in game theory where no player can benefit from changing strategies, keeping the other player's strategy constant. In this sense, Nash equilibriums are stable. I'll use the word stable interchangeably with Nash equilibrium.

Ships was credible. In World War II, strategic bombing took the concept of deterrence to new heights.[2] The firebombing of Dresden on the night of February 14, 1945, killed at least 22,700 people, rendered more than 100,000 homeless and effectively destroyed the entire city. The Allies lost only eight of the more than two thousand warplanes sent against Dresden.[3]

The enormous damage caused by Allied bombing raids in 1945 obscures the earlier experience of World War II. When Germany (or England) had active fighter defenses, the conduct of bombing raids came at a significant cost.[4] In the British Bomber Command, 55,573 of around 125,000 total aircrew were killed during the war. The American Eighth Air Force, also tasked with bombing Nazi territory, suffered 47,000 casualties, of which 26,000 were fatal. It was not unusual for 10% of air crews to be lost in a single raid. The bombing campaign also required massive investments in ground personnel, war materiel, and aviation fuel. In short, it isn't clear that the Allied bombing campaign warranted its use of scarce wartime resources.[5] Conventional bombing would not be a credible strategic deterrent in the post-war era.

The lack of credible threat posed by strategic bombing was known by the Superpowers. They needed to develop a new method of creating destruction. This need for credibility led to the development of ICBMs. As opposed to bombers, which could be shot out of the sky before dropping their payloads, ICBMs can be stationed in North Dakota and still reach central Russia. Flying at many multiples of the speed of sound, and with a tiny cross section, ICBMs could not be destroyed in flight.[6] To further increase credibility, each ICBM soon contained **multiple independent reentry vehicles**

---

2. Or, more accurately, depths.
3. I'm not opining on the morality of the Dresden raid, or the even-more-deadly Tokyo raid, or the eventual dropping of the atomic bombs. But their military value as a deterrent is beyond doubt.
4. This disagreed with the famous quote from Stanley Baldwin, British Prime Minister in the 1930s, who said that "the bomber will always get through." This belief, which became British policy, explains why Britain faced devastating bombing raids. Baldwin starved Britain's fighter defense because he thought it would be of little use. Neville Chamberlain is better known today, but he inherited the weakness of his predecessor's military. Baldwin, despite leaving power long before the war began, did more to lose it than any other Allied leader.
5. At least until destruction of the German Luftwaffe greatly reduced the cost.

(MIRVs). Above the top of the atmosphere, an ICBM could release a dozen MIRVs, along with decoys and who knows what else. Each individual MIRV carried massive destructive power, enough to destroy a city. Each launch therefore created multiple threats, further decreasing the likelihood of repelling the strike.

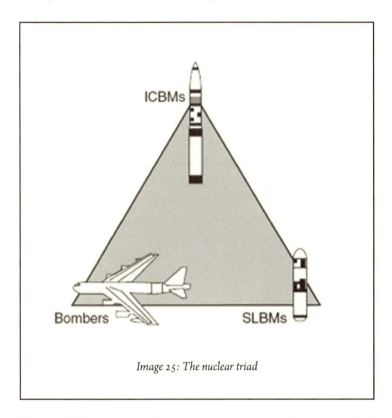

ICBMs

Bombers

SLBMs

Image 25: The nuclear triad

Land-based ICBMs were, however, still vulnerable to attack. If you know where your opponent keeps their missiles, you might try to destroy them using your ICBMs, in a first strike. Everybody started looking for places to hide their missiles. They were kept deep underground or on specialized trucks, in order to remain mobile. But the best hiding spot was below water, and nuclear-armed submarines became the key to deterrence. By 1961, nuclear weapons were de-

---

6. At least not with 1960s technology. And even if you shoot down a few, those that got through your defenses would still be catastrophic. An ICBM also cost much less than a strategic bomber. Of course, unlike bombers, an ICBM is a single-use item.

ployed on both American and Soviet submarines. Destroying one nuclear submarine was challenging enough; destroying a fleet, impossible. Simultaneously destroying your opponent's bomber force, submarine force, and land-based ICBMs is a fool's errand. This credible strategic deterrence became known as the **nuclear triad**.

By 1965, both sides had thousands of missiles arranged in their nuclear triads. A successful attack from the other side would be certain to draw a response, called a **second strike**. American planners thought a second strike equivalent to 400 million tons of TNT would be enough to destroy the Soviet Union's capability to make war; the Soviet Union likely had similar estimates.[7] Given that each side possessed around 10,000 million tons of bombs by the end of the 1960s, both sides had more than enough firepower. Both sides had a highly credible threat; a successful nuclear strike would return a strike in kind. This is **mutually assured destruction**, also known by its acronym, MAD. Game theory tells us MAD should prevent nuclear war. In theory.

WHAT ARE THE PROBLEMS WITH MAD?

We've talked a lot about the "D," destruction. We've also seen that *both* superpowers had the ability to annihilate the other in a successful strike, hence the "M," mutual. Which leaves us with the trickiest letter: "A" for assured. To consider it, we'll leave the historical path and return to game theory.

Let's go back to our game of Chicken. We can translate it into a game of nuclear strategy: from Swerve Last to Fire First and Swerve First to Fire Second—but there is a problem. In the first version of the game, the outcome where you swerve first is not a terrible result. You are the chicken, but you will survive. In global thermonuclear war, the situation where your opponent fires first and you fire second is extremely bad. We need to modify the utility table:

---

7. "How much nuclear weapons tonnage did the Soviet Union think it needed in 1965" returns precisely one result, this piece in its original form.

When will you shoot your nukes?		USSR	
		Second	First
USA	Second	1, 1	-15, -5
	First	-5, -15	-10, -10

Figure 38: Global Thermonuclear War

We can debate about the values in this table, but what matters is that any nuclear war is really bad. I have assumed you would rather be the victim of a second-strike than a first. What really matters, and should make you feel a bit better, is that the situation where neither side fires first is stable. In this game, neither side will rationally start a war. Deterrence has worked. This is what we hoped MAD would do.

Unfortunately, there is a problem. In the real world, both sides have a third option: Never Fire. There are several reasons why a superpower might not actually conduct a second strike. For example, their weapons could malfunction—not a remote scenario if 400 million tons of TNT has just been detonated in your territory. The ability to detect launches was not trivial in the 1960s. If you can't know whether the other guy fired his missiles, how can you be sure you'll strike back?

Let's look at our game again, including the option not to retaliate:

		USSR		
		First	Retaliate	Never
USA	First	-10,-10	-5,-15	5,-20
	Retaliate	-15,-5	1,1	1,1
	Never	-20,5	1,1	1,1

Figure 39: Thermonuclear War: A third choice

The four outcomes in the bottom-right corner of Figure 39 represent situations where nobody fires their bombs first. If nobody ever fires first, then there is never a nuclear war, and everybody wins. The other outcomes show what happens after the three possible responses to an attack. If you retaliate, you end up in the same situation as in Figure 38. But if you don't retaliate, in this version, you are even worse off than if you had. In this scenario, your opponent would be better off than if the war had never happened, since he now dominates the world.

In this version, when both sides play Never, the outcome is still stable. However, we can also see that the game is unstable if both sides plan Never. If you know he will not respond, you maximize your utility by firing your missiles immediately, winning the war. Fortunately, in game theory, players are always rational. Retaliate always performs as well or better than Never. Therefore, no rational player will ever choose Never, and we are safe.[8]

Is this a good description of the real world? Consider the situation where you are facing an imminent incoming strike and must decide what to do. Whatever you choose, the attack will destroy your country, perhaps killing half of your population and rendering your land uninhabitable. Given that this a certainty, no matter what you do, are you absolutely sure you would fire back? If you hold fire, your country will be destroyed, but your opponents' will survive. Not a great outcome but firing back will kill millions more and possibly re-

---

8. Well, as safe as we can be in a world with gigatons of nuclear weapons scattered around.

sult in the extinction of humanity. It's not so easy to push that button. If you think you might be better off not retaliating, it leads to a new table.

		USSR		
		First	Retaliate	Never
USA	First	-15, -15	-10, -15	5, -10
	Retaliate	-15, -10	1, 1	1, 1
	Never	-10, 5	1, 1	1, 1

Figure 40: Nuclear War, with extinction

The key difference in Figure 40 is that choosing Never is no longer entirely irrational. But, as we saw, if one player chooses Never, the other will immediately launch a full strike. This means that, even if you aren't sure you will Retaliate, survival depends on making your opponent think you will. And, if you suspect your opponent of weakness, you must consider Firing First.[9]

Let's go back to the 1960s. Put yourself in the seat of President Kennedy or Chairman Khrushchev. In both countries, the power to fire nuclear weapons sat with one person. If either Kennedy or Khrushchev chose to fire first, no Congress, Presidium, or military leadership could have stopped them.[10] There was plenty of mutual distrust keeping tensions elevated. Kennedy used the CIA to sponsor a coup against Soviet-aligned Cuba. Khrushchev attempted to force the capitulation of West Berlin by provoking another crisis at that Cold War flashpoint. Sitting at the White House and at the Kremlin, they are both buffered by military, political, domestic, and

---

9. We were dangerously close to this situation in the Cold War. The Soviet Union, allegedly, considered a first-strike policy on the theory that the weak-kneed Americans wouldn't fire back.

10. This is still true today. There is no way to stop a President of the United States from launching a nuclear strike. The order must be transmitted via the Secretary of Defense, but ignoring such a direct order would cause the offending Secretary to be instantaneously replaced by somebody more pliant.

foreign policy advisors, each with their own agenda. They have met in person only once, a tense one-day summit in Vienna. To keep the world safe (or at least stable), each must convince the other of their willingness to end the human race, should the situation arise.

Brinksmanship is the strategy of pushing conflicts to the edge of disaster without quite crossing the line into nuclear war. It became de facto American policy under President Eisenhower, whose Secretary of State, John Foster Dulles, said "the ability to get to the verge without getting into the war is the necessary art." President Truman intervened in the Korean War, but specifically prohibited the use of nuclear weapons. In 1961, American and Soviet tanks stared each other down over Checkpoint Charlie, at the gates of Berlin. A false move by a private manning a turret could have led to nuclear holocaust. Most dangerously, ballistic missiles in Cuba upset the strategic balance and were unacceptable to U.S. security interests. Kennedy had to eliminate this threat without escalating past the point of no return.

Brinksmanship was dangerous, but it served a purpose: communication. Defending your interests in the most far-flung parts of the world left little doubt that you would defend your own homeland. If you are crazy enough to fly in every morsel of food and pound of coal needed to supply West Berlin for fifteen months, clearly you are not to be trifled with.[11] On the other hand, both Superpowers made it clear that attacks on their personnel could lead to terrible consequences. Therefore, the Soviets did not shoot down a single one of the 200,000 vulnerable supply flights during the Berlin Airlift. The American quarantine of Cuba went to great lengths to avoid firing a live shot.

Of course, any good brinksmanship player would play the game far from their own home. Both superpowers had plenty of proxies around the world to use as battlefields in these brush wars. Like most games of chess, this usually didn't work out well for the pawns. An estimated two million Vietnamese lost their lives during twenty years of American involvement in southeast Asia. Perhaps as many Afghans were killed during the nine years of Soviet incursion there;

---

11. More than two million tons of supplies were airlifted in total. Coal was the largest component.

we don't really know. Fully one third of the Afghan population became refugees by the time the Soviets pulled out of the Bear Trap, leaving a complete power vacuum behind. The Taliban was able to take power, with far-reaching consequences.[12]

WILL THIS GAME WORK IN THE MODERN NUCLEAR PARADIGM?

Mutually assured destruction worked well enough when it was two superpowers facing off.[13] Never before in human history have nations possessing the best and the biggest weapons refrained from using them. Game theory, MAD, brinksmanship, and other forms of communication just barely managed to keep the missiles in their silos.

As we have seen, MAD requires several prerequisites in order to be strategically effective. Each participating nation must have the ability to destroy utterly its opponent. Each must also know that his opponent is able—and willing—to conduct a devastating retaliatory strike. Clear and consistent lines of communication are important; you need to be able to talk in order to convince the other guy that you are not playing the dreaded Never card. Redundancy, such as that created via a nuclear triad, ensures second-strike capability to go with the willingness to use it.

The world's nuclear paradigm has changed since the fall of the Soviet Union. Do these prerequisites of MAD hold in the modern age?

India and Pakistan

India and Pakistan have fought three major wars since their partition and independence in 1947.[14] India first conducted a successful nuclear test in 1974; Pakistan likely had a working weapon shortly after, although their first test wasn't until 1998. Since that time, two

---

12. The Taliban were "our guys" at the time. Not the greatest decision we've ever made.
13. Source: you are reading this in a currently inhabitable world rather than some type of post-apocalyptic nuclear winter wasteland.
14. There have also been many smaller skirmishes, mostly about the fate of the disputed Kashmir region. These are still ongoing today, with occasional casualties.

nations with significant unresolved border issues, as well as some slight differences with respect to religion, have had the bomb. This is a not great situation.

The India-Pakistan nuclear game doesn't look like the MAD we know and love. Both have only 100 total nuclear weapons, with yields significantly less than one megaton each. India has a nascent nuclear triad, but with just two nuclear submarines. Pakistan has no triad at all. Neither country can credibly claim destructive second-strike power. As we've seen, this has the counterintuitive effect of making the weapons easier to use. Bilateral communication between these long-time antagonists is strained at best.

There is, however, some good news in south Asia. Both countries keep their weapons in a non-deployed state. Both countries have clear "no first strike" policies in place. Both have clear statements of purpose for their nuclear arsenals: "minimum credible deterrence" for Pakistan and "credible minimum deterrence" for India.[15] Both have stated and published fairly clear statements about what type of action would provoke a nuclear response. Overall tensions between the two countries have calmed in the last two decades. The big risk is that, in the case of another general conflict, battlefield commanders could be delegated the ability to launch a tactical nuclear response. In this situation, game theory is no help.

Israel

Israel's nuclear arsenal is the world's worst kept secret. Israel follows a policy of "nuclear ambiguity"; basically, if you ask Israel about its nuclear arsenal, they tell you how nice the beaches are in Tel Aviv. Israel has said it will not "introduce" nuclear weapons to the Middle East; I don't know exactly what they think this word means.

It gets worse. Because Israel won't confirm it has nuclear weapons, it can't clarify the conditions under which they will use them. Israel has historically had some disputes with its neighbors. It is entirely possible for one of them to accidentally stumble across an Israeli nuclear red line. It is commonly understood that, during the 1973 Yom Kippur War, Israel came close to using nuclear weapons

---

15. Apparently, these are not the same thing. India's version involves a somewhat greater retaliatory capacity.

against Egyptian or Syrian military headquarters. Such an attack would not have been against remote desert fortresses, but rather downtown Cairo or Damascus. And let's not forget that Israel is one of the few countries that officially contemplates conducting pre-emptive war.[16]

Fortunately, after the initial shock, Israeli forces quickly turned the tide of battle in 1973. The weapons went back into storage. Some believe that the deployment was a bluff—if so, it worked. After their satellites detected the deployment, the Soviet Union cautioned Egypt against advancing further, and the U.S. began a massive resupply. Today, Israel has signed peace treaties with Egypt and Jordan. The risk of conventional invasion by its direct neighbors is thus greatly reduced. Israel is highly integrated to the global economy and concerned with its public image. Outside of survival being at stake, it's hard to imagine a situation where Israel would launch a first strike.

An unconventional attack is a different story. Israel has said that it would respond to an attack by weapons of mass destruction with everything in its arsenal. It has also reserved the right to strike against other nations' nuclear development capacities. The lack of a clear red line is, again, troubling.

North Korea

When we look at the nuclear weapons on the northern half of the Korean peninsula, game theory is of less help. In theory, a nation should fear the stigma of conducting a nuclear sneak attack. In theory, a nation should fear global isolation. In theory, a nation should fear second-strike capacity. In theory, a nation should fear the inevitable invasion by a U.S.-led international coalition, bringing to bear the enormous capabilities of the advanced militaries of the world, hell bent on deposing its leader, little concerned with civilian casualties, willing to use its entire arsenal including tactical nuclear devices, and planning to establish some type of military government

---

16. I'm not saying they are wrong to do so. Israel is a narrow strip of land, surrounded by about a dozen hostile countries with combined populations fifty times greater than hers. Imagine trying to defend Delaware against a joint attack by New York, New Jersey, Pennsylvania, and Maryland.

for an indefinite period while working to deprogram every one of the citizens from seventy years of devastating and devastatingly effective propaganda. To de-escalate the nuclear Korean peninsula, we'll need to devise a new game.

—§—

Two great Cold War movies have plots living in the intersection between nuclear war and game theory. Both add more insight to our topic than one might expect, warranting discussion here.

The key to maintaining a stable game of MAD involves convincing your opponent that you will always retaliate against a nuclear first strike. You need to communicate this as a certainty despite retaliation not necessarily being the optimal strategy. As President or Chairman, with just minutes to make the decision, on your own, will you really decide to destroy the world? Wouldn't it be helpful to be able to say that the response will be automatic? In other words, if an attack is detected, the response will occur, with no opportunity for human weakness. This is the Doomsday Device from Dr. Strangelove, or the War Operation Process Response (WOPR) from WarGames. In theory, if you have one of these devices, it will always be irrational for your opponent to start a war.

As these movies showed, such devices can also cause their own problems. To serve as a deterrent, you must tell the world about your doomsday device. If you announce it before it is operational, there is an incentive for your opponent to launch an attack before it comes online. If you turn it on today and tell the world later, you risk making a non-proportional response to a rogue attack. The world ends.[17]

Perhaps your WOPR has a bit more nuance. It might use artificial intelligence to consider optimal strategies, thinking about the outcomes before blindly firing back with everything you have. In this case, you are still susceptible to a mistaken detection or an incursion into your system. And you can never build in a manual override for your WOPR, as that would make your threat is no longer credible. A WOPR that can be turned off sounds like exactly the kind of thing a "never fire" superpower would own.[18]

---

17. This is the plot to Dr. Strangelove.

How do we eliminate—or at least reduce—the threat of nuclear war? People smarter than I am have been working on this since August 1945. Since we haven't had a nuclear war yet, they have been successful so far. I can offer my thoughts on where to go next.

Preventing further proliferation is critical. Doing so involves a long-term game of carrots and sticks, as well as soft power. The **Non-Proliferation Treaty** (NPT), while not perfect, has been largely successful. All nations but five have signed it. No signatory has developed nuclear capabilities. The NPT works via trust alone: there is no enforcement mechanism and any state can leave at any time without penalty.[19] However, this does not make the treaty ineffective. Nuclear weapons are very expensive to develop. If all your enemies, potential enemies, rivals, neighbors, and so forth are NPT signatories, it is rational for you to sign on too. Everybody can then deploy their resources more productively.

We also need to create clear rewards for those nations who decrease or eliminate their arsenals. The only nation to voluntarily eliminate its nuclear program so far is South Africa.[20] Along with the end of the abhorrent system of apartheid, elimination of its nuclear arsenal brought South Africa into the community of nations. The last twenty-five years have treated her far better than if she hadn't changed her ways. Sticks must also be imposed: economic sanctions, aid to neighbors, and disengagement. The recent treaty with Iran is another attempt at the carrot and stick approach. Its success is far from certain; skepticism is warranted. But if a framework such as this is not effective, there is no solution in Iran short of invasion. The threat of invasion is exactly the reason given by Iran for wanting to join the nuclear club.

Once we deal with proliferation, we are left with the stockpiles in the existing nuclear states. Here, there is again hope, even if dis-

---

18. This is the actual plot of WarGames. You should see both—you've invested so much time learning about nuclear war, you've earned some time in front of the TV.

19. North Korea in fact did withdraw from the NPT. That's not a great data point for its efficacy.

20. Several former Soviet Republics had nuclear weapons when they became independent and voluntarily gave them up. This was different from what happened in South Africa: Belarus never had a nuclear program, just some bombs that happened to be sitting around.

tant and disjointed. Bilateral and multilateral treaties over the past fifty years have significantly lowered the threat. The Comprehensive Nuclear-Test-Ban Treaty is still in the process of ratification, but only one nation has tested weapons since 1998. The United States and Russian Federation each retain around 7,000 nuclear weapons in their stockpiles. This is an enormous reduction from Cold War peaks of 30,000 and 37,000 weapons, respectively. Most of these remaining weapons are not actively deployed. Both plan to reduce stockpiles by half again in the next decade, joined by reductions in the U.K. and China. For the first time in a half century, the world should soon have fewer than 10,000 nuclear weapons. That's a start.

After these goals are achieved, it will get harder. The remaining number of weapons will still create a game of Mutually Assured Destruction, but just barely. Further reductions from these levels will eliminate second-strike capabilities, invalidating MAD. The path from the end of MAD to a nuclear-free world necessarily involves a period of high instability. I don't know how to travel this road. I do know that doing so successfully will require an innumerate number of small steps, each of which involves communication between nations, building trust. I am hopeful, because there is no nation today that doesn't wish for a verifiably nuclear-free world. Even though we've agreed on this goal, the nuclear knot we've created will take a generation or more to untie. I do believe it can be done.

ONE MORE VOLUME
HEALTH INSURANCE, PART V
THE THEORY OF HEALTH CARE

"Nobody knew health care could be so complicated."
—Donald J. Trump

"It's the prices, stupid."
—Uwe Reinhardt

It seems like health reform will be with us even after we've solved all our other problems. It's not my expertise to predict the future, and the future of the uniquely American health care system is as difficult to predict as it has ever been.

To even take a guess at its future, we should first consider why health care is so hard. It poses a special challenge to those who would apply normal economic principles: choice, competition, and the market taking care of itself. There are precisely zero examples of modern, successful health care systems based on unregulated free markets.

Perhaps health care has a few specificities—perhaps it doesn't fit neatly into Economics 101. Maybe this fundamentally different problem requires a fundamentally different solution.

- Why is health insurance hard?
- How do other nations provide their citizens with health care?
- How would you stabilize the United States' current health care system?
- What are the structural, underlying problems in our system? Is it possible to fix them?

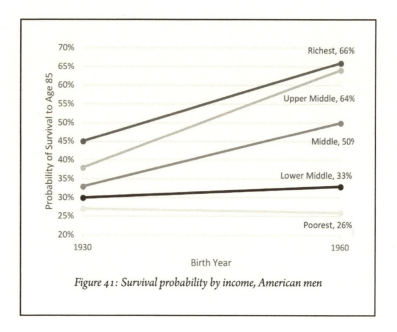

Figure 41: Survival probability by income, American men

WHY IS HEALTH INSURANCE HARD?

Economics was born in 1776, when Adam Smith published *The Wealth of Nations*. Of course, people had long tried to understand the mechanics of production and consumption, but only after Smith's work could economics be considered remotely scientific. He was the first to understand and express how free markets can self-regulate. He foresaw the potential that would soon be released by free markets and free labor and was far ahead of his time in envisioning the necessary steps to achieve this potential. His invisible hand is still at work today, controlling prices and production.

Consider bread.[1] Imagine a fictional, ideal market with just this one product and cash with which to buy it. There are several bakers, each working independently to maximize their personal profitability. The amount of bread produced is the economy's output. Consumers buy bread at the prevailing price; all bread is eaten every day, so consumption equals output.[2] Prices and production levels will

---

1. Apologies to our gluten-free readers.
2. There is no inventory in our fictional world. Who wants day-old bread?

stabilize quickly and remain consistent over time, unless something changes in the environment.

One possible change is an increase in the population. More people means more buyers of bread. Producers will be able to raise their prices, increasing their profitability. But because baking bread is now more profitable, they will produce more of it. This causes them to lower the price in order to sell the additional quantity counteracting some, but not all, of the previous price increase. The economy will reach a new equilibrium, with larger quantities of bread sold at higher prices. This is a **demand shock**.

Another possibility is a bad harvest, causing wheat prices to increase. Bakers will increase bread prices to remain profitable. At these higher prices, however, consumers will buy less bread.[3] Bakers will therefore bake less bread, reacting to this lower demand. An equilibrium will again be reached, this time with higher prices but lower output. This is a **supply shock**.[4]

In both of these cases, markets stabilize without external intervention, just by letting individuals pursue their best interests. A baker can't unilaterally raise prices; her customers will buy cheaper bread next door. A baker can't unilaterally lower quality. Unless accompanied by lower prices, he will again lose customers. Adam Smith was the first to show the resiliency of markets to maintain equilibrium.

Unfortunately, real markets are not straightforward and ideal. There are many factors in a free market system that limit its ability to reach equilibrium in the manner described by Smith. For example:

- If the bakers collude rather than compete, they can raise prices without fear of competition. This is called a **monopoly**.
- Alternatively, buyers of bread can create an organization and negotiate lower prices. This is called a **monopsony**.

---

3. They might buy more rice or corn instead, in what is called **substitution**. As people shift to buy more of these products, their price will increase.
4. An example of supply shock is what happens to oil prices when exporters reduce production. Initially, prices will spike as shortages create lines at gas stations. Consumers will buy less oil at the higher price, counterbalancing this somewhat. An equilibrium will be reached, with higher prices and less consumption, as expected.

- If a baker uses sawdust instead of flour, he will earn enormous profits for a little while, until his treachery is discovered. This is an example of **information asymmetry**.
- A baker can also lower his costs by dumping toxic bread waste into bucolic Bread River. He will earn larger profits, while the cost of cleaning up will be borne by the entire society. This is called a **negative externality**, creating costs paid for by others.[5]
- If a buyer is starving and must buy bread immediately, the baker can charge any price he wants. This unfortunate buyer is called a **price taker**.

Fortunately, markets for most everyday goods—those for bread, apples, and books, as well as cars and houses—operate with reasonable efficiency. This is due (in part) to well-planned government regulation. Anti-trust laws have broken up monopolies, in industries ranging from crude oil to telephone service. Car manufacturers must post window stickers with all relevant information about the vehicle, limiting asymmetry. Companies are fined for dumping toxic waste.[6] The further the market for a specific good is from ideal, the greater the need for government-enforced rules to ensure efficiency.

Which brings us to health care. In the span of a single ambulance ride, we see that its market is far from ideal and efficient.

You experience a medical event and call 911. They send an ambulance to your home to pick you up. There is no competition in the ambulance market; you're going to ride in whatever shows up. This is a monopoly. If you are like 91% of American adults under 65, you have health insurance, which will ultimately pay for the ambulance. Among other purposes, health insurance companies operate as an organization of buyers of health care, or, monopsonies. I doubt your hospital posts the costs of their treatments on some type of menu. Even if they did, when you get dropped off at the emergency room, a menu wouldn't help much, as nobody can predict in advance the type of treatment you will need. This is information asymmetry. In-

---

5. Efforts to fight negative externalities are called Pigovian Taxes, after English economist Arthur Pigou. A fine for littering is a Pigovian Tax. So is a charge levied when a power plant releases global-warming-causing carbon dioxide.
6. But we don't charge people for releasing carbon dioxide into the air, which is causing more negative externalities than all other wastes.

surance companies are incentivized to reject claims, lowering their costs.[7] If they succeed at doing so, somebody else will pay for the care given. This is a negative externality. From the time you unconsciously enter the ambulance, to your emergency surgery, to your time in the ICU and then until discharge, you are unlikely to price shop—the world's best example of a price taker.

We could stop here. The market for health care clearly does not follow the same rules as the market for bread, and therefore cannot be left unregulated. Unfortunately, the nature of health means our problem is even more complex.

In 2013, 50% of U.S. medical costs were incurred by just 3% of patients. For people in this group, the average cost of medical care was $200,000. The median national income is around $59,400 and the median American adult has a total net worth of around $60,000. Clearly, we have a problem: people with high medical costs will be unable to pay for them on their own. Fortunately, we know how to address this problem.

The population experiencing high health costs is like other groups of people who have fallen on hard times. Only a small percentage of all houses catch fire in a given year. Few people experience severe automobile accidents. Fewer than 1 out of 500 American adults between the ages of 35 and 44 will pass away in the next year. These calamities all have one thing in common: they are things that we buy insurance against. The risk of outsized, negative outcomes is pooled among the population. Each person pays the *expected cost* for an average member of the population, rather than his or her *actual cost*. The concept of insurance is precisely that we all pay premiums, but most of us won't get anything back. It still makes sense for people to buy insurance because, while they can afford the annual premiums, they can't afford the low-probability catastrophe. Because medical costs are skewed in a similar way, a system based on insurance makes sense.

Insuring against medical costs has a fundamental difference from insuring against a fire or auto accident. You can determine the expected cost of providing homeowner's insurance via a few variables,

---

7. The Affordable Care Act eliminated many pathways previously used by insurance companies to reject valid claims.

such as the property's location, size, proximity to a fire station, and replacement cost. Beyond these, the chance of an individual home being damaged in a given year is almost entirely random. Importantly, the owner's ability to predict future insurance claims is little better than the insurance company's. The process of determining the risk factors to properly price insurance is called **underwriting**. Underwriting homeowner's insurance is comparatively straightforward.[8]

On the other hand, medical costs are not random; counterintuitively, this makes insuring against them more complex. People have a strong ability to predict their future medical costs. Perhaps you take medication regularly or require ongoing physical therapy. Perhaps you are planning to have a child (or are already pregnant). Perhaps you have a serious, ongoing, and expensive-to-treat medical condition like cancer, lupus, or diabetes. There are unexpected costs too, ranging from new conditions to skiing accidents, but addressing them constitutes a minority of total medical spending.

Before the ACA, insurers in the individual market underwrote by looking for these non-random factors. Then, they used this information to price their policies. But, this is a problem; people with expensive conditions cannot afford the expected costs of their own health care. If a person's current condition is taken into account when determining premiums, via what is called **medical underwriting**, health insurance will be available to only the healthy. If we want an insurance-based system, we need to average everybody's expected costs together. Premiums will then be based on the cost of insuring the entire population.[9]

Because insurance is a pooling of risk, it will, in a sense, have winners and losers. Insurance payments made to those who get into car accidents are subsidized by those who did not. Similarly, those with few medical problems will subsidize those with many. To have a

---

8. In the case of homeowner's insurance, underwriting is also easier because incentives are aligned. People generally don't want their homes flooded, even if the insurance company will foot the bill. This is why insurance companies fear arson, which breaks the incentive alignment.

9. Insurers won't do this unless they are forced to; it is more profitable for them to find and refuse coverage to the most expensive patients.

health system based on insurance, the younger and healthier among us must subsidize the older and sicker.

Because American health care costs per capita are around $9,000, health insurance premiums will cost around $9,000 on average. Even after pooling the risks, many people are unable to afford even this average amount. It is an impossible burden, even for some households above the median national income of $56,000. Therefore, in our health insurance system, the rich must also subsidize the middle class and poor. Whatever the mechanism, if society's goal is for everybody to have access to health care, these subsidies must exist.

Proceeding from economic principles, we've shown certain requirements that any health payment system must have. Because almost nobody can afford unexpected, high medical costs, we must use insurance. Because some people can't afford their personal expected cost, we must average insurance premiums across large risk pools. Because many can't afford this average, there must also be subsidies of some sort based on income. The question is not whether a successful system must have these features, only how they are designed.

HOW DO OTHER NATIONS PROVIDE THEIR CITIZENS WITH HEALTH CARE?

We've demonstrated many reasons why an unregulated free market does not work for the provision of health care. Governments must get involved, or health care will be unavailable to many.

No two nations have identical health care payment systems. Other than the United States, other systems were designed to meet specific societal goals. Like the United States, once a health system is in place, changes are difficult to achieve. With this in mind, we can conduct a quick world tour, looking at how various countries have set up their health care systems, and how they perform.

France

Key Health Statistics:

Life Expectancy:	82.4 years
Infant Mortality:	3.3 per 1000 births
Adult Mortality:	101 per 1000 adult males
Health Spending ($ per capita):	$4,407
Health Spending (% GDP):	11.5%

Many people envy the French health system. Others use France as a scary example of "socialized medicine." Contrary to popular belief, medicine in France is not run by the government. Like the United States, the French health care system is a mix of public entities, private players, and public-private partnerships.

The core of France's health care financing is a small group of private, non-profit, highly regulated insurance companies. Every French citizen is required to buy health insurance from one of these five companies.[10] Premiums are paid out of taxes levied on employers' cost of labor and the capital gains of high-income individuals. Therefore, although the requirement to have coverage applies to individuals, there is no incremental cost for an individual to have insurance. The government sets the prices paid to providers, which has helped control costs. Most French doctors work for private companies, while most hospitals are publicly owned. Almost all doctors accept the rates set by the government; almost every provider is in the network.[11]

Another misconception of the French system is that it is very generous. In fact, the level of co-pays and deductibles in France is simi-

---

10. A tiny number of people are exempt from this requirement.
11. Generally, French doctors earn revenues of around 60% of what comparable physicians are paid in the United States. However, their costs are also significantly lower. Medical school in France costs less than 1,000 Euros per year, and doctors are paid comparatively well during their internship. Malpractice insurance is inexpensive, not because of less litigation, but because it is provided by a central fund. There are even a few tax breaks to get doctors to join the system. There is no shortage of good French doctors.

lar to those in the U.S. Many French employers provide supplemental health insurance to help cover these costs; these policies are offered by private, for-profit insurance companies. For those without supplemental plans, the amount of cost sharing depends on the total cost of care for a given beneficiary. Those with significant health issues will spend less out of pocket on a percentage basis.

Virtually 100% of the French have comprehensive health insurance. Generally, the French love their health care system.

United Kingdom

Key Health Statistics:

Life Expectancy:	81.2 years
Infant Mortality:	4.3 per 1000 live births
Adult Mortality:	85 per 1000 adult males
Health Spending ($ per capita):	$4,003
Health Spending (% GDP):	9.1%

The U.K. has socialized medicine. No country in the world has greater government control over its health care system.[12] The government collects taxes and uses them to fund the National Health Service (NHS). The NHS provides universal health care access to all permanent residents. Hospitals are owned by the NHS; doctors are employed by the NHS. It therefore has a strict control on the costs of care.[13] Cost-sharing is very low, consisting of small charges for outpatient prescription drugs and services like dentistry.

Another unique aspect of the NHS is that it operates on a strict budget. Private insurers in other countries must pay out all legally valid claims, even if they lose money in the process. The NHS's total annual expenditures are set during Parliament's budgeting process.[14] One way in which this budget is managed is by controlling salaries.

---

12. There must be some obscure counter-example to this statement, but I'm not aware of it.
13. There is a group of private insurers and private doctors, but it is too small to be relevant to our discussion.

Typical U.K. doctors earn between £75,000 and £100,000 per year ($100,000-$135,000 at current exchange rates). There is a popular belief—expounded by the U.K. press—that wait times for NHS appointments and procedures are onerously long. Statistics do not bear this out; while the wait can be longer for procedures that are not time-sensitive, there is no sign that the British are not getting timely care for urgent issues. They have made a choice, accepting triage in their system in exchange for massively lower costs.

Every British citizen has comprehensive health insurance. The British, generally, love their health care system.[15]

Japan

Key Health Statistics:

Life Expectancy:	83.7
Infant Mortality:	2.0 per 1000 live births
Adult Mortality:	72.6 per 1000 adult males
Health Spending ($ per capita):	$4,150
Health Spending (% GDP):	10.2%

Japan leads the world in many health metrics including life expectancy. They have achieved this despite spending a percentage of GDP on health that is near the average among developed countries. This is an excellent level of efficiency in health care provision. Clearly, their system is of interest in our review.

Japanese health care is not as simple as many other successful systems. Prices and standards for care are set by the national government. However, much decision making is delegated to Japan's 47 provinces (prefectures). Payments to providers are made by the

---

14. This makes the NHS budget a political football. For example, proponents of the U.K. leaving the E.U. said that Brexit would allow for greater NHS spending. After winning the referendum, the Leave campaign revealed that this was, in fact, a lie.

15. Fun fact: the NHS is one of the five largest employers in the world, along with the U.S. Department of Defense, Chinese People's Liberation Army, Wal-Mart, and McDonald's.

highly regulated members of Japan's public health insurance system. But proponents of single-payer systems should take note: Japan's excellent system has 3,500 insurers providing coverage.[16] Like many other countries with universal coverage, there is a small system outside of the government mandate that provides supplemental insurance for various uncovered items.

Japan's health system involves significant point-of-sale cost sharing. Typically, co-payments are 30% of total cost, although the cap on maximum out-of-pocket spending is low. Cost sharing is also subject to exemptions for age or disability status as well as income-based subsidies. Despite this cost sharing, Japanese citizens visit their doctors more often than citizens of almost all other countries. This odd response to incentives is another way in which health care does not following the usual rules of economics.

Virtually 100% of Japanese citizens have comprehensive health insurance. The Japanese, generally, love their health care system.

Canada

Key Health Statistics:

Life Expectancy:	82.2 years
Infant Mortality:	4.6 per 1000 live births
Adult Mortality:	81.4 per 1000 adult males
Health Spending ($ per capita):	$4,608
Health Spending (% GDP):	10.4%

First of all: no, Canadians are not flocking over the border to gain access to the American health care system.[17]

---

16. Japan is aware that having many small insurers is inefficient, but there seems to be little political will to address the problem.
17. This myth just won't die, no matter the evidence. The best available statistics say that one out of approximately every 2,000 Canadians goes abroad for health care annually. This is identical to the number of Americans who go abroad for medical care. The most often-cited reason for Canadians traveling for health care is to receive elective procedures.

At a glance, the Canadian system is similar to the French system. Tax revenue pays for basic, comprehensive, universal coverage for all residents. Most providers work for private companies, with private hospitals being slightly more common in Canada than in France. Most Canadians carry supplemental insurance to cover services not provided by the government, such as prescription drugs, dental care, and vision care. Long-term care (i.e., nursing home care) is also not covered by the Canadian system. Prices for all services are strictly negotiated by the government.[18]

Unlike the French system, Canadian health insurance is directly managed by the government.[19] Compared to France, Canada has very little cost-sharing. Excepting those services that are not covered, Canadians have never heard of co-pays and deductibles. Classical economic theory would say this would cause Canadians to use their system more. In practice, this does not happen. Efficiency of billing is a strong lever in Canada's successful cost control efforts. Canadian doctors send all bills to one payer, greatly simplifying their offices.

Despite lower compensation than what is available in their southern neighbor, almost all Canadian doctors participate in the national system. In Canada, there is almost no way for individuals to pay more and go outside the system. As a nation, they have intentionally made a trade-off: effective, efficient, and comprehensive care is achieved by preventing the wealthiest from paying more for greater convenience.

All Canadians have comprehensive health insurance. Canadians, generally, love their health care system.

---

18. Canada's system is also federalized, with each of Canada's provinces and territories managing its own program. There are slight differences depending on the province in which one lives. Contrary to the text, one province, Quebec, does cover prescription drugs.
19. It's called Medicare, which frequently leads to confusion for those who write pieces comparing the health system of Canada and the United States.

HOW WOULD YOU STABILIZE THE UNITED STATES' HEALTH CARE SYSTEM IN THE SHORT TERM?

The original sin of Republican attempts to repeal and replace the ACA is they don't know what problem they are trying to solve. You can't write a law without knowing what you want it to achieve. Repealing Obamacare is not a policy goal; it's just a catchphrase. An inability to explain, realistically, exactly how to improve our system is a key reason why the GOP has failed (so far) to make any substantive changes.

To take an obvious example, Republicans have not been clear on whether reducing the number of people without health insurance should be, in and of itself, a policy goal. They talk about health insurance as if it's a choice: some people choose to buy health insurance, others choose to go without. Describing health insurance as a choice demonstrates an utter lack of understanding about how our health care system works. We've already talked about how risk sharing must be part of any health care system. American insurance companies also have a role in negotiating prices, as well as in the operations of patient care. This means that, more than most, our system only takes care of those with health insurance. Almost no rational American chooses to go without health insurance.[20]

Once we accept the value of having health insurance, I can state my short-term goal: get more people health insurance that is more comprehensive, at the lowest possible cost to society. Making structural changes to the health care system is difficult; we should avoid unnecessary change. Employer-based insurance isn't going anywhere—not for a long time. Neither are for-profit insurance companies, drug companies, hospitals, or doctors. In this section, we consider only changes that would not be highly disruptive to the overall system. We think about our stakeholders, who are (usually) just doing their best to fight their way through an imperfect system.

---

20. If there were really 30 million people who would choose to give up their health care (as Paul Ryan would have you believe), then you probably would have met some of them.

Obamacare, excepting its intentional subversion by the Trump Administration, is not failing. It is not entering a death spiral. Anybody who is willing to look at the data can easily see this. In a failing health insurance system, the number of people covered by insurance decreases rapidly; this is not happening. A death spiral is a real thing, not just a scary-sounding made-up word. You are in a death spiral when there is a correlation between premium increases and coverage losses; this is also not happening. Importantly, insurance companies are making money from their exchange-based business. Even Donald Trump has said that insurance companies "have made a fortune with Obamacare."[21] A system based on private insurers must have the ability for them to turn a profit. It took time to reach an equilibrium, but we've achieved this important measure of stability.

In proposing changes, I've also tried to consider the politics. Republicans will not willingly agree to large increases in government health insurance programs. Republicans are going to exist and have a say in the government for the foreseeable future. However, their previous strategy of eliminating Obamacare via neglect may also have run its course.[22] They recognize that, controlling Congress and the Presidency, they are responsible for the health care system, and will be held to account by the voters. Therefore, I will assume that both parties are incentivized to improve the system within the structure of the ACA. Using this standard, while my proposed changes will be Democratic-leaning, they could plausibly achieve a grudging signoff from enough Republicans in Congress to become law.[23]

---

21. Trump, of course, didn't know what he was talking about. Through 2016, the experience of insurers had been unprofitable. In the first half of 2017, however, the medical loss ratio in the individual market dropped to 75% of premiums from 86-88% previously. This means that the markets have now stabilized and could be expected to remain stable. At least, until the Trump team got involved.
22. As this book was going to publication, the Republican tax cut bill has been signed, and it includes a repeal of the individual mandate. I fear some of our members of Congress could gain by reading this book.
23. I should note that there are many lists of ACA fixes from which I have borrowed ideas, in whole or in part. There are so many lists that I'm not able to attribute individual ideas with their initial proponents.

Encouraging Competition

You've probably heard about the lack of participants on the ACA's insurance exchanges. The situation isn't nearly as dire as it sounds in the press. Each exit of an insurer from a state exchange is treated as breaking news; insurers joining exchanges are ignored. In 2018, there are no "bare counties," where people will have no options on the health insurance exchanges. However, competition has become uneven between jurisdictions. Oklahoma had only one exchange insurer in 2017, while New York had 14. States supportive of the ACA tend to have more competition than those opposed; larger states with urban populations are usually more attractive health insurance markets.[24] There are some simple fixes that would help smooth these imbalances and improve the marketplaces nationwide.

The decision by the administration to cancel cost-sharing reduction (CSR) payments added pointless risk to participating insurers. Counterintuitively, by not paying the subsidies, costs to the government also increased.[25] However, state insurance regulators, as well as the providers, quickly responded to this subversive Trump action. In another sign that Obamacare markets are generally stable, they quickly reached equilibrium in a new paradigm. Restoring CSR payments now would not help the market; more changes and regulatory uncertainty could be harmful.

On the other hand, we should undo a different vindictive GOP action by funding the **risk corridors**. Risk corridors were a sort of reinsurance, whereby insurers who get lucky on the cost of their enrollees pay excess gains into a pool, which is paid out to their unlucky counterparts. The risk corridor system decreases the risk for insurers. Insurers don't like risk. Less risk means lower premiums. Lower insurance premiums mean fewer subsidies. Again, the system is improved, and the government saves money.

Most people are aware of the Medicare Advantage program, where Medicare services are provided by private companies. Med-

---

24. This rule has exceptions, of course. Wisconsin, a medium-sized state whose governor has done everything possible to oppose the law, leads the way with 15 insurers.
25. Because ACA subsidies are linked to premium levels, they cost the government more as premiums increase. This is what happened when Trump cancelled CSR payments. The CBO has analyzed the issue and confirmed this effect.

icaid has a similar program, where private insurance companies bid to provide Medicaid services. Both managed services are profitable business lines for private insurers. Two states, Nevada and New York, have made exchange participation a prerequisite to bid for the managed Medicaid program. This has encouraged competition and should be copied in the other states.[26]

A few states have specific insurance regulation quirks, by which they shoot themselves in the foot. One example is Tennessee, which permits its Farm Bureau to sell health insurance outside of the ACA's regulations. Because it is not subject to community rating requirements, the Farm Bureau cherry-picks the healthiest enrollees. The remaining risk pool is therefore degraded, leading to higher premiums on comprehensive insurance. Tennessee should end this loophole. Those currently buying Farm Bureau insurance would see their premiums increase, but they will be able to find insurance if they later become sick. The affected people would also potentially be eligible for premium subsidies. This means that, for many, the new, comprehensive insurance will be little more expensive than their current plan. Several other states, notably Iowa, have similar self-defeating health insurance regulations.

If these changes don't create sufficient competition, then we need to consider the public option. The public option would be a government-sponsored plan that competed on the exchanges. Applicants would have a choice: public or private insurer. Nobody would force them to buy the government-sponsored product. It would compete on a level playing field. Debated at length before the law's passage, the public option did not end up in the ACA. Lawmakers were concerned that private companies would be unable to compete. This is an untenable argument for anybody who complains about lack of competition on exchanges today. A public option could be made available everywhere, or, as a compromise, only in regions that lack competition based on some metric. Because it would operate under the identical system of guaranteed issue and community rating, a public option would not create a negative selection bias for private insurers.

---

26. Because Medicare is a federal program, states can't unilaterally create similar requirements to participate in Medicare Advantage. Of course, if Congress wanted to pass the analogous law, I'd be in favor of that too.

Extending subsidies

There two types of subsidies in the Obamacare exchange system:

- Advance Premium Tax Credits (APTC) help people afford premiums. They are available for households with incomes between 100% and 400% of the federal poverty line (FPL). Their amount is set so that a benchmark plan doesn't exceed a percentage of household income as shown in Table 4.

Household Income (% of FPL)	Maximum Benchmark Net Premium (% of income)
Up to 138% of FPL	2% of income
138 - 150%	3 - 4%
150 - 200%	4 - 6.3%
200 - 250%	6.3 - 8.05%
250 - 300%	8.05 - 9.5%
300 - 400%	9.5%

Table 4: ACA maximum premium by income

- Cost-Sharing Reduction (CSR) subsidies cap out-of-pocket costs. They are available to households with incomes between 100% and 250% of the FPL. For an individual or family, once the out-of-pocket maximum is reached, the insurance provider will bill the government for the balance. CSR limits are again based on household income, as shown in Table 5:

Household Income (% FPL)	Minimum Actuarial Value[27]	Out-of-pocket Max (Individual / Family)
100—150% of FPL	94%	$2,350 / $4,700
150—200%	87%	$2,350 / $4,700
200—250%	73%	$5,700 / $11,400
Above 250%	70%	$7,150 / $14,300

Table 5: CSR calculations

Let's run through a quick example of how this works. Consider a family of four with a total income of $50,000 per year, which is 201% of FPL. The maximum premium for this family for the benchmark plan would be 6.3% of income, or $3,150 annually ($262 monthly). If the unsubsidized cost of this plan were $9,000, the APTC subsidy amount would be the difference between this and the maximum benchmark allowed, or $5,850. The family could apply this subsidy to any plan on the exchange. They would also be eligible for CSR payments, which would cap their out-of-pocket maximum at $11,400.[28]

I would recommend making several adjustments to the subsidy calculations. First, I would extend APTC subsidies to all levels of income, so that no household pays more than 10% of its income on insurance premiums. This would end a current problem for households with incomes close to 400% of FPL. A few dollars of extra income, pushing the family to 401% of FPL, causes them to lose their entire subsidy. Even worse, they will only find out about this loss of subsidies when the file their tax returns the following April; they are then forced to pay them back. The cost of this extension would be small, less than $2 billion per year.[29]

High out-of-pocket costs are a frequent complaint about ACA plans. But there are only two ways to decrease co-pays and deductibles for all plans in the market. We can either introduce regulations to reduce the maximum cost sharing allowed, or we can offer (more) subsidies to offset them. I recommend doing a bit of both. Currently, the actuarial value of a bronze plan is 60%. For a silver

---

27. Recall that actuarial value is the amount of expected total medical costs paid by a given insurance plan. If total expected medical costs are $1,000 and expected out-of-pocket costs are $200, the insurance company is paying $800, making the plan's actuarial value 80%.

28. Note that if the family's income had been 199% of FPL, the cap on out-of-pocket spending would have been $4,700 rather than $11,400. APTC subsidies have sliding scales, but for some reason CSR subsidies have these strict cutoffs. This feature of CSR subsidies should also be changed.

29. As a reference, total spending on ACA subsidies in 2017 is around $46 billion. While my proposals are to increase subsidies, if doing so caused more people to buy insurance, improving the quality of the risk pool, higher subsidies could actually result in the government saving money.

plan, it is 70%.[30] Both should be increased by 5%, lowering out-of-pocket costs by 12% and 16%, respectively. We could also extend CSR subsidies to incomes up to 400% of FPL and make the table more generous at lower income levers. Depending on the details, these changes would cost the government about $5 billion per year. However, I should note that this cost to the government would be savings for individuals. The net cost to society would be negligible.

Changing the Mandates

Polling on the ACA is consistent. People love it—except for the part where they are forced to have insurance (or pay a fine) or employers are forced to provide insurance (or pay a fine).

Let's eliminate the employer mandate. While it was a sensible idea, compliance has proven tedious and expensive. For those who want to decrease the prevalence of employer-sponsored coverage, eliminating a requirement for employers to provide such coverage is obviously a necessary step. Elimination of this mandate would also help gain Republican support for some of our other changes.

Ending the employer mandate is expensive for the government. We don't how many companies would stop sponsoring insurance, but many of the people who lost coverage would be eligible for subsidies for exchange-based plans. As an estimate, if 3% of employers stopped offering health insurance, subsidy costs might increase by $12 billion per year. In addition, the government will no longer collect annual mandate penalties of $20 billion.

On the other hand, many people working for companies who ended their health benefits would be better off for it. Cash compensation for these employees should increase. With subsidies, many will find coverage on the exchanges at a lower cost. Those below 250% of the FPL will see less out-of-pocket cost due to CSR subsidies. The transition will be challenging; if such a change were made, legislators must consider ways to mitigate the uncertainty.[31]

---

30. Gold and platinum plans have actuarial values of 80% and 90% respectively, but almost nobody buys these. Medicaid has almost no cost sharing, with an actuarial value between 95 and 100%.

31. As well as the political blowback as some people are forced to move to different coverage.

Since we are doing one thing people will like, we'll do another they won't: make the individual mandate tougher. Currently, the mandate penalty is \$695 per adult or 2.5% of household income, whichever is greater. Approximately 6.5 million people paid the mandate penalty in 2015. If the penalty were increased to \$1,000 or 3% of income, many of these people will buy insurance. With several million new enrollees, the risk pool would improve, and premiums would decrease. The government would lose the mandate penalty revenue but would pay fewer subsidies; the net cost should be roughly neutral. Thus, a significant population will be newly insured at no cost to the federal government.[32]

Fixing Bugs

With seven years of hindsight, we have learned that some features of the ACA were poorly conceived. Most are easy to fix.

One well-intentioned provision hasn't worked as expected. Under the ACA, people who are offered insurance from their employer are not eligible for exchange subsidies. The idea was to prevent people from turning down employer-sponsored insurance, taking public subsidy money to buy their own policies instead. The problem is that some people are offered insurance from their employer at a cost much higher than they would pay for an exchange policy. They would be better off if their employer cancelled their program entirely. Changing the rule for what qualifies as a real offer of employer-based insurance would fix this problem.

The second glitch also involves the relationship between employer-based coverage and exchange subsidies. If an employer offers insurance to the employee, but *not to his or her family*, then the family is not eligible for subsidies. It appears this was not an intended feature in the law, rather a drafting error. Fixing these two glitches will help around two million people gain affordable health insurance.

---

32. I suppose that people paying the new, larger mandate penalty won't like this change. Come on people, get insured. According to a recent study, 54% of people paying the mandate penalty could have bought a health plan for less than the amount of their penalty. In other words, they would have kept more money and still had health insurance. An exchange plan is better than no plan; many essential health benefits are available at no cost. Even if you don't think you'll use your plan at all, at least it's there in case of catastrophe.

One "problem" with the ACA that I do not recommend fixing is the so-called Medicaid gap. The ACA provides no exchange subsidies for households below 100% of the FPL, as they were expected to gain coverage through Medicaid expansion. As we've already noted, some states, inexplicably, have chosen not to provide their citizens with health care at the expense of the federal government. In these non-expansion states, 2.8 million people are eligible for neither Medicaid nor ACA subsidies. As pointless as this situation is, I do not recommend extending subsidies to populations earning less than the FPL. This is because it would discourage states from expanding their Medicaid programs. Some states might end their existing expansions to take advantage of this new subsidy money. Because Medicaid provides more generous coverage at a lower cost, moving people from Medicaid to private insurance is bad. I wish I had a proposal to help the working poor unfortunate enough to live in states whose leaders prioritize scoring political points over their constituents' well-being.[33]

At its core, Obamacare was intended to eliminate the disparity between those who get health insurance from their employer and those who don't. I can think of no policy rationale for subsidizing the health care of Person A, who works for a large company, but not for Person B, who is identical in every way except for being self-employed. The fact that those receiving employer-sponsored insurance tend to have higher incomes means that, even with Obamacare, government health insurance subsidies are higher for Americans who earn more. This makes no sense and is a major cause of overall inefficiency in our system. It is why health outcomes in the United States are so dependent on income, as was starkly shown in Figure 41 at the start of this chapter.

I grow tired of saying (and hearing) how Obamacare has real problems. Of course it does; everything has problems. I think I've demonstrated here that many of its problems can be ameliorated with simple changes that won't bust either the budget or the blood vessels of your local Republican Congressperson. Taken together, the number of uninsured could be reduced to less than 5% of the population.

---

33. They should vote for people who will expand Medicaid.

The most important thing that can be done in the short term to improve our health care system is also the simplest. The GOP needs to stop sabotaging health insurance markets. As of October 2017, we seem to have reached the end of the seven-year Obamacare repeal saga.[34] However, the actions of the Trump administration haven't been honest, intelligent attempts to improve the system. They are trying to undermine it. Once Obamacare's benefits have been taken away, people will have less reason to support the law itself. The fact that people will die in the process doesn't seem to affect their thinking.[35]

WHAT ARE THE STRUCTURAL, UNDERLYING PROBLEMS IN OUR SYSTEM? IS IT POSSIBLE TO FIX THEM?

The American health care system is not like that of any other country. As we've discussed throughout this book, our system was not "designed" at all. It grew out of World War II-era wage controls and loopholes through which corporations decrease their tax bills. Over time, government programs have been bolted on, usually to address a specific problem, often without considering effects on the broader system.

The ACA is another in a half-century of these patchwork fixes to the system. Its major health provisions directly affect only about 20% of the population: those who were uninsured and those buying insurance through the non-group market. The focus of the legislation was on reducing the number of people without insurance. Lowering costs is a far more difficult problem and was treated as a secondary issue. But we know that these two goals are related; Medicare will save $716 billion due to the greater levels of health coverage achieved via Obamacare.[36] A massive savings, but still a drop in the

---

34. Although there are rumblings that it might come back.
35. Based on a study in the New England Journal of Medicine, the coverage losses due to Obamacare repeal would cause 44,000 incremental deaths per year.
36. It is always important to note that, despite what you may have heard, these savings were not a cut to Medicare benefits. Medicare will cover the exact same services as before. The savings resulted from two areas. First, hospitals expected uncompensated care to decrease, so they were able to lower prices for services. Second,

bucket toward getting our nation on track to achieving the health care efficiency other nations have achieved.

These linked goals, higher coverage and lower cost, inform our larger thinking of what outcomes would improve our system. I've complained about Republicans' failure to state what they would like to change about our health system. While I've alluded to my goals in the previous section, the best way for me to avoid falling victim to my own criticism is to provide a clear statement of what I want to achieve:

- Cost control: As of 2015, health spending accounted for 18% of total U.S. GDP. An aging population will, on its own, cause this number to rise over coming decades. This is not sustainable. I want to decrease medical inflation to be roughly equal to overall inflation.
- Comprehensive, universal coverage: The United States is the only advanced country in the world where significant numbers of people lack access to health care. This is indefensible from either a moral or economic perspective.
- Consistency: Change is expensive. We shouldn't change things that we don't need to change. Initiatives must provide real benefits to be worth the upheaval they would require.
- Transparency: All countries ration health care. Every country but one communicates how and why this rationing is necessary.

One way to bend the cost curve is to look for specific areas of inefficiency. In other words, where does all the extra money in the American system go? The cash is not being lit on fire or buried in the ground; somebody is receiving it in exchange for goods and services provided. If the United States is spending nearly twice as much as other countries on the health of its citizens, there must be actors in the system turning a handy profit. Who are these people? Are they adding value to the system and improving health outcomes?

For-profit insurance companies are an obvious target. As we've discussed, government programs, such as Medicare, Medicaid and

---

payments made to private firms via Medicare Advantage were reduced. This program was intended save money by unleashing the magic of the free market. It has not worked out this way.

the Veterans' Administration, have long provided high-quality care at a significantly lower cost than private insurers. One of the major reasons why private programs have higher costs is that they spend more on administration, as we see in Figure 42.

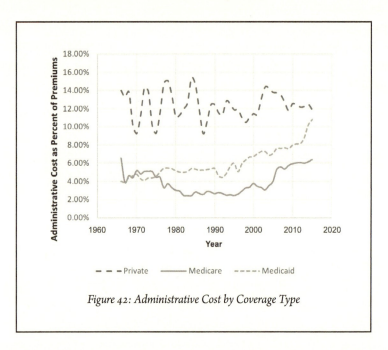

Figure 42: Administrative Cost by Coverage Type

Even this chart, which relies on data from the National Health Expenditures (NHE) survey, understates the difference in administrative costs for public health insurance plans compared to private. You may notice a spike in costs for Medicare around 2005; this was due to the introduction of private Medicare Advantage plans, which have proven less efficient.[37] For traditional Medicare, the administrative costs remain closer to 2%, significantly lower than private plans.[38]

---

37. The spike in Medicaid administration cost in 2014 was also largely due to the increased prevalence of private providers, but there is an additional factor. The influx of healthier enrollees due to the ACA's Medicaid expansion, made the pool of beneficiaries became less costly on a per-person basis. This increased administrative costs as a percentage of total costs. My best estimate is that true, total Medicaid administration costs are around 5% of premiums.

38. Government-sponsored programs do not have lower costs because they use other governmental departments to do their work. When Medicare relies on the IRS to collect its funding via withholding taxes, the IRS sends Medicare a bill, which is included in Medicare's administrative costs.

One way to reduce system costs would be to take advantage of the administrative efficiency of government systems.[39] These administrative cost savings have been achieved by other countries, without any reduction in the quality of care.[40]

Another big reason why our health care costs so much is that the prices are so high. This may seem obvious, but not to policy makers, many of whom focus on reducing the amount of health care consumed, rather than the price paid. They believe that our system is expensive because Americans go to the doctor too much. This isn't true, as we see in Figure 43.

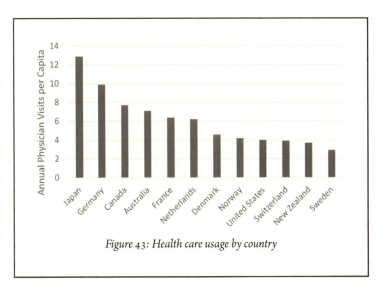

Figure 43: Health care usage by country

Other metrics, such as the number of physicians or hospital beds per capita, also show the United States consumes a below-average amount of health care.[41] Overuse is not the reason why we spend so

39. This does not require lowering reimbursement rates to Medicare levels.
40. Of course, a lot of people work in health insurance and your wasteful overhead is their rent and food. There are around 500,000 people working directly in the American health insurance industry, and some would lose their jobs in exchange for gains in efficiency. We could probably find work for these people that is more fulfilling than sending me stacks of bills for $1.78 to an address I lived at nine years ago, eventually turning me over to a collection agency for said amount, which is something that actually happened.
41. The major exception is that we use the most prescription drugs per capita. Even there, we are not an outlier compared to other countries.

much on health care. Therefore, if we are trying to look more like the rest of the world, reducing usage is the wrong path. We should probably focus on the price of the health care services we use already.

Prescription drugs are an area where American consumers pay far more than the rest of the developed world. The exact amount paid for drugs depends on whether they are bought as individuals, or if an insurance company is paying, or a hospital is buying in bulk. Because of this, it is difficult to know exactly how much we pay for prescription drugs on average. With that caveat, let's look at the annual cost of one of the world's best-selling drugs, Humira, in various countries:[42]

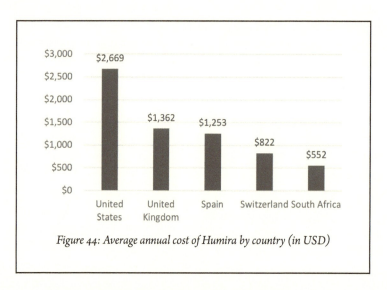

Figure 44: Average annual cost of Humira by country (in USD)

It goes without saying that the Humira used by Americans is not any better than that used by Spaniards or South Africans. So why does it cost so much more? The answer has to do with the way we negotiate drug prices. To learn how we can do it better, we can look to the example of Singapore.

Proponents of maintaining private control over our health care system often point to Singapore as a model. We didn't consider Singapore in our world tour, but it has an interesting and unique sys-

---

42. I chose Humira randomly. American pharmaceutical overpayment varies depends on the drug, but Humira is a fair representative of many best-selling brand-name drugs.

tem. Like the United States, Singapore relies on a group of for-profit, private health insurance companies. With this system, Singapore has achieved true competition between these insurers, leading to a system that is highly efficient.[43] If Singapore has achieved this success via the free market, why can't we?

In addition to ignoring the obvious differences in providing health care to an island nation of six million people in a single metropolitan area, Republicans who long for Singapore's health system completely miss the point. A stable system of private insurers requires government regulations. Singapore's health insurance plans are very highly regulated and must include critical protections such as community rating. Singapore also has a punitive individual mandate, which, along with generous subsidies, creates near-universal health coverage. The Singaporean health system is Obamacare on steroids.

Most importantly, Singapore's system has another feature that goes far beyond Obamacare and has been critical in reducing costs: prices for health care are set by the central government. In this sense, there is little difference between Singapore and countries with socialized medicine. By negotiating as a unit, Singapore gains significant leverage and keeps prices low. In the United States, of course, each benefit provider negotiates separately; individually, they are not large enough to get the best price.

Federally sponsored insurance programs, such as Medicare, are larger than many whole countries and have been able to drive a hard bargain when they try to. Amazingly, we often fail to use this leverage. Famously, when prescription drug benefits were added to Medicare, there was a strict prohibition against negotiating prices with drug makers. As a result, according to a 2007 study, Medicare pays 58% more for prescription drugs than the Veterans Administration, which has no such prohibition. There is just no reason for this; the United States shouldn't pay more for its drugs than the rest of the developed world.

The discrepancy in pricing persists beyond prescription drugs.[44] In every country that has had success controlling its health care cost,

---

43. This is a difference from insurance companies in France and Japan. In these countries, the incredibly strict regulation means insurance plans do not compete in the traditional sense.

the government sets the prices of health care delivery. As with Singapore, this can be achieved via private health insurance or by government-sponsored programs. Centralized price setting doesn't necessarily put us on the road to single payer. But, until we have such price-setting in place, we are not being serious about controlling our costs.

So far, the changes I've mentioned will be largely painless for consumers. But we can only get so far toward our efficiency goals without consumers noticing. To go further, we will need to change the way we ration health care. As I've said, health care is already rationed in the United States. Our rationing is based on a person's ability to afford, or the type of employer they have, rather than on need, or whether a given treatment works. We don't need to do it this way, and we can change it if we want to. Rationing care based on efficacy and necessity doesn't mean we need to go as far as Canada, where there is virtually no market to pay more for better care. But there is a clear correlation between a country's willingness to ration care and its ability to control costs.

Some levers which ration health care will have virtually no effect on consumers. You know those billboards that hospitals put up on the Interstates, showing off their latest futuristic piece of equipment? Well, just because they are futuristic doesn't mean they are useful. It does mean they are expensive, requiring patients (or their insurance companies) to pay their costs. Hospitals also heavily market their emergency rooms, over the less-profitable provision of ongoing, comprehensive care. Even more intrusive in your daily live is the inundation of ads for the latest drug, from your favorite multinational pharmaceutical company. They probably have exclusive rights to the drug due to their shiny, new patent. This doesn't necessarily mean their drug is better than previously existing one. But it usually means it is more expensive.

I'm not saying that providers are evil. They are following the incentive structure that we, as a society, have created for them. Remember from our discussion of economics; people act in their own best interest. We need to change the incentive structure, reducing

---

44. As context, prescription drugs compromise around 10% of all U.S. health care spending.

spending that does not efficiently improve health outcomes. The free market will not do this on its own.

As a society, we can spend only so much of our national wealth on health care; the United States is likely not far from its limit. If the previous 30 years have featured an explosion of health costs due to new types of care, the next generation must adopt a better understanding and application of how we can deliver the best and most efficient results for all our citizens. In other words, our societal values will need to become better aligned with how we ration our care. But ration care we always have, and ration care we always must. We need to change how we do it.

If the market for health care were like the market for bread, life would be grand. The government could step back, the free market could be free, and we could all be insured, healthy, and happy. Unfortunately, we have shown that this is nothing like the world we live in. It is proscribed by individual self-interest, the very force that created the free market in the first place. Once you state the goal of giving everybody access to medical care, your choices for setting up a health care system narrow quickly. Unhealthy people can't afford the actual cost of care, requiring a system of insurance. Middle class people can't afford their expected cost of care, requiring risks to be pooled and premiums subsidized.

The trade-offs in insurance regulations and subsidies should reflect a nation's values, as decided by the results of a vigorous public debate. Pooling risks necessarily means some groups will subsidize others; the details of these subsidies are a country's statement of who needs help and who can help. Which is itself a statement of how a society treats its vulnerable members.

In the United States, the elderly (and some disabled) are the largest recipients of health subsidies. Those over 65 receive their health insurance via Medicare. Medicare is heavily subsidized for all enrollees, but especially those of lower income. This makes sense; very few seniors would be able to afford full-priced health insurance.

After seniors, the largest health subsidies are paid to those above the median income level. As we saw in "Fiscal Policy, Part I: Taxes," deductibility of health insurance premiums costs the federal government $210 billion per year. This amount is nothing more than subsidies paid only to people who receive health insurance from their employer. Such people tend to have higher incomes. The fact that so many Americans receive health insurance through their employer was never an intentional part of our system, but rather a historical accident. Reducing the importance of employers in the health insurance game is a worthy goal, but also an enormous shock to a complex system. We should do this slowly and carefully.

Obamacare is not a disaster; it has survived vicious Republican-led sabotage to do what it was designed to do. The sabotage needs to stop. Nobody gains when people don't have health insurance; stop discouraging them from signing up. Nobody gains when insurers leave the market due to uncertainty; stop undermining this critical public-private partnership. The never-ceasing, misleading yelling is self-reinforcing; the system relies on trust in the system. It also makes it impossible to compromise toward the types of changes we've discussed. If you've said for the better part of a decade that something can't be fixed, it is hard to try honestly to fix it.[45]

People's lives depend on the stability of our health care system and our health insurance system. For every 830 people who lose health insurance, there will be one additional death every year. There will be one bankruptcy every year for every 80 people who are uninsured. Every other nation in the world has found a better way to design a health care system, spending less for better results. Maybe we don't want to copy their systems, but we can't ignore their blueprints.

And nowhere does a successful health care blueprint, one that achieves our goals of lower cost and universal coverage, involve getting the government out of health care.

---

45. Having accused the other party of trying to kill your grandparents also does little to promote compromise.

CONCLUSION

Well, I hope you found this as challenging to read as I did to write. And as enjoyable, too.

As we discussed, our universe is unimaginably big. So far as we can tell, to get from one end to the other you'd need to travel 93 billion light years. One light year is further than you could travel in 1,000 generations. We go to work, eat and sleep, and live our lives seldom thinking about what is going on out in this vast space and how it all affects us. We will never be able to observe or understand even the smallest fraction of what exists or what is possible.

Which is another way of saying that we shouldn't expect important topics to be simple. We have already figured out solutions to most of our simple problems. Like pre-sliced bread.

When applied to government policy, the complexity of the universe should make you wary when you are told our problems are easy to solve. The best ideas, those without any losers, were figured out long ago. For example, our National Parks were relatively easy to establish, and are maintained efficiently by the excellent National Park Service. They have no losers, only winners.[1] They've also been around for more than a century.

At this point in our nation's history, improving our citizens' lives further will involve trade-offs. We must honestly consider and prioritize our goals, determine creative solutions by which to reach them, and consistently update our plans based on what we learn. Information—that which helps us gain knowledge—is our only guide.

Those who tell us about magic plans that will make everything better for everybody are the enemy of progress in our society. Those that honestly admit and explain trade-offs are our friends. Listen to

---

1. Just as this book was moving to publication, the current administration began considering doubling entrance fees for many National Parks. Thus, proving that it is easy to create simple policies with only losers and no winners.

your friends even when you disagree, correct them when they are wrong, and support them in their own search for more information.

These attempts to implement slogans as serious solutions to difficult problems are a great cause of concern to me. Their growing prevalence is why I started this project in the first place. Our society features a disdain of expertise and increasingly of knowledge itself. Faulty logic and a misunderstanding of the scientific method are used to impeach individual experts, entire disciplines, and even the difference between truth and lies. This is very dangerous. Once you discard truth as a guide, you can tell anybody anything, and they can't prove you wrong. In an alternative-fact-based world, two plus two indeed equals five.

Progress in society isn't a given. We are, today, in an unprecedented period of improvement of the human condition. For perhaps 500 years, and especially the last 200 years, human lives have improved with only small steps back. This has never happened previously in the history of our species. No previous era of human success has persisted so long without falling prey to barbarians or the plague. The recent global financial crisis, unprecedented in scope and global effect, did not lead to famine and revolution. In less than five years, a speck in the timeline of history, we recovered everything we had lost and more.

This ongoing societal progress is not guaranteed. In the long run, our only effective weapons against backsliding are reason and logic. If they are lost, we risk ice ages, bubonic plague, feudalism, nuclear holocaust, and worse.

There are also great reasons to be optimistic—greater reasons than ever. When human society has faced dark times in the past, it often resulted from an uninformed populace. In 2018, we have the tools to combat this. There is more information available today, to more people, than ever before. In the time it takes you to read this paragraph, you could find summaries of health insurance risk pool calculations or climate data going back thousands of years. You could read newspapers from anywhere in the world or nearly any book that has ever been published, for a small fee.[2] Even in my

---

2. Also, you can see many pictures of cats. Progress is truly a great thing.

youth, let alone the lives of my grandparents or their grandparents, this would have been utterly unimaginable.

This plethora of information comes with a cost; those that have undeclared (or falsely declared) biases can put their false information out there just as easily as anybody else. Those with evil intentions can reach their audience in ways that we have no means of preventing. Intentionally misleading information isn't labelled as intentionally misleading. Separating good information from bad is difficult. You need to put in effort. You need to want to know.

Basing our debates on facts should not and does not limit discussion. You and I can look at the same set of data and come to conflicting, equally valid, conclusions. You and I can come to the same conclusions but retain major philosophical differences. Everybody should work as hard as they wish to convince others that their philosophy is the best one, and that their solutions should be the winner in the marketplace of ideas. But if some people enter the debate buoyed by information that is false, then it isn't a debate at all. It's just a shouting match. Somebody who does not care about the truth cannot be convinced by evidence or logic.

So if I can close by imparting one last thing, it is to implore you to consider where your information came from and why somebody put in all that time to create it and put it in front of your eyes. Start this process with this book and me, the person who wrote it. I've tried to be objective, and to differentiate facts from opinions. An honest communicator can only hope to understand and explain how their view of the world affects what they write and say. I've honestly attempted to do so here. If you agree, then I've succeeded in my primary task, encouraging you to tackle challenging subjects and understand my point of view. This is the way I think, and this story is my story.

NOTES AND SOURCES

INTRODUCTION

The joke in Footnote 3 is, unfortunately, not of my own creation. It has been around a long time. I have no idea who originally wrote it.

HEALTH INSURANCE, PART I

Originally Published as "Volume 2: Health Care in the US, Part I" on November 26, 2016.

Statistics on joint replacements are from American Academy of Orthopaedic Surgeons, *2.5 Million Americans Living with an Artificial Hip, 4.7 Million with an Artificial Knee,* 2014.

All of the data on the status of health insurance from 2009 are from the Census Bureau. Private insurance figures are from U.S. Department of Commerce; U.S. Census Bureau, *Income, Poverty and Health Insurance in the United States: 2008,* 2009, p. 23.

The 1948 Democratic and 2016 Republican platforms are available on the Internet at American Presidency Project, *Political Party Platforms,* 1999-2017 and GOP.com, *Republican Platform,* n.d., respectively.

For a summary of the health financing situation of seniors in the 1960s, I like the Politifact overview at Louis Jacobsen, *Were the early 1960s a golden age for health care?,* 2012.

Medicaid enrollment details in Figure 1 are from the Centers for Medicare and Medicaid Services at Centers for Medicare and Medicaid Services, *2014 CMS Statistics,* 2014. Calculations in Figure 2 are mine, based on the Census Bureau. Historical health care inflation in Table 1 is from Catlin & Cowen, *History of Health Spending in the United States, 1960 - 2013*, 2015. Figure 3 is from Gould, *Health Insurance Coverage Continues to Decline in a New Decade*, 2012, based on data from U.S. Census Bureau, *Current Population Survey Annual Social and Economic Supplement (CPS-ASEC)*, n.d..

Employment statistics for Medicaid are from Schubel, *No Need for Work Requirements in Medicaid*, 2015. CBPP is a stated "nonpartisan research and policy institute" but should probably be referred to as Democratic-leaning.

Statistics on cost sharing in Medicaid are from the National Women's Law Center in *Medicaid 101: The Federal-State Health Care Partnership*, 2006, with underlying data from FY 2006 Federal Register, *Federal Financial Participation in State Assistance Expenditures*, 2004, pp. Volume 69, Number 226.

Interactive data on CHIP/S-CHIP are available from the Kaiser Family Foundation at Kaiser Family Foundation, *Total Number of Children Ever Enrolled in CHIP Annually*, n.d.. The data in Figure 3 on the slow demise of ESI is from Long, Rae, Claxton, & Damico, *Trends in Employer-Sponsored Insurance Offer and Coverage Rates, 1999-2014*, 2016

A lot of data on health insurance in the U.S. are available at the invaluable ACASignups.net, managed by Charles Gaba. Data on sources of health insurance for the population are from Gaba, *SHOW YOUR WORK: Healthcare Coverage Breakout for the Entire U.S. Population in 1 Chart*, 2016.

Statistics on federal workforce from Office of Personnel Management at Office of Personnel Management, *Historical Federal Workforce Tables: Executive Branch Civilian Employment Since 1940*, n.d..

For the story of the disaster that was New York's guaranteed issue regulation, see Kliff, *Here's why health insurance premiums are tumbling in New York*, 2013.

The Atlantic offered a full accounting of the medical debt we faced as a populace in Khazan, *Why Americans Are Drowning in Medical Debt*, 2014.

The data on health spending and life expectancy in Figure 4 come from the databases at the OECD and World Bank, respectively. Both have highly-useful databases for all types of information, but I've specifically used Organization for Economic Co-Operation and Development, *Health Spending* and World Bank, *Life expectancy at birth, total (years)*, n.d..

A TALE OF TWO ALABAMA GOVERNORS

Originally published as "Two Alabama Governors" on April 13, 2017.

The most famous telling of the Don Siegelman story was on 60 Minutes, at Pelley, *The Prosecution of Don Siegelman*, 2008. The local Huntsville, Alabama CBS affiliate did not show the segment, claiming technical difficulties.

For a case of corruption, Robert Bentley's story was easy to investigate and prove. Because of this it has been told at length in many publications. A useful overview, in the format of a timeline, is available at Phillips, *Former Alabama governor Robert Bentley's year from hell, a timeline*, 2017.

HEALTH INSURANCE, PART II

Originally published as "Volume 4: Health Insurance, Part II" on December 21, 2016.

For a debunking of the "Canadians coming across the border" myth, see Lee, *Trump's claim about Canadians traveling to the United States for medical care*, 2016.

Data on national health spending from Organization for Economic Co-Operation and Development, *Health Spending* .

My favorite rendition of the three-legged stool story is Krugman, *Revenge of the Three-Legged Stool*, 2012. It is also available in cartoon form at Obamacare Facts, *ObamaCare Guaranteed Issue*, n.d..

Health care spending by user is from Kaiser Family Foundation, *Health Care Costs: A Primer*, 2012. The analogue for alcohol is interesting and available at Haden, *How Much Do the Top 10 Percent Drink? More Than You Ever Imagined*, 2014.

The statistic on Americans with pre-existing conditions is from Kaiser Family Foundation, *An Estimated 52 Million Adults Have Pre-Existing Conditions That Would Make Them Uninsurable Pre-Obamacare*, 2016.

For details on the implementation of Obamacare's guaranteed issue and community rating, see Section 45 of the Code of Federal Regulations, specifically: 45 CFR 147.102, 45 CFR 147.104 and 45 CFR 148.122. 26 USC 5000A covers the individual mandate.

To calculate Obamacare subsidies on your own, use the widget at Kaiser Family Foundation, *Health Insurance Marketplace Calculator*, 2016.

Kaiser Family Foundation, *Summary of Coverage Provisions in the Patient Protection and Affordable Care Act*, 2012 and Obamacare Facts, *Summary of Provisions in The Patient Protection and Affordable Care Act* both have longer explanations of what is in the ACA. The latter is an especially robust list.

There is a lot of information out there about the relative efficiency of Medicare/Medicaid versus private insurance. The KFF study mentioned is available at Lisa Clemans-Cope, *Medicaid Spending Growth Compared to Other Payers: A Look at the Evidence*, 2016. Jacobson, *Barbara Boxer says Medicare overhead is far lower than private insurers' overhead*, 2011 weighed in on Senator Barbara Boxer's claim that Medicaid had lower costs. I've written on this topic myself at Cohen N. , *In Which I Pick a Fight with the Cato Institute*, 2017. There are many surveys comparing Medicaid approval to private insurance, but a good example is provided by U.S. News and World Report, *Medicare Beats Private Plans for Patient Satisfaction: Survey*, 2012.

Pre-Obamacare Medicaid eligibility by state is from Kaiser Family Foundation, *Where Are States Today? Medicaid and CHIP Eligibility Levels for Children, Pregnant Women, and Adults*, 2017 and expansion status at Obamacare Facts, *ObamaCare Medicaid Expansion* .

For more on Medicare cost savings, see Carey, *FAQ: Decoding The $716 Billion In Medicare Reductions*, 2012. For progress on cost cutting, see Mangan, *Obamacare program generates 'substantial' Medicare savings*, 2015.

Past Republican support for the basic structure of the ACA can be found in many places. The original thesis is available at Butler, *Assuring Affordable Health Care for All Americans*, 1989. See also reporting in Cooper, *Conservatives Sowed Idea of Health Care Mandate, Only to Spurn It Later*, 2012 and description at Commonwealth of Massachusetts, *The Top Ten Facts about Massachusetts Health Care Reform* .

Studies on uninsured from Obamacare Facts, *ObamaCare: Uninsured Rates* and Cohen, Martinez, & Zammitti, *Health Insurance Coverage: Early Release of Estimates From the National Health Interview Study, January-March 2016*, 2016. The chart projecting overall state of health insurance is Gaba, *SHOW YOUR WORK: Healthcare Coverage Breakout for the Entire U.S. Population in 1 Chart*, 2016.

FOUR MONTHS IN 1933

Originally published as "Volume 5: Four Months in 1933" on January 18, 2017.

No discussion of Interwar Germany, or at-war Germany, would be complete without copious thanks to William Shirer. My understanding of Weimar and the rise of the Nazis is based on Shirer, *The rise and fall of the Third Reich: A history of Nazi Germany*, 1960. If Rise and Fall's girth scares you, go for Shirer, *Berlin Diary*, 1941.

For background on the Weimar Republic, one of my key sources is from BBC, *Germany 1918-1939*, 2017, the BBC's study guide for the British GSCE exam. Unfortunately, much of its Weimar resources are now archived.

The entire Weimar Constitution is available online, in what I can only guess is an accurate translation into English, at PSM-Data "Geschichte", *Weimar Constitution*, 2001. If you want a summary, I can recommend the article at Wikipedia, *Weimar Constitution*, n.d..

For the full telling via my favorite version of Weimar's hyperinflation, go to Ahamed, *Lords of Finance: The Bankers Who Broke the World*, 2009. See pages 116-129.

Finding quality economic data from an obscure Republic from almost a century ago was a challenge for me. The best listing of number of unemployed came from Trueman, *Weimar Republic And The Great Depression*, 2015. Growth rates come from Räth, *Rezessionen in historischer Betrachtung*, 3/2009. For the fallacy of the link between hyperinflation and the rise of the Nazis, see The Economist, *Germany's hyperinflation-phobia*, 2013.

For the full article about Hitler's release from Landsberg, see New York Times Company, *Hitler Tamed by Prison*, 1924.

ORBITAL MECHANICS AND THE MARTIAN

Originally published on March 16, 2017.

The delta-v information is from the map produced at Carrion, *I made a delta-v subway map of the Solar System*, 2017.

I've created a handy public Google Sheet that you can use to play around with the variables used in the Mars Ascent Vehicle calculations. It's available at Cohen N. , *Martian - MAV Calcs (Google Sheets)*, n.d.

Lunar Module and Saturn V specifications are both available on Wikipedia, *Apollo Lunar Module*, n.d. and Wikipedia, *Saturn V*, n.d.

The Martian is available for purchase at a retailer of fine books near you Weir, *The Martian*, 2014.

HEALTH INSURANCE, PART III

Originally published as "Volume 6: Health Insurance, Part III" on January 31, 2017.

For more on Politifact's rating system, see Tampa Bay Times, *About Politifact*, n.d..

There are many sources out there for information about Obamacare. As expected, they tend to have partisan slants, one way or another. I attempted to be even more careful than usual in the sourcing for this piece.

I used several sources specifically to consider the question of plan cancellations. A description of cancellations that happened "because" of Obamacare is available at Obamacare Facts, *ObamaCare: Health Insurance Cancellation*, n.d.. It also includes a partial list of Obamacare protections that existing plans did not meet. A list of various surveys and methodologies to nail down the number affected is at Robertson, *'Millions' Lost Insurance*, 2014.

The initial CBO report on Obamacare is Congressional Budget Office, *Estimates for the Insurance Coverage Provisions of the Affordable Care Act Updated for Recent Supreme Court Decision*, 2012. The effect on the budgets in Figure 7 are from Congressional Budget Office, *Letter to John Boehner re: H.R. 6079*, 2012.

The Washington Post's take on the labor market effects of the ACA is Kessler, *No, CBO did not say Obamacare will kill 2 million jobs*, 2014. For information on voluntary vs. involuntary part-time work, see Schierholtz, *Positive Jobs Trend*, 2014.

Charles Gaba's fantastic pie chart showing current insurance coverage by provider is at Gaba, *ACASignups.net estimates of total U.S. healthcare coverage as of March 2016*, 2016. His chart of Open Enrollment results is at Gaba, *ACA EXCHANGE Qualified Health Policy (QHP) Enrollments:*, 2017.

For comparison of premiums in the exchange and employer-sponsored markets, see Johnson C. Y., *Skyrocketing Obamacare premiums still lower than employer-sponsored insurance*, 2016. Standard and Poor's take on the possibility of a death spiral is available at Banerjee, *The ACA Individual Market: 2016 Will Be Better than 2015, But Achieving Target Profitability Will Take Longer*, 2016.

Figure 8 combines information from several different sources. There were two relevant reports from the CBO, Congressional Budget Office, *Federal Subsidies for Health Insurance Coverage for People Under Age 65: 2016-2026*, 2016 and Congressional Budget Office, *Updated Esti-*

mates of the Insurance Coverage Provisions of the Affordable Care Act, 2015. As usual, KFF provided valuable translation to everyday English in Levitt & Claxton, *How Much Financial Assistance Are People Receiving Under the Affordable Care Act?*, 2014. I compiled the data myself and translated it into the format displayed here.

A humorous summary of seven years of the Republicans failing to produce a replacement plan is available at Linkins, *A Brief History Of The Republican Alternative To Obamacare: Your Sunday Morning Conversation,* 2014.

Most of the "Obamacare Victims" stories are laughably easy to deconstruct. For example, Julie Boonstra, into whose story Americans for Prosperity pumped enormous advertising money, was quickly found to be saving $1,200 under the ACA; see Kessler, *A hard-hitting anti-Obamacare ad makes a claim that doesn't add up,* 2014. Many claimed the ACA was at fault for actions taken by their private insurance company, as described in Cesca, *Another Obamacare 'Horror Story' Debunked; and, No, the President Didn't Lie About the Law,* 2013. The Atlantic describes victims as people who lacked information and chides the conservative press for not checking out their stories in John, *Lessons from the Obamacare 'Horror Stories',* 2014. I encourage you to go search for more; nothing will better convince you of the success of the ACA than the mendacity required to create its supposed victims.

THE RULE OF BAYES

Originally published as "Volume 7: Bayes Theorem" on February 14, 2017.

Both the leading quote and Image 11 are from XKCD.com: A webcomic of romance, sarcasm, math and language. For the original version, please see Monroe, *Frequentists vs. Bayesians,* n.d..

As mentioned in the text, Image 10 is probably not Thomas Bayes. However, it is also the only image I have ever seen used for Bayes. So far as I can tell, it was first used to represent Bayes in O'Donnell, *History of Life Insurance in Its Formative Years,* 1936.

The quote demonstrating our lack of knowledge about Bayes is from his Wikipedia page at Wikipedia, *Thomas Bayes, n.d.*. At best, we have a biographical sketch of Bayes; we probably know more about his father, in fact. I first learned about the billiards table thought experiment from McGrayne, *The Theory That Would Not Die: How Bayes' Rule Cracked the Enigma Code, Hunted Down Russian Submarines, and Emerged Triumphant from Two Centuries of Controversy*, 2012.

The simplest proof of Bayes Theorem I can find is Allison, *Proof of Bayes Theorem* . There are many places to see the complexity of drug tests when Bayesian logic is used. One I especially liked was Gross, *Drug testing Example for Conditional Probability and Bayes Theorem*, n.d..

HEALTH INSURANCE, PART IV

Originally published as "Volume 8: Health Insurance, Part IV" on February 27, 2017.

The distribution of tax reductions from a repeal of the ACA are from Debot, Huang, & Marr, *ACA Repeal Would Lavish Medicare Tax Cuts on 400 Highest-Income Households*, 2017. The effects of repeal through reconciliation are from Blumberg, Buettgens, & Holahan, *Implications of Partial Repeal of the ACA through Reconciliation*, 2016.

For a more thorough explanation of the Senate reconciliation procedures, see Matthews, *Budget reconciliation, explained*, 2016. A good summary of then-Representative Price's health insurance regulation bill is available at Kodjak, *5 Things To Know About Rep. Tom Price's Health Care Ideas*, 2016. The information in Figure 9 is based on my assumptions and calculations, which are in turn based on data from Gaba, *ACASignups.net estimates of total U.S. healthcare coverage as of March 2016*, 2016.

For costs of average plans, I received my data from HealthPocket, *Silver Plan*, 2016. To compute the values in Figure 10, I used the summary of the Empowering Patients First Act at Pianin, *8 Big Changes Under Tom Price's Obamacare Replacement Plan*, 2016 and the subsidies calculated by the Kaiser Family Foundation widget at Kaiser Family Foundation, *Health Insurance Marketplace Calculator*, 2016. I used U.S. Average, with FPL of $12,000. Everything is based on a single-member household. Disclaimer: health insurance is highly dependent on a person's individual circumstances, so this is a rough calculation.

If you are interested in Georgia's experience allowing other states' plans to be offered therein, it is told in a number of places. Some that I found insightful are at Miller A. , *Interstate Health Insurance Sales Has A Tryout In Georgia But No Takers*, 2016 and Ungar, *Georgia Cross-State Health Insurance Sales Law A Major Bust*, 2012.

Statistics on pre-existing conditions from Claxton, Cox, Damico, Levitt, & Pollitz, *Pre-existing Conditions and Medical Underwriting in the Individual Insurance Market Prior to the ACA*, 2016. You might be interested in what used to be considered pre-existing conditions. Each insurer maintained its own list, but one example can be found at Illinois Health Agents, *BlueCross BlueShield of Illinois – Pre-Existing Condition Exclusions*, 2012. Kaiser also has a good summary of pre-ACA high-risk pools available at Schwartz, *State High-Risk Pools: An Overvieew*, 2010. Estimates for proper funding levels of high-risk pools have huge variations; we really don't know. Some reputable guesstimates are available at Park, *Trump, House GOP High-Risk Pool Proposals a Failed Approach*, 2016 and Hall, *Why a National High-Risk Insurance Pool Is Not a Workable Alternative to the Marketplace*, 2014.

For an overview of the comparison of the cost of Medicaid against private insurers, see my piece again, at Cohen N. , *In Which I Pick a Fight with the Cato Institute*, 2017.

FISCAL POLICY, PART I
TAXES

Originally published as "Volume 9: Fiscal Policy, Part I: Taxes" on March 14, 2017.

There are many places that discuss President Obama's effect on the deficit. Politifact addresses the issue head-on at Sanders, *Barack Obama claims deficit has decreased by two-thirds since taking office*, 2015.

For data on fiscal policy (and many other things), the Federal Reserve Economic Data (FRED) is an invaluable resource. Fiscal data can be found at Federal Reserve Bank of St. Louis, *Federal Govern-*

ment Data, n.d.. Be careful: FRED is a rabbit hole. It claims to have 498,343 data series at the time of publication. The data for Figure 11 is from FRED.

The amounts raised by various taxes comes from Chantrill, *Government Revenue Details*, 2017, which processes and reformats data from the Congressional Budget Office. The CBO has its own summaries of tax receipts at Congressional Budget Office, *Taxes*, n.d.. All figures are from fiscal year 2016. Current income tax brackets are available in many places, but I used Orem, *2017 Federal Income Tax Brackets*, 2017.

The list of tax expenditures in Table 2 is from Tax Policy Center, *What are the largest tax expenditures?*, n.d.. The Tax Policy Center is a partnership of the Urban Institute and the Brookings Institution. The former is properly described as left-leaning. The latter is, in my opinion, a good example of a non-partisan, centrist think tank. Underlying data for the Tax Policy Center's Analysis is from Office of Tax Policy, *Tax Expenditures*, 2016. Note that the Office of Tax Policy's model does not consider behavioral changes resulting from eliminating tax expenditures.

For information on the distribution of capital gains on the among different groups, see Flowers, *The Top 1 Percent Earns A Lot From Cashing In On Investments*, 2015, Lenzner, *The Top 0.1% Of The Nation Earn Half Of All Capital Gains*, 2011, and Sahadi, *Top 400 taxpayers' average income jumps to $336 million*, 2015.

Information on corporate tax rates comes from Trading Economics, *List of Countries by Corporate Tax Rate*, n.d.. Data on corporate tax collections vis-à-vis GDP is from Organization for Economic Co-Operation and Development, *Revenue Statistics - OECD countries: Comparative tables*, n.d..

Note: as the book was heading to publication, the "Tax Cuts and Jobs Act" was signed into law. Its effects are not mentioned in this book. If you want to know more about it, I recommend Avi-Yonah, et al., *The Games They Will Play: An Update on the Conference Committee Tax Bill*, 2017.

TAXES AND GROWTH RATES AND PLENTY OF CHARTS

Originally published on March 20, 2017.

The Laffer Curve Napkin is part of the collection of the National Museum of American History, part of the Smithsonian Institution. The image is from their site at National Museum of American History, *Laffer Curve Napkin,* 1979.

Data on GDP Growth is from the World Bank at World Bank Group, *GDP growth (annual %),* n.d.. Unemployment statistics are from the Bureau of Labor Statistics, available at Bureau of Labor Statistics, *Databases, Tables & Calculators by Subject,* n.d.. Raw data for taxes as a percentage of GDP are from the OECD at Organization for Economic Co-Operation and Development, *Tax revenue,* n.d.. Historical marginal tax rates are from the Tax Foundation, Tax Foundation, *U.S. Federal Individual Income Tax Rates History, 1862-2013 (Nominal and Inflation-Adjusted Brackets),* n.d.. Calculations and regressions are all by the author, so any errors are my own.

CONGRESS

Originally published as "Volume 11: Congress" on April 5, 2017.

For Article I of the U.S. Constitution, see Legal Information Institute, *U.S. Constitution > Article I .* You could have found this yourself, but I had to get in a plug for The Legal Information Institute (LII). A project of the Cornell University Law School, LII is a fantastic online repository for governmental documents of all types. I'm continually amazed by the breadth of what they have available.

A non-technical summary of Apportionment Paradoxes is available at Wikipedia, *Apportionment paradox,* n.d..

For information on rejected use of the Commerce Clause in gun regulation, see *United States v. Lopez,* 1995.

For more on the Conference process, see Rybicki, *Conference Committee and Related Procedures: An Introduction,* 2015. Congressional Research Service also explains Congressional Ping-Pong at Rybicki, *Amendments Between the Houses: Procedural Options and Effects,* 2015 and lists Senate Confirmable positions at Davis & Greene, *Presidential Appointee Positions Requiring Senate Confirmation and Committees Handling Nominations*, 2017.

THE POINCARÉ CONJECTURE

Originally published as "Volume 12: The Poincaré Conjecture" on April 23, 2017.

There are many resources that show lists and descriptions of topological invariants. For a technical list, see Crainic, *Inleiding Topologie 2011*, 2011, pp. 63-82 and Viro, Ivanov, Netsvetaev, & Kharlamov, *Elementary Topology: Problem Textbook*, 2008. Of course, there is also a concise list at Wikipedia, *Topological property*, n.d..

For more on the BOOMERanG project, see Caltech, *Boomerang*, 2010. Apparently, there is actually a thing called the National Scientific Balloon Facility, which you can learn about at Johnson M. , *Columbia Scientific Balloon Facility*, 2017.

We mentioned the Clay Mathematics Institute (CMI), whose prize of $1,000,000 was turned down by Gregori Perelman. CMI maintains a portal with links to information about the Conjecture and Perelman's proof at Clay Mathematics Institute, *Perelman's Solution*, n.d.. Perelman's proof itself consists of three papers: Perelman, *The entropy formula for the Ricci flow and its geometric applications*, 2002, Perelman, *Ricci flow with surgery on three-manifolds*, 2002, and Perelman, *Finite extinction time for the solutions to the Ricci flow on certain three-manifolds*, 2003. If you don't have an advanced degree in mathematics, you are unlikely to understand these; I certainly don't.

Edgar Allen Poe's involvement in cosmology is one of those strange historical interludes that seem to pop up. Somehow, he considered concepts of relativity, expansion of the universe and the Big Bang decades before the work of Einstein, Hubble and Lematre. See Poe, *Eureka, A Prose Poem: Or the Physical and Metaphysical Universe*, 1848.

FISCAL POLICY, PART II
SPENDING

Originally published as "Volume 13: Fiscal Policy, Part II: Spending" on May 9, 2017.

General information on federal spending comes from the Congressional Research Service at Levitt, Austin, & Stupak, *Mandatory Spending Since 1962*, 2015. CRS reports that its data are from OMB, the Budget and the CBO.

A summary of items in President Obama's budget that had no chance of implementation are available at Fox, *Here Are Seven Things in Obama's Budget That Are Never Going to Happen*, 2015. The CBO maintains a useful portal of presidential budgets on their website at Congressional Budget Office, *President's Budget* . The NIH's budget is available on its website at National Institutes of Health, *Budget*, 2017.

Saturno, Heniff, & Lynch, *The Congressional Appropriations Process: An Overview*, 2016 is a complete overview of the appropriations process. For more on the 2017 omnibus, see McCrimmon, *Omnibus Agreement Details $1 Trillion in FY 2017 Spending*, May and Hess & Reilly, *2 contentious air provisions hitch ride on omnibus*, 2017.

In an attempt to promote clarity at a slight cost in consistency, I used an amalgam of sources for the final spending figures by type. These included: InsideGov, *2016 United States Budget*, 2016; Congressional Budget Office, *The Federal Budget in 2016*, 2016; Havelund, *Expenditures in the United States Federal Budget*, 2012; Center on Budget and Policy Priorities, *Policy Basics: Where Do Our Federal Tax Dollars Go?*, 2016; Chantrill, *FY18 Federal Budget Spending Actuals*, 2017; and Office of Management and Budget, *Historical Tables* . As mentioned in the text, different methods between these sources cause difficulty in achieving a single, comprehensive, precise overview of federal spending. The calculations, simplifications, clarifications, and errors made are my own.

For one of the many pieces as to the relative compensation of public against private-sector employees, see Volokh, *Are public-sector employees "overpaid"?*, 2014.

For one comparison of infrastructure spending against where it should be, see VanderMay & Rapp, *Here's How Bad U.S. Infrastructure Has Become*, 2017. This is a huge long-term problem. Information on the gasoline tax is from Pomerleau, *How High are Other Nations' Gas Taxes?*, 2015, with data from the OECD.

For more on the Antideficiency Act and its enforcement, see U.S. Government Accountability Office, *Antideficiency Act*, n.d.. You can also find examples there of how the Act is enforced.

GAME THEORY AND THE NUCLEAR AGE, PART I

Originally published as "Volume 14: Game Theory and the Nuclear Age, Part I" on May 23, 2017.

The examples of historical usage of game theory in conflict are from Ross, *Game Theory*, 2014.

You can find game theory's foundational text at von Neumann & Morgenstern, *Theory of Games and Economic Behavior: 60th Anniversary Commemorative Edition*, 2007.

GERRYMANDERING

Originally published as "Volume 15: Gerrymandering" on June 8, 2017.

To go further into the life of Elbridge Gerry, I recommend his official Senate bio, Hatfield, *Vice Presidents of the United States, 1789-1993*, 1997, pp. 63-68.

The Supreme Court cases described, obviously, can be researched via many different avenues; I used several sources for background research, including private notes. If you are interested in looking into these cases, I recommend the following starting points:

- Baker v. Carr: C-SPAN Specials, *Supreme Court Landmark Case Baker v. Carr*, 2015
- Reynolds v. Sims: McBride, *Reynolds v. Sims (1964)*, n.d.
- Davis v. Bandemer: Brennan Center for Justice, *Earlier Partisan*

Gerrymandering Cases, 2016
- Shaw v. Reno, and the other travails of the North Carolina 12th: Cohen & Gilkeson, *North Carolina Redistricting Cases: the 1990s*, 2003
- Vieth v. Jubelirer: Legal Information Institute, *VIETH V. JUBELIRER (02-1580) 541 U.S. 267 (2004)*, n.d.

As discussed, gerrymandering is an area where we can expect significant developments, legislative and judicial, soon. I based current descriptions of ongoing events on the following sources:

- Ohio's ballot initiative: Associated Press, *Congressional Redistricting in Ohio Takes Another Step Ahead*, 2017
- North Carolina's power grab: Stern, *Court Blocks Most of North Carolina GOP's Legislative Coup, Including Election-Board Power Grab*, 2017 and Graham, *North Carolina's 'Legislative Coup' Is Over, and Republicans Won*, 2016
- Gill v. Whitford: Brennan Center for Justice, *Gill v. Whitford*, 2017

For a summary of redistricting procedures by state (including Ohio and North Carolina), see Ballotpedia, *State-by-state redistricting procedures*, n.d.. This portal leads to significant detail for each federal and state methodology. Loyola Law School also has an important and useful resource, Levitt J. , *All About Redistricting*, 2017.

For more on the GOP's REDMAP project, see Daley, *The House the GOP Built: How Republicans Used Soft Money, Big Data, and High-Tech Mapping to Take Control of Congress and Increase Partisanship*, 2016.

The question of the mathematical importance of redistricting—who gains seats, where, and why—is a subject of significant debate. For the statistics on Ohio's Congressional Election of 2012, see Wikipedia, *United States House of Representatives elections in Ohio, 2012*, n.d., which recompiles data from the Ohio Secretary of State, Husted, *2012 Elections Results*, n.d.. Other studies I reviewed include New York Times, *Imbalance of Power*, 2013, Vaughn, Bangia, Bridget Dou, & Mattingly, *Quantifying Gerrymandering @Duke University* , Gersh & Staff, *Gerrymandering Increasingly Defies the Will of Voters*, 2016, and Chen & Cottrell, *Evaluating partisan gains from Congressional gerrymandering: Using computer simulations to estimate the effect of gerry-*

mandering in the U.S. House, 2016. There are many others, but the mode of the studies is around a 25-seat gain for Republicans in the 2012 House elections.

GAME THEORY AND THE NUCLEAR AGE, PART II

Originally published as "Volume 16: Game Theory and the Nuclear Age, Part II" on June 29, 2017.

Casualty figures from Bomber Command and the Eighth Air Force are quoted from Roberts, *High courage on the axe edge of war,* 2017, which quotes from Bishop, *Bomber Boys: Fighting Back 1940-1945,* 2008 and Miller D. , *The Eighth Air Force: The American Bomber Crews in Britain,* 2007. There is also an online resource with very detailed (but not yet complete) by-raid data for the Eighth Air Force at Philo, *Eighth Air Force Combat Losses,* 1976-2017.

Most of the data on nuclear arsenal sizes and details comes from Ploughshares Fund. If you want to learn more, see Ploughshares Fund, *World Nuclear Weapon Stockpile,* 2016.

ONE MORE VOLUME
HEALTH INSURANCE, PART V

The data in Figure 41 comes from National Academies of Sciences, Engineering and Medicine, *The Growing Gap in Life Expectancy by Income: Implications for Federal Programs and Policy Responses,* 2015, via analyses from Sheiner, *Implications of the growing gap in life expectancy by income,* 2015 and Ehrenfreund, *The stunning — and expanding — gap in life expectancy between the rich and the poor,* 2015.

A great, but long, overview of various national health care systems is available from the Commonwealth Fund at Mossialos & Martin Wenzl, *2015 International Profiles of Health Care Systems,* 2016. Life expectancy is from the World Health Organization at World Health Organization, *Life expectancy data by country,* 2016; infant mortality from the CIA World Factbook, Central Intelligence Agency, *Country Comparison: Infant Mortality Rate,* n.d.; adult mortality from the World Bank, World Bank, *Mortality rate, adult, male (per 1,000 male adults)*, n.d.; health spending from Organization for Economic Co-Operation and Development, *Health expenditure and financing*, 2017 and as percentage of GDP from World Bank, *Health expenditure, total (% of GDP)*, n.d..

U.K. doctor salaries can be found at NHS Employers, *Pay and Conditions Circular (M&D) 1/2017*, 2017. To learn more about the qualitative experience of using the NHS, see Edwards, *What the NHS 'A&E crisis' looks like in comparison to America's private healthcare*, 2015. For a qualitative study of the topic generally, which unfortunately does not include the United States, see Nina Viberg, *International comparisons of waiting times in health care – Limitations and prospects*, 2013.

Japanese doctor visit per capita data comes from Organization for Economic Co-Operation and Development, *Health at a Glance, 2015; Health care activities, Consultations with doctors*, 2015.

The data on Canadians coming to the U.S. for treatments is imperfect. The most rigorous survey, which is unfortunately based on data twenty years old, is available at Katz, Cardiff, Pascali, Barer, & Evans, *Phantoms In The Snow: Canadians' Use Of Health Care Services In The United States*, May 2002. It found that out of 18,000 Canadians surveyed, only 20, or 0.1%, travelled to the United States specifically to receive medical care. A more recent analysis by the conservative Fraser Institute found that 0.15% of Canadians travelled abroad in 2015 at Barua & Ren, *Leaving Canada for Medical Care, 2015*, March 2015. I don't like their methodology: at a glance, they assume that Canadians travel abroad as frequently for routine procedures as they do for specialists. This is akin to saying that you are as likely to go the Mayo Clinic for your next physical as you are for a complex cancer treatment. In any case, taking their numbers at face value, a maximum of 1 out of every 600 Canadians travels abroad for care in each year, and not all of these go to the United States.

Evidence of a Canadian doctor surplus is Blackwell, *Untrained and unemployed: Medical schools churning out doctors who can't find residencies and full-time positions*, 2015; I don't put stock in this idea, but I find even the fact that it is out there to be relevant.

Determining the exact additional amount the United States pays for prescription drugs is difficult. Pharmacy benefit managers, the largest buyers of pharmaceuticals, negotiate discounts from list prices and these are not public. One article that provides a good estimate of the difference, including these discounts, is available at Langreth, Migliozzi, & Gokhale, *The U.S. Pays a Lot More for Top Drugs Than Other Countries*, 2015. On the difference in prescription drug cost between Medicare and the VA, see Families USA, *No Bargain: Medicare Drug Plans Deliver High Prices*, 2007.

Data on medical loss ratios and insurance company margin from Levitt & Cox, *Individual Insurance Market Performance in Early 2017*, 2017.

For Charles Gaba's analogue to my short-term fix list, see Gaba, *UPDATED: If I Ran The Zoo: 20 repairs/improvements for Obamacare 2.0*, 2017. He specifically includes a longer description of the glitches in the current ACA subsidy eligibility system. For a full picture of exchange participation, see Kaiser Family Foundation, *Number of Issuers Participating in the Individual Health Insurance Marketplaces*, 2014-2017.

I don't think much of the argument against the public option, but if you really want to see it, an example is available at Cannon, *Fannie Med? Why a "Public Option" Is Hazardous to Your Health*, 2009. I responded to this argument at length, again at Cohen N. , *In Which I Pick a Fight with the Cato Institute*, 2017.

There are a lot of resources for researching and calculating subsidies. Kaiser Family Foundation, *Explaining Health Care Reform: Questions About Health Insurance Subsidies*, 2006 is a good overview, and the kff.org website has a number of fun tools.

There is a lot of polling on individual components of the Affordable Care Act. For a representative example, see Bialik & Geiger, *Republicans, Democrats find common ground on many provisions of health care law*, 2016.

The cost estimates for changes to the health system are my own, based on the sources included in this section. I'm not aware of any official scoring of these exact provisions, other than the refusal to pay for the CSR subsidies.

Morbidity due to lack of insurance is from Millhiser, *Here's how many people could die every year if Obamacare is repealed*, 2016 and Himmelstein & Woolhandler, *Repealing the Affordable Care Act will kill more than 43,000 people annually*, 2017, which relies on data from Sommers, Baicker, & Epstein, *Mortality and Access to Care among Adults after State Medicaid Expansions*, 2012.

For information on the $716 billion in Medicare savings, see Kliff, *Romney's right: Obamacare cuts Medicare by $716 billion. Here's how*, 2012. The National Health Expenditure Survey data used in Figure 42 are available for download from Centers for Medicare and Medicaid Services, *National Health Expenditure Data*, 2014. A longer description of the two benchmarks for Medicare/Medicaid administrative costs can be found at McCanne, *Important: What are Medicare's true administrative costs?*, 2013. Medicaid's administrative costs are from Office of the Actuary, Centers for Medicare and Medicaid Services, *2015 Actuarial Report on the Financial Outlook for Medicaid*, 2015; Medicare's are available at Boards of Trustees, Federal Hospital Insurance and Federal Supplementary Medical Insurance Trust Funds, *2017 Annual Report of the Boards of Trustees*, 2017.

For Paul Ryan and "skin in the game," see Newell, *Paul Ryan, About Seven Years Too Late, Explains Why Full Repeal Would Be a Disaster*, 2017.

Health care usage per capita is from Organization for Economic Co-Operation and Development, *Health at a Glance, 2015; Health care activities, Consultations with doctors*, 2015.

FURTHER READING

There are a lot of different ways to use sources. You can directly quote them. Or you can use somebody else's work to help develop a theme, or as a jumping off point for your discussion. Or contextualize the analyses created by others. Or you can use a source's raw data, run your own analysis, and present that.

Then there are the sources from which you received your background knowledge. Maybe you didn't quote it, refer to it, use it as a foundation, or borrow their data. But there is also little doubt that the source's narrative and logic permeated your thinking. Your piece couldn't have been written without it.

This is especially true for me. What I write is prompted by something I've read. Some pieces are specific responses to books I've recently finished. Other times the process is more general. I always find myself wishing I could express a point as well as my predecessor did.

In any case, I wanted to list sources like these that were of general use, but not specifically cited. As they are mostly books, a suggested reading list seemed apropos. This way, if you want to know more about a subject, you have a handy list of recommendations.

HEALTH INSURANCE, PART I

The Emperor of All Maladies is a stunning look at the early history of cancer. Today, we know about the medical options available to cancer sufferers: surgery, chemotherapy, radiation, and pharmaceuticals. It was not so long ago that only the first of these had been discovered.

ORBITAL MECHANICS AND THE MARTIAN

Well, I mean you should still read *The Martian*, even if I have some issues with its spacecraft design assumptions.

FOUR MONTHS IN 1933

The Rise and Fall of the Third Reich is one of the most important books of history, on any topic. It is infinitely readable; William Shirer was a journalist first, and this clean style comes through in his masterwork. Despite its significant girth, it is worth the effort. You should also read Shirer's *Berlin Diaries*.

Lords of Finance is one of those books that look at history in a new light. Before picking it up, I'd never considered the perspective of the major central bankers. Ahamed tells many good tales, Weimer inflation chief among them. I do recommend a base knowledge of economics or monetary policy before picking it up.

THE RULE OF BAYES

Bill Bryson's *At Home* was my inspiration to begin my story of Bayesian probability with the story of Bayesian England. Bryson's book tells you about everything you'll find in, well, your home. The author himself lived in an old countryside English parsonage, which caused him to do as I have, spending an equally inappropriate portion of his work discussing the fascinating people who inhabited such abodes 200 years ago.

My favorite telling of the life of Bayes, as well as the history of his rule as it repeatedly fell into disfavor and was rediscovered, is *The Theory That Would Not Die: How Bayes' Rule Cracked the Enigma Code, Hunted Down Russian Submarines, and Emerged Triumphant from Two Centuries of Controversy*, by Sharon McGrayne. In addition to discussing the Theorem and its applications, McGrayne provides a fascinating, in-depth story of its history. She also discusses how the Theorem owes as much to both Richard Price and Pierre-Simon Laplace as to Bayes himself. Price discovered Bayes' notes, without which we would never have heard his name. Little known today, Price also made important contributions toward American independence. When he received an honorary doctorate from Yale in 1781, the other recipient was George Washington. Laplace, who is sometimes called France's Isaac Newton, doesn't lack historical recognition. However, while better known for his work in astronomy and his eponymous transform, no portion of Laplace's work resonates more than his extension of Bayesian principles. To say that Laplace's 1812 *Théorie analytique des probabilités* launched serious study of both probability and statistics as mathematical disciplines is only a slight exaggeration.

There are many good books that talk about the relationship between math and gambling. I enjoyed *Fortune's Formula: The Untold Story of the Scientific Betting System That Beat the Casinos and Wall Street*, which is about the Kelly Criterion, an implementation of Bayesian logic. Edward Thorp applied these same ideas to both betting and financial markets. His classic, *Beat the Dealer: A Winning Strategy for the Game of Twenty-One*, as well as his recent autobiography, *A Man for All Markets: From Las Vegas to Wall Street, How I Beat the Dealer and the Market*, will let you into his fascinating mind.

Of course, the godfather of all these topics is Claude Shannon, founder of the Information Age. Shannon's *The Mathematical Theory of Communication* is approachable even if you have no mathematical background past high school algebra. There is also a new biography about Shannon, *A Mind at Play, How Claude Shannon Invented the Information Age*, by Jimmy Soni and Rob Goodman, which I highly recommend.

FISCAL POLICY, PART I
TAXES

For more on fairness, within tax policy and without, the John Rawls classic, *A Theory of Justice* is a must read. If you enjoyed this piece, but wish it was many times longer and included more charts and graphs, see *Taxing Ourselves*, by Joel Slemrod and Jon Bakija, whose fifth edition is hot off the press.

CONGRESS

The minutiae of Congress, the small deals made and missed, the parliamentary procedures used and opposed, and the personalities of the people sitting in each chair could—and does—take up a library. If you are ready to take a first step into the topic, my recommendation is Robert Caro's *The Years of Lyndon Johnson: Master of the Senate*.

THE POINCARÉ CONJECTURE

For more on Poincaré, his problem, and its solution, I recommend *Poincaré's Prize: The Hundred-Year Quest to Solve on of Math's Greatest Puzzles*. It requires no more mathematical knowledge than reading this book. If you want to know more about the universe, how it started, and how it might end, I recommend *A Universe from Nothing*, by Lawrence M. Krauss.

GAME THEORY AND THE NUCLEAR AGE, PART I

I thought of this topic due to having read Richard Rhodes' *The Making of the Atomic Bomb*, which details the period from Rutherford to Trinity. You would never think that a fifty-year search for invisible atomic particles could be gripping, but it is. The Vemork raid was mentioned only briefly, but if a story of Norwegians spies dashing around on skis and possibly saving the world in the process, *The Winter Fortress: The Epic Mission to Sabotage Hitler's Atomic Bomb*, by Neal Bascomb, is for you.

GERRYMANDERING

The last half century of voting rights is defined by the Voting Rights Act of 1965, which is itself defined by Lyndon Johnson, without whom it would never have happened. To understand what voting was like before the VRA, go back to Robert Caro and read *The Years of Lyndon Johnson: Passage of Power*.

GAME THEORY AND THE NUCLEAR AGE, PART II

Mutually assured destruction didn't begin with the Bomb; its concepts existed earlier, forming a critical (and disastrous) portion of England's strategy in the lead up to World War II. To see it from the perspective of Winston Churchill, read *The Last Lion, Winston Spencer Churchill: Alone, 1932-1940*. For more about the results of the bombing, its strategic effects, and its cost, see *The Bombing War, Europe 1939-1945*.

BIBLIOGRAPHY

Ahamed, L. (2009). Lords of Finance: The Bankers Who Broke the World. New York: Penguin Press.

Allison, J. (n.d.). Proof of Bayes Theorem. University of Pennsylvania, http://www.hep.upenn.edu/~johnda/papers.html.

American Academy of Orthopaedic Surgeons. (2014, March 14). 2.5 Million Americans Living with an Artificial Hip, 4.7 Million with an Artificial Knee. Retrieved from AAOS.org: http://newsroom.aaos.org/media-resources/Press-releases/25-million-americans-living-with-an-artificial-hip-47-million-with-an-artificial-knee.htm

American Presidency Project. (1999-2017). Political Party Platforms. Retrieved from The American Presidency Project: http://www.presidency.ucsb.edu/ws/?pid=29599

Anrig, G. (2004, December 14). Twelve Reasons Why Privatizing Social Security is a Bad Idea. Retrieved from The Century Foundation: https://tcf.org/content/commentary/twelve-reasons-why-privatizing-social-security-is-a-bad-idea/

Associated Press. (2017, May 30). Congressional Redistricting in Ohio Takes Another Step Ahead. Retrieved from US News: https://www.usnews.com/news/best-states/ohio/articles/2017-05-30/congressional-redistricting-in-ohio-takes-another-step-ahead

Avi-Yonah, R., Batchelder, L., Fleming, J. C., Gamage, D., Glogower, A., Hemel, D. J., . . . Viswanathan, M. (2017). The Games They Will Play: An Update on the Conference Committee Tax Bill. SSRN.

Ballotpedia. (n.d.). State-by-state redistricting procedures. Retrieved from ballotpedia.org: https://ballotpedia.org/State-by-state_redistricting_procedures

Banerjee, D. (2016, December 22). The ACA Individual Market: 2016 Will Be Better than 2015, But Achieving Target Profitability Will Take Longer. Retrieved from Morning Consult:

https://morningconsult.com/wp-content/uploads/2016/12/12-22-16-The-ACA-Individual-Market-2016-Will-Be-Better-Than-2015-But-Achieving-Target-Profitability-Will-Take-Longer.pdf

Barua, B., & Ren, F. (March 2015). Leaving Canada for Medical Care, 2015. Fraser Research Bulletin, 1-7.

BBC. (2017). Germany 1918-1939. Retrieved from GSCE - History - Modern World History: http://www.bbc.co.uk/education/topics/zcqs6fr

Bialik, K., & Geiger, A. (2016, December 8). Republicans, Democrats find common ground on many provisions of health care law. Retrieved from Pew Research Center: http://www.pewresearch.org/fact-tank/2016/12/08/partisans-on-affordable-care-act-provisions/

Bishop, P. (2008). Bomber Boys: Fighting Back 1940-1945. London: HarperCollins Publishers.

Blackwell, T. (2015, June 14). Untrained and unemployed: Medical schools churning out doctors who can't find residencies and full-time positions. Retrieved from National Post: http://nationalpost.com/health/untrained-and-unemployed-medical-schools-churning-out-doctors-who-cant-find-residencies-and-full-time-positions

Blumberg, L. J., Buettgens, M., & Holahan, J. (2016, December 6). Implications of Partial Repeal of the ACA through Reconciliation. Retrieved from Urban Institute: http://www.urban.org/research/publication/implications-partial-repeal-aca-through-reconciliation

Boards of Trustees, Federal Hospital Insurance and Federal Supplementary Medical Insurance Trust Funds. (2017, July 13). 2017 Annual Report of the Boards of Trustees. Retrieved from CMS.gov: https://www.cms.gov/Research-Statistics-Data-and-Systems/Statistics-Trends-and-Reports/ReportsTrustFunds/downloads/tr2017.pdf

Brennan Center for Justice. (2016, June 13). Earlier Partisan Gerrymandering Cases. Retrieved from Brennan Center for Justice: https://www.brennancenter.org/analysis/major-partisan-gerrymandering-cases

Brennan Center for Justice. (2017, September 6). Gill v. Whitford. Retrieved from Brennan Center for Justice: https://www.brennancenter.org/legal-work/whitford-v-gill

Bryson, B. (2010). At Home: A short history of private life. Toronto: Doubleday Canada.

Bureau of Labor Statistics. (n.d.). Databases, Tables & Calculators by Subject. Retrieved from BLS.gov: https://data.bls.gov/timeseries/LNS14000000

Butler, S. (1989, October 1). Assuring Affordable Health Care for All Americans. Retrieved from The Heritage Foundation: http://www.heritage.org/social-security/report/assuring-affordable-health-care-all-americans

Caltech. (2010, February 25). Boomerang. Retrieved from astro.caltech.edu: http://www.astro.caltech.edu/~lgg/boomerang/boomerang_front.htm

Cancryn, A. (2015, November 11). The short life and inevitable decline of the ACA's CO-OP program. Retrieved from SNL Financial: https://www.snl.com/InteractiveX/Article.aspx?cdid=A-34293461-12590

Cannon, M. F. (2009, August 6). Fannie Med? Why a "Public Option" Is Hazardous to Your Health. Retrieved from Cato.org - Policy Analysis: https://object.cato.org/sites/cato.org/files/pubs/pdf/pa642.pdf

Carey, M. A. (2012, August 17). FAQ: Decoding The $716 Billion In Medicare Reductions. Retrieved from KFF.org: http://khn.org/news/faq-716-billion-medicare-reductions/

Caro, R. A. (2002). Master of the Senate. New York: Alfred A. Knopf.

Carrion, U. (2017, June 29). I made a delta-v subway map of the Solar System. Retrieved from Reddit: https://www.reddit.com/r/space/comments/29cxi6/i_made_a_deltav_subway_map_of_the_solar_system/

Catlin, A. C., & Cowen, C. A. (2015, November 19). History of Health Spending in the United States, 1960 - 2013. Retrieved from CMS.gov: https://www.cms.gov/Research-Statistics-Data-and-Systems/Statistics-Trends-and-Reports/NationalHealthExpendData/Downloads/HistoricalNHEPaper.pdf

Center on Budget and Policy Priorities. (2016, March 4). Policy Basics: Where Do Our Federal Tax Dollars Go? Retrieved from Center on Budget and Policy Priorities: https://www.cbpp.org/research/federal-budget/policy-basics-where-do-our-federal-tax-dollars-go

Center on Budget and Policy Priorities. (2016, October 25). Social Security Keeps 22 Million Americans Out of Poverty: A State-By-State Analysis. Retrieved from Center on Budget and Policy Priorities: http://www.cbpp.org/research/social-security/social-security-keeps-22-million-americans-out-of-poverty-a-state-by-state

Centers for Medicare and Medicaid Services. (2014). 2014 CMS Statistics. Retrieved from CMS.gov: https://www.cms.gov/Research-Statistics-Data-and-Systems/Statistics-Trends-and-Reports/CMS-Statistics-Reference-Booklet/Downloads/CMS_Stats_2014_final.pdf

Centers for Medicare and Medicaid Services. (2014). National Health Expenditure Data. Retrieved from CMS.gov: https://www.cms.gov/Research-Statistics-Data-and-Systems/Statistics-Trends-and-Reports/NationalHealthExpendData/Downloads/NHE2015.zip

Central Intelligence Agency. (n.d.). Country Comparison: Infant Mortality Rate. Retrieved from CIA.gov: https://www.cia.gov/library/publications/the-world-factbook/rankorder/2091rank.html

Cesca, B. (2013, November 6). Another Obamacare 'Horror Story' Debunked; and, No, the President Didn't Lie About the Law. Retrieved from HuffPost: http://www.huffingtonpost.com/bob-cesca/another-obamacare-horror-_b_4229439.html

Chantrill, C. (2017, August 21). FY18 Federal Budget Spending Actuals. Retrieved from usgovernmentspending.com: http://www.usfederalbudget.us/federal_budget_detail_2016bs22016n_0040_652#usgs302

Chantrill, C. (2017, August 7). Government Revenue Details. Retrieved from usgovernmentrevenue.com: http://www.usgovernmentrevenue.com/year_revenue_2016USbn_18bs1n_101112303340466063F0F1E0#usgs302

Chen, J., & Cottrell, D. (2016). Evaluating partisan gains from Congressional gerrymandering: Using computer simulations to estimate the effect of gerrymandering in the U.S. House. Electoral Studies, pp. 329-340.

Claxton, G., Cox, C., Damico, A., Levitt, L., & Pollitz, K. (2016, December 12). Pre-existing Conditions and Medical Underwriting in the Individual Insurance Market Prior to the ACA. Retrieved from KFF.org: http://www.kff.org/health-reform/issue-brief/pre-existing-conditions-and-medical-underwriting-in-the-individual-insurance-market-prior-to-the-aca/

Clay Mathematics Institute. (n.d.). Perelman's Solution. Retrieved from CMI: http://www.claymath.org/millennium-problems-poincar%C3%A9-conjecture/perelmans-solution

Cohen, G., & Gilkeson, B. (2003, July 8). North Carolina Redistricting Cases: the 1990s. Retrieved from senate.mn: https://www.senate.mn/departments/scr/REDIST/Redsum/ncsum.htm

Cohen, N. (2017, June 16). In Which I Pick a Fight with the Cato Institute. Retrieved from LobbySeven Commentary: http://www.lobbyseven.com/single-post/2017/06/16/In-Which-I-Pick-a-Fight-with-the-Cato-Institute

Cohen, N. (n.d.). Martian - MAV Calcs (Google Sheets). Retrieved from docs.google.com: https://docs.google.com/spreadsheets/d/1gu8vH1vD36UYrs85Ws_yzc8zfiQGUoOJmH3UK1BkTXQ

Cohen, R. A., Martinez, M. E., & Zammitti, E. P. (2016). Health Insurance Coverage: Early Release of Estimates From the National Health Interview Study, January-March 2016. National Center for Health Statistics, https://www.cdc.gov/nchs/data/nhis/earlyrelease/insur201609.pdf.

Commonwealth of Massachusetts. (n.d.). The Top Ten Facts about Massachusetts Health Care Reform. Retrieved from mass.gov: http://www.mass.gov/eohhs/docs/eohhs/healthcare-reform/top-10-facts.pdf

Congressional Budget Office. (2012, July 24). Estimates for the Insurance Coverage Provisions of the Affordable Care Act Updated for Recent Supreme Court Decision. Retrieved from CBO.gov: http://www.cbo.gov/sites/default/files/cbofiles/attachments/43472-07-24-2012-CoverageEstimates.pdf

Congressional Budget Office. (2012). Letter to John Boehner re: H.R. 6079. Washington: Congressional Budget Office.

Congressional Budget Office. (2015, January). Updated Estimates of the Insurance Coverage Provisions of the Affordable Care Act. Retrieved from CBO.gov: https://www.cbo.gov/sites/default/files/114th-congress-2015-2016/reports/49892/49892-breakout-AppendixB.pdf

Congressional Budget Office. (2016, March). Federal Subsidies for Health Insurance Coverage for People Under Age 65: 2016-2026.

Retrieved from CBO.gov: https://www.cbo.gov/sites/default/
files/114th-congress-2015-2016/reports/51385-
healthinsurancebaselineonecol.pdf

Congressional Budget Office. (2016). The Federal Budget in 2016.
Retrieved from CBO.gov: https://www.cbo.gov/sites/default/
files/cbofiles/images/pubs-images/52xxx/52408-Land-
Budget_Overall.png

Congressional Budget Office. (2017, March 13). American Health
Care Act. Retrieved from CBO.gov: https://www.cbo.gov/
publication/52486

Congressional Budget Office. (2017, May 24). H.R. 1628, American
Health Care Act of 2017. Retrieved from CBO.gov:
https://www.cbo.gov/publication/52752

Congressional Budget Office. (2017, June 26). H.R. 1628, Better
Care Reconciliation Act of 2017. Retrieved from CBO.gov:
https://www.cbo.gov/publication/52849

Congressional Budget Office. (2017, July 19). H.R. 1628,
Obamacare Repeal Reconciliation Act of 2017. Retrieved from
CBO.gov: https://www.cbo.gov/publication/52939

Congressional Budget Office. (n.d.). President's Budget. Retrieved
from CBO.gov: https://www.cbo.gov/topics/budget/presidents-
budget

Congressional Budget Office. (n.d.). Taxes. Retrieved from
CBO.gov: https://www.cbo.gov/topics/taxes

Cooper, M. (2012, February 14). Conservatives Sowed Idea of
Health Care Mandate, Only to Spurn It Later. The New York
Times.

Crainic, M. (2011). Inleiding Topologie 2011. Retrieved from
staff.science.uu.nl: http://www.staff.science.uu.nl/~crain101/
topologie11/lecture-notes.pdf

C-SPAN Specials. (2015, December 7). Supreme Court Landmark
Case Baker v. Carr. Washington, District of Columbia, USA.

Daley, D. (2016, April 24). The House the GOP Built: How
Republicans Used Soft Money, Big Data, and High-Tech
Mapping to Take Control of Congress and Increase Partisanship.
Retrieved from NYMag.com: http://nymag.com/daily/
intelligencer/2016/04/gops-house-seats-are-safe-heres-why.html

Davis, C., & Greene, M. (2017). Presidential Appointee Positions Requiring Senate Confirmation and Committees Handling Nominations. Washington: Congressional Research Service.

Debot, B., Huang, C.-C., & Marr, C. (2017, January 12). ACA Repeal Would Lavish Medicare Tax Cuts on 400 Highest-Income Households. Retrieved from Center on Budget and Policy Priorities: https://www.cbpp.org/research/federal-tax/aca-repeal-would-lavish-medicare-tax-cuts-on-400-highest-income-households

Economic Policy Institute. (2014, September 26). Per capita Social Security expenditures and the elderly poverty rate, 1959–2015. Retrieved from Economic Policy Institute: http://www.stateofworkingamerica.org/chart/swa-poverty-figure-7r-capita-social-security/

Edwards, J. (2015, November 12). What the NHS 'A&E crisis' looks like in comparison to America's private healthcare. Retrieved from Business Insider: http://www.businessinsider.com/comparison-uk-nhs-v-us-private-heathcare-2015-1

Ehrenfreund, M. (2015, September 18). The stunning — and expanding — gap in life expectancy between the rich and the poor. Retrieved from The Washington Post: https://www.washingtonpost.com/news/wonk/wp/2015/09/18/the-government-is-spending-more-to-help-rich-seniors-than-poor-ones

Families USA. (2007). No Bargain: Medicare Drug Plans Deliver High Prices. Families USA.

Federal Reserve Bank of St. Louis. (n.d.). Federal Government Data. Retrieved from FRED: https://fred.stlouisfed.org/categories/5

Feldstein, M. (1997, January 31). Cato Institute Social Security Choice Paper No. 7. Retrieved from Cato Project on Social Security Choice: https://object.cato.org/sites/cato.org/files/pubs/pdf/ssp7.pdf

Fichtner, J. (2016, November 7). Opinion: The retirement age for Social Security needs to rise to 70. Retrieved from MarketWatch: http://www.marketwatch.com/story/the-retirement-age-for-social-security-needs-to-rise-to-70-2016-11-02

Fiedler, M., & Adler, L. (2017, March 16). How will the House GOP health care bill affect individual market premiums? Retrieved from Brookings: https://www.brookings.edu/blog/

up-front/2017/03/16/how-will-the-house-gop-health-care-bill-affect-individual-market-premiums/

Fiesta, R. (2016, October 19). Social Security, Medicare and the 3rd Presidential Debate. Retrieved from AFL-CIO: https://aflcio.org/2016/10/19/social-security-medicare-and-3rd-presidential-debate

Flowers, A. (2015, January 20). The Top 1 Percent Earns A Lot From Cashing In On Investments. Retrieved from FiveThirtyEight: https://fivethirtyeight.com/datalab/the-top-1-percent-earns-a-lot-from-cashing-in-on-investments/

Fox, L. (2015, February 2). Here Are Seven Things in Obama's Budget That Are Never Going to Happen. Retrieved from The Atlantic: https://www.theatlantic.com/politics/archive/2015/02/here-are-seven-things-in-obamas-budget-that-are-never-going-to-happen/445716/

FY 2006 Federal Register. (2004). Federal Financial Participation in State Assistance Expenditures. Washington: Federal Register.

Gaba, C. (2015, November 11). Risk Corridor Massacre: The Autopsy. Retrieved from ACASignups.net: http://acasignups.net/15/11/11/risk-corridor-massacre-autopsy

Gaba, C. (2016, March). ACASignups.net estimates of total U.S. healthcare coverage as of March 2016. Retrieved from ACASignups.net: http://acasignups.net/sites/default/files/2016_total_coverage_pie_chart.jpg

Gaba, C. (2016, March 28). SHOW YOUR WORK: Healthcare Coverage Breakout for the Entire U.S. Population in 1 Chart. Retrieved from ACAsignups.net: http://acasignups.net/16/04/18/show-your-work-healthcare-coverage-breakout-entire-us-population-1-chart

Gaba, C. (2017). ACA EXCHANGE Qualified Health Policy (QHP) Enrollments:. Retrieved from ACASignups.net: http://acasignups.net/graphs

Gaba, C. (2017, July 18). UPDATED: If I Ran The Zoo: 20 repairs/improvements for Obamacare 2.0. Retrieved from ACASignups.net: http://acasignups.net/17/07/25/updated-if-i-ran-zoo-20-repairsimprovements-obamacare-20

Garfield, R., & Damico, A. (2016, October 19). The Coverage Gap: Uninsured Poor Adults in States that Do Not Expand Medicaid. Retrieved from KFF.org: http://www.kff.org/uninsured/issue-brief/the-coverage-gap-uninsured-poor-adults-in-states-that-do-not-expand-medicaid/

Gersh, M., & Staff, N. (2016, November 30). Gerrymandering Increasingly Defies the Will of Voters. Retrieved from NCEC.org: http://ncec.org/articles/20161130-gerrymandering-widens-gap

Golshan, T., Scott, D., & Stein, J. (2017, June 16). We asked 8 Senate Republicans to explain what their health bill is trying to do. Retrieved from Vox: https://www.vox.com/policy-and-politics/2017/6/16/15810524/senate-ahca-explain-please

GOP.com. (n.d.). Republican Platform. Retrieved from www.gop.com: https://www.gop.com/platform/renewing-american-values/

Gould, E. (2012, December 5). Health Insurance Coverage Continues to Decline in a New Decade. EPI Briefing Paper, p. #353.

Graham, D. A. (2016, December 16). North Carolina's 'Legislative Coup' Is Over, and Republicans Won. Retrieved from The Atlantic: https://www.theatlantic.com/politics/archive/2016/12/north-carolinas-republicans-succeed-in-power-grab/510950/

Gross, L. (n.d.). Drug testing Example for Conditional Probability and Bayes Theorem. Retrieved from University of Tennessee: http://www.tiem.utk.edu/~gross/math151fall07/drug.test.pdf

Haden, J. (2014, October 7). How Much Do the Top 10 Percent Drink? More Than You Ever Imagined. Retrieved from INC.com: https://www.inc.com/jeff-haden/the-top-10-percent-drink-way-more-than-you-think.html

Hall, J. P. (2014). Why a National High-Risk Insurance Pool Is Not a Workable Alternative to the Marketplace. The Commonwealth Fund.

Hatfield, M. O. (1997). Vice Presidents of the United States, 1789-1993. Washington, D.C.: U.S. Government Printing Office.

Havelund, L. (2012). Expenditures in the United States Federal Budget. Retrieved from wikipedia.org: https://en.wikipedia.org/wiki/Expenditures_in_the_United_States_federal_budget#/media/File:Discretionary_Spending_FY2013.svg

HealthPocket. (2016, December 20). Silver Plan. Retrieved from HealthPocket: https://www.healthpocket.com/individual-health-insurance/silver-health-plans

Hess, H., & Reilly, S. (2017, May 1). 2 contentious air provisions hitch ride on omnibus. Retrieved from E&E News: https://www.eenews.net/stories/1060053850

Himmelstein, D., & Woolhandler, S. (2017, January 23). Repealing the Affordable Care Act will kill more than 43,000 people annually. Retrieved from The Washington Post: https://www.washingtonpost.com/posteverything/wp/2017/01/23/repealing-the-affordable-care-act-will-kill-more-than-43000-people-annually/

Husted, J. (n.d.). 2012 Elections Results. Retrieved from sos.state.oh.us: https://www.sos.state.oh.us/elections/election-results-and-data/2012-elections-results/

Illinois Health Agents. (2012). BlueCross BlueShield of Illinois—Pre-Existing Condition Exclusions. Retrieved from Illinois Health Agents: http://www.ilhealthagents.com/bluecross-blueshield-illinois/pre-existing-condition-exclusions/

InsideGov. (2016). 2016 United States Budget. Retrieved from InsideGov: http://federal-budget.insidegov.com/l/119/2016

Jacobson, L. (2011, May 30). Barbara Boxer says Medicare overhead is far lower than private insurers' overhead. Retrieved from Politifact.com: http://www.politifact.com/truth-o-meter/statements/2011/may/30/barbara-boxer/barbara-boxer-says-medicare-overhead-far-lower-pri/

John, A. (2014, January 6). Lessons from the Obamacare 'Horror Stories'. Retrieved from The Atlantic: https://www.theatlantic.com/politics/archive/2014/01/lessons-obamacare-horror-stories/356728/

Johnson, C. Y. (2016, September 19). Skyrocketing Obamacare premiums still lower than employer-sponsored insurance. Retrieved from The Washington Post: https://www.washingtonpost.com/news/wonk/wp/2016/09/19/skyrocketing-obamacare-premiums-still-lower-than-employer-sponsored-insurance

Johnson, M. (2017, August 23). Columbia Scientific Balloon Facility. Retrieved from csbf.nasa.org: https://www.csbf.nasa.gov/

Kaiser Family Foundation. (2006, November 1). Explaining Health Care Reform: Questions About Health Insurance Subsidies. Retrieved from KFF.org: http://www.kff.org/health-reform/issue-brief/explaining-health-care-reform-questions-about-health/

Kaiser Family Foundation. (2012, May 1). Health Care Costs: A Primer. Retrieved from KFF.org: http://www.kff.org/report-section/health-care-costs-a-primer-2012-report/

Kaiser Family Foundation. (2012, July 12). Summary of Coverage Provisions in the Patient Protection and Affordable Care Act. Retrieved from KFF.org: http://www.kff.org/health-costs/issue-brief/summary-of-coverage-provisions-in-the-patient/

Kaiser Family Foundation. (2014-2017). Number of Issuers Participating in the Individual Health Insurance Marketplaces. Retrieved from KFF.org: http://www.kff.org/other/state-indicator/number-of-issuers-participating-in-the-individual-health-insurance-marketplace/

Kaiser Family Foundation. (2016, December 12). An Estimated 52 Million Adults Have Pre-Existing Conditions That Would Make Them Uninsurable Pre-Obamacare. Retrieved from KFF.org: http://www.kff.org/health-reform/press-release/an-estimated-52-million-adults-have-pre-existing-conditions-that-would-make-them-uninsurable-pre-obamacare/

Kaiser Family Foundation. (2016). Health Insurance Marketplace Calculator. Retrieved from KFF.org: http://www.kff.org/wp-content/themes/vip/kaiser-foundation-2016/static/subsidy-calculator-widget.html

Kaiser Family Foundation. (2017, March 15). Where Are States Today? Medicaid and CHIP Eligibility Levels for Children, Pregnant Women, and Adults. Retrieved from KFF.org: http://www.kff.org/medicaid/fact-sheet/where-are-states-today-medicaid-and-chip/

Kaiser Family Foundation. (n.d.). Total Number of Children Ever Enrolled in CHIP Annually. Retrieved from KFF.org: http://www.kff.org/other/state-indicator/annual-chip-enrollment/

Katz, S. J., Cardiff, K., Pascali, M., Barer, M. L., & Evans, R. G. (May 2002). Phantoms In The Snow: Canadians' Use Of Health Care Services In The United States. Health Affairs, 19-31.

Kessler, G. (2014, February 20). A hard-hitting anti-Obamacare ad makes a claim that doesn't add up. Retrieved from The Washington Post: https://www.washingtonpost.com/news/fact-checker/wp/2014/02/20/a-hard-hitting-anti-obamacare-ad-makes-a-claim-that-doesnt-add-up

Kessler, G. (2014, February 14). No, CBO did not say Obamacare will kill 2 million jobs. Retrieved from The Washington Post: https://www.washingtonpost.com/news/fact-checker/wp/2014/02/04/no-cbo-did-not-say-obamacare-will-kill-2-million-jobs

Khazan, O. (2014, October 8). Why Americans Are Drowning in Medical Debt. The Atlantic.

Kliff, S. (2012, August 14). Romney's right: Obamacare cuts Medicare by $716 billion. Here's how. Retrieved from The Washington Post: https://www.washingtonpost.com/news/wonk/wp/2012/08/14/romneys-right-obamacare-cuts-medicare-by-716-billion-heres-how/

Kliff, S. (2013, July 17). Here's why health insurance premiums are tumbling in New York. The Washington Post.

Kodjak, A. (2016, November 29). 5 Things To Know About Rep. Tom Price's Health Care Ideas. Retrieved from Shots - Health News From NPR: http://www.npr.org/sections/health-shots/2016/11/29/503720671/5-things-to-know-about-rep-tom-prices-health-care-ideas

Krugman, P. (2012, September 9). Revenge of the Three-Legged Stool. Retrieved from The New York Times: https://krugman.blogs.nytimes.com/2012/09/09/revenge-of-the-three-legged-stool

Langreth, R., Migliozzi, B., & Gokhale, K. (2015, December 18). The U.S. Pays a Lot More for Top Drugs Than Other Countries. Retrieved from Bloomberg: https://www.bloomberg.com/graphics/2015-drug-prices/

Lee, M. Y. (2016, October 11). Trump's claim about Canadians traveling to the United States for medical care. Washington Post.

Legal Information Institute. (n.d.). U.S. Constitution > Article I. Retrieved from Cornell Law School: https://www.law.cornell.edu/constitution/articlei

Legal Information Institute. (n.d.). VIETH V. JUBELIRER (02-1580) 541 U.S. 267 (2004). Retrieved from law.cornell.edu: https://www.law.cornell.edu/supct/html/02-1580.ZC.html

Lenzner, R. (2011, November 20). The Top 0.1% Of The Nation Earn Half Of All Capital Gains. Retrieved from Forbes: https://www.forbes.com/sites/robertlenzner/2011/11/20/the-top-0-1-of-the-nation-earn-half-of-all-capital-gains/#7c7dc6787893

Levitt, J. (2017, June 16). All About Redistricting. Retrieved from redistricting.lls.edu: http://redistricting.lls.edu/

Levitt, L., & Claxton, G. (2014, March 27). How Much Financial Assistance Are People Receiving Under the Affordable Care Act? Retrieved from KFF.org: http://www.kff.org/health-reform/issue-brief/how-much-financial-assistance-are-people-receiving-under-the-affordable-care-act/

Levitt, L., & Cox, C. (2017, July). Individual Insurance Market Performance in Early 2017. Retrieved from KFF.org: http://files.kff.org/attachment/Issue-Brief-Individual-Insurance-Market-Performance-in-Early-2017

Levitt, M. R., Austin, D. A., & Stupak, J. M. (2015, March 18). Mandatory Spending Since 1962. Retrieved from Congressional Research Service: https://fas.org/sgp/crs/misc/RL33074.pdf

Linkins, J. (2014, Mar 2). A Brief History Of The Republican Alternative To Obamacare: Your Sunday Morning Conversation. Retrieved from Huffington Post: http://www.huffingtonpost.com/2014/03/02/republican-alternative-to-obamacare_n_4877100.html

Lisa Clemans-Cope, U. I. (2016, April 13). Medicaid Spending Growth Compared to Other Payers: A Look at the Evidence. Retrieved from KFF.org: http://www.kff.org/report-section/medicaid-spending-growth-compared-to-other-payers-issue-brief/

Long, M., Rae, M., Claxton, G., & Damico, A. (2016, March 21). Trends in Employer-Sponsored Insurance Offer and Coverage Rates, 1999-2014. Retrieved from KFF.org: http://www.kff.org/private-insurance/issue-brief/trends-in-employer-sponsored-insurance-offer-and-coverage-rates-1999-2014/

Louis Jacobsen. (2012, January 30). Were the early 1960s a golden age for health care? Retrieved from Politifact: http://www.politifact.com/truth-o-meter/article/2012/jan/20/was-early-1960s-golden-age-health-care/

Mangan, D. (2015, May 4). Obamacare program generates 'substantial' Medicare savings. Retrieved from CNBC.com: http://www.cnbc.com/2015/05/04/obamacare-program-generates-substantial-medicare-savings.html

Matthews, D. (2016, November 23). Budget reconciliation, explained. Retrieved from Vox: https://www.vox.com/policy-and-politics/2016/11/23/13709518/budget-reconciliation-explained

McBride, A. (n.d.). Reynolds v. Sims (1964). Retrieved from pbs.org: https://www.pbs.org/wnet/supremecourt/rights/landmark_reynolds.html

McCanne, D. (2013, February 19). Important: What are Medicare's true administrative costs? Retrieved from Physicians for a National Health Program: http://pnhp.org/blog/2013/02/19/important-what-are-medicares-true-administrative-costs/

McCrimmon, R. (May, 1 2017). Omnibus Agreement Details $1 Trillion in FY 2017 Spending. Retrieved from Roll Call: https://www.rollcall.com/politics/omnibus-spending-bill-budget-trump-agenda

McGrayne, S. B. (2012). The Theory That Would Not Die: How Bayes' Rule Cracked the Enigma Code, Hunted Down Russian Submarines, and Emerged Triumphant from Two Centuries of Controversy. New Haven: Yale University Press.

Medicaid. (n.d.). Cost Sharing Out of Pocket Costs. Retrieved from medicaid.gov: https://www.medicaid.gov/medicaid/cost-sharing/out-of-pocket-costs/index.html

Miller, A. (2016, December 8). Interstate Health Insurance Sales Has A Tryout In Georgia But No Takers. Retrieved from Kaiser Health News: http://khn.org/news/interstate-health-insurance-sales-has-a-tryout-in-georgia-but-no-takers/

Miller, D. (2007). The Eighth Air Force: The American Bomber Crews in Britain. London: Aurum Press Ltd.

Millhiser, I. (2016, December 7). Here's how many people could die every year if Obamacare is repealed. Retrieved from Think Progress: https://thinkprogress.org/heres-how-many-people-could-die-every-year-if-obamacare-is-repealed-ae4bf3e100a2/

Monroe, R. (n.d.). Frequentists vs. Bayesians. Retrieved from xkcd.com: https://xkcd.com/1132/

Mossialos, E., & Martin Wenzl, e. (2016, January). 2015 International Profiles of Health Care Systems. Retrieved from Commonwealth Fund: http://www.commonwealthfund.org/~/media/files/publications/fund-report/2016/jan/1857_mossialos_intl_profiles_2015_v7.pdf?la=en

Mukherjee, S. (New York). The Emperor Of All Maladies: A Biography Of Cancer. 2010: Scribner.

National Academies of Sciences, Engineering and Medicine. (2015). The Growing Gap in Life Expectancy by Income: Implications for Federal Programs and Policy Responses. Retrieved from National Academies Press: https://www.nap.edu/catalog/ 19015/the-growing-gap-in-life-expectancy-by-income-implications-for

National Institutes of Health. (2017, March 6). Budget. Retrieved from NIH.gov: https://www.nih.gov/about-nih/what-we-do/ budget

National Museum of American History. (1979, September 14). Laffer Curve Napkin. Retrieved from americanhistory.si.edu: http://americanhistory.si.edu/collections/search/object/ nmah_1439217

National Women's Law Center. (2006). Medicaid 101: The Federal-State Health Care Partnership. Washington: National Women's Law Center.

New York Times. (2013, February 2). Imbalance of Power. Retrieved from The New York Times: http://www.nytimes.com/ interactive/2013/02/03/sunday-review/imbalance-of-power.html

New York Times Company. (1924, December 21). Hitler Tamed by Prison. The New York Times.

Newell, J. (2017, March 9). Paul Ryan, About Seven Years Too Late, Explains Why Full Repeal Would Be a Disaster. Retrieved from Slate: http://www.slate.com/blogs/the_slatest/2017/03/09/ paul_ryan_uses_a_powerpoint_presentation_to_sell_his_ailing _health_care.html

NHS Employers. (2017, August 11). Pay and Conditions Circular (M&D) 1/2017. Retrieved from nhsemployers.org: http://www.nhsemployers.org/~/media/Employers/ Documents/Pay%20and%20reward/ FINAL%20Pay%20and%20Conditions%20Circular%20MD%20 12017.pdf

Nina Viberg, B. F. (2013). International comparisons of waiting times in health care—Limitations and prospects. Health Policy, 53-61.

OASDI Trustees. (2015). 2015 OASDI Trustees Report; Projections of Future Financial Status. Retrieved from SSA.gov: https://www.ssa.gov/oact/tr/2015/II_D_project.html

Obamacare Facts. (n.d.). ObamaCare Guaranteed Issue. Retrieved from Obamacare Facts: https://obamacarefacts.com/ guaranteed-issue/

Obamacare Facts. (n.d.). ObamaCare Medicaid Expansion. Retrieved from Obamacare Facts: https://obamacarefacts.com/obamacares-medicaid-expansion/

Obamacare Facts. (n.d.). ObamaCare: Health Insurance Cancellation. Retrieved from Obamacare Facts: https://obamacarefacts.com/health-insurance-cancellation/

Obamacare Facts. (n.d.). ObamaCare: Uninsured Rates. Retrieved from Obamacare Facts: https://obamacarefacts.com/uninsured-rates/

Obamacare Facts. (n.d.). Summary of Provisions in The Patient Protection and Affordable Care Act. Retrieved from Obamacare Facts: https://obamacarefacts.com/summary-of-provisions-patient-protection-and-affordable-care-act/

O'Donnell, T. (1936). History of Life Insurance in Its Formative Years. Chicago: American Conservation Co.

Office of Management and Budget. (n.d.). Historical Tables. Retrieved from obamawhitehouse.archives.gov: https://obamawhitehouse.archives.gov/omb/budget/Historicals

Office of Personnel Management. (n.d.). Historical Federal Workforce Tables: Executive Branch Civilian Employment Since 1940. Retrieved from OPM.gov: https://www.opm.gov/policy-data-oversight/data-analysis-documentation/federal-employment-reports/historical-tables/executive-branch-civilian-employment-since-1940/

Office of Tax Policy. (2016, September 28). Tax Expenditures. Retrieved September 18, 2017, from treasury.gov: https://www.treasury.gov/resource-center/tax-policy/Documents/Tax-Expenditures-FY2018.pdf

Office of the Actuary, Centers for Medicare and Medicaid Services. (2015). 2015 Actuarial Report on the Financial Outlook for Medicaid. Retrieved from medicaid.gov: https://www.medicaid.gov/medicaid/financing-and-reimbursement/downloads/medicaid-actuarial-report-2015.pdf

Orem, T. (2017, May 14). 2017 Federal Income Tax Brackets. Retrieved from nerdwallet: https://www.nerdwallet.com/blog/taxes/federal-income-tax-brackets/

Organization for Economic Co-Operation and Development. (2015). Health at a Glance, 2015; Health care activities, Consultations with doctors. Retrieved from OECD Health

Statistics 2015: http://www.oecd-ilibrary.org/social-issues-migration-health/data/oecd-health-statistics_health-data-en

Organization for Economic Co-Operation and Development. (2017, October 04). Health expenditure and financing. Retrieved from stats.oecd.org: http://stats.oecd.org/Index.aspx

Organization for Economic Co-Operation and Development. (n.d.). Health Spending. Retrieved from OECD Data: https://data.oecd.org/healthres/health-spending.htm

Organization for Economic Co-Operation and Development. (n.d.). Revenue Statistics - OECD countries: Comparative tables. Retrieved from OECD: http://stats.oecd.org/Index.aspx?QueryId=21699

Organization for Economic Co-Operation and Development. (n.d.). Tax revenue. Retrieved from OECD: https://data.oecd.org/tax/tax-revenue.htm

Park, E. (2016, November 17). Trump, House GOP High-Risk Pool Proposals a Failed Approach. Retrieved from Center on Budget and Policy Priorities: https://www.cbpp.org/blog/trump-house-gop-high-risk-pool-proposals-a-failed-approach

Pattison, D. (2015). Social Security Trust Fund Cash Flows and Reserves, Social Security Bulletin, Vol 75, No 1. Retrieved from Social Security Office of Retirement and Disability Policy: https://www.ssa.gov/policy/docs/ssb/v75n1/v75n1p1.html

Pear, R., & Kaplan, T. (2016, December 15). G.O.P. Plans to Replace Health Care Law With 'Universal Access'. The New York Times, p. A20.

Pelley, S. (2008, February 21). The Prosecution of Don Siegelman. 60 Minutes. New York, NY, USA: Continental Broadcasting System.

Perelman, G. (2002). The entropy formula for the Ricci flow and its geometric applications. arXiv:math/0211159.

Perelman, G. (2002). Ricci flow with surgery on three-manifolds. arXiv:math/0303109.

Perelman, G. (2003). Finite extinction time for the solutions to the Ricci flow on certain three-manifolds. arXiv:math/0307245.

Phillips, A. (2017, April 10). Former Alabama governor Robert Bentley's year from hell, a timeline. Retrieved from The Washington Post: https://www.washingtonpost.com/news/the-fix/wp/2017/04/08/the-long-strange-affair-saga-of-alabama-gov-robert-bentley-is-about-to-get-serious

Philo, T. (1976-2017). Eighth Air Force Combat Losses. Retrieved from Tom Philo Photography: http://www.taphilo.com/history/8thaf/8aflosses.shtml

Pianin, E. (2016, November 30). 8 Big Changes Under Tom Price's Obamacare Replacement Plan. Retrieved from The Fiscal Times: http://www.thefiscaltimes.com/2016/11/30/8-Big-Changes-Under-Tom-Price-s-Obamacare-Replacement-Plan-0

Ploughshares Fund. (2016, March 2). World Nuclear Weapon Stockpile. Retrieved from Ploughshares Fund: https://www.ploughshares.org/world-nuclear-stockpile-report

Poe, E. A. (1848). Eureka, A Prose Poem: Or the Physical and Metaphysical Universe. New York: Leavitt, Trow and Co.

Pomerleau, K. (2015, March 3). How High are Other Nations' Gas Taxes? Retrieved from Tax Foundation: https://taxfoundation.org/how-high-are-other-nations-gas-taxes/

PSM-Data "Geschichte". (2001). Weimar Constitution. Retrieved from zum.de: http://www.zum.de/psm/weimar/weimar_vve.php

Räth, D. N. (3/2009). Rezessionen in historischer Betrachtung. Volkswirtschaftliche Gesamtrechnungen, 206.

Roberts, A. (2017, March 31). High courage on the axe edge of war. The Times.

Robertson, L. (2014, April 11). 'Millions' Lost Insurance. Retrieved from factcheck.org: http://www.factcheck.org/2014/04/millions-lost-insurance/

Ross, D. (2014, December 9). Game Theory. Retrieved from Stanford Encyclopedia of Philosophy: https://seop.illc.uva.nl/entries/game-theory/

Rybicki, E. (2015). Amendments Between the Houses: Procedural Options and Effects. Washington: Congressional Research Service.

Rybicki, E. (2015). Conference Committee and Related Procedures: An Introduction. Washington: Congressional Research Service.

Sahadi, J. (2015, April 8). Top 400 taxpayers' average income jumps to $336 million. Retrieved from CNN.com: http://money.cnn.com/2015/04/08/pf/taxes/top-400-taxpayers-2012/

Sanders, K. (2015, January 20). Barack Obama claims deficit has decreased by two-thirds since taking office. Retrieved from Politifact: http://www.politifact.com/truth-o-meter/statements/2015/jan/20/barack-obama/barack-obama-claims-deficit-has-decreased-two-thir/

Saturno, J. V., Heniff, B., & Lynch, M. S. (2016, November 30). The Congressional Appropriations Process: An Overview. Retrieved from Congressional Research Service: https://fas.org/sgp/crs/misc/R42388.pdf

Schierholtz, H. (2014, August 13). Positive Jobs Trend. Retrieved from Economic Policy Institute: http://www.epi.org/publication/positive-jobs-trend-involuntary-part-time/

Schubel, J. (2015, May 1). No Need for Work Requirements in Medicaid. Retrieved from Center on Budget and Policy Priorities: http://www.cbpp.org/blog/no-need-for-work-requirements-in-medicaid

Schwartz, T. (2010). State High-Risk Pools: An Overvieew. Kaiser Commission on Medicaid and the Uninsured.

Sheiner, L. (2015, September 18). Implications of the growing gap in life expectancy by income. Retrieved from Brookings: https://www.brookings.edu/blog/health360/2015/09/18/implications-of-the-growing-gap-in-life-expectancy-by-income/

Shirer, W. L. (1941). Berlin Diary. London: H. Hamilton.

Shirer, W. L. (1960). The rise and fall of the Third Reich: A history of Nazi Germany. New York: Simon and Schuster.

Social Security Administration. (1996, July). Research Note #3: Details of Ida May Fuller's Payroll Tax Contributions. Retrieved from SSA.gov: https://www.ssa.gov/history/idapayroll.html

Social Security Administration. (2005, April 5). Presidential Statements - George W. Bush - 2nd Quarter, 2005. Retrieved from Social Security Online: https://www.ssa.gov/history/gwbushstmts5b.html#04052005

Social Security Administration. (2010, February). Annual Statistical Supplement to the Social Security Administration. Retrieved from Social Security Administration: https://www.ssa.gov/policy/docs/statcomps/supplement/2009/supplement09.pdf

Social Security Administration. (2016). Social Security Beneficiary Statistics. Retrieved from SSA.gov: https://www.ssa.gov/oact/STATS/OASDIbenies.html

Social Security Administration Office of the Chief Actuary. (2017, February 28). Summary of Provisions that Would Change the Social Security Program. Retrieved from Social Security Administration: https://www.ssa.gov/oact/solvency/provisions/summary.pdf

Social Security Administration. (n.d.). Social Security History. Retrieved from Social Security History: https://www.ssa.gov/history/index.html

Social Security Administration. (n.d.). Social Security Trust Fund Data. Retrieved from Social Security Administration: https://www.ssa.gov/oact/progdata/funds.html

Social Security and Medicare Boards of Trustees. (2017). A Summary of the 2017 Annual Reports. Retrieved from Social Security Administration: https://www.ssa.gov/oact/TRSUM/index.html

Sommers, B. D., Baicker, K., & Epstein, A. M. (2012). Mortality and Access to Care among Adults after State Medicaid Expansions. The New England Journal of Medicine, 1025-1034.

Stern, M. J. (2017, March 18). Court Blocks Most of North Carolina GOP's Legislative Coup, Including Election-Board Power Grab. Retrieved from Slate: http://www.slate.com/blogs/the_slatest/2017/03/18/north_carolina_legislative_power_grab_blocked_in_court.html

Tampa Bay Times. (n.d.). About Politifact. Retrieved from Politfact: http://www.politifact.com/about/

Tax Foundation. (n.d.). U.S. Federal Individual Income Tax Rates History, 1862-2013 (Nominal and Inflation-Adjusted Brackets). Retrieved from Tax Foundation: https://taxfoundation.org/us-federal-individual-income-tax-rates-history-1913-2013-nominal-and-inflation-adjusted-brackets/

Tax Policy Center. (2017, May 3). Household Income Quintiles. Retrieved from Tax Policy Center: http://www.taxpolicycenter.org/statistics/household-income-quintiles

Tax Policy Center. (n.d.). What are the largest tax expenditures? Retrieved from Tax Policy Center (Briefing Book):

http://www.taxpolicycenter.org/briefing-book/what-are-largest-tax-expenditures

Tergesen, A. (2016, November 12). Retirement Policy Under Donald Trump? Unclear, but There Are Clues. Retrieved from The Wall Street Journal: https://www.wsj.com/articles/retirement-policy-under-donald-trump-unclear-but-there-are-clues-1478952001

The Economist. (2013, November 15). Germany's hyperinflation-phobia. The Economist.

Trading Economics. (n.d.). List of Countries by Corporate Tax Rate. Retrieved from Trading Economics: https://tradingeconomics.com/country-list/corporate-tax-rate

Trueman, C. N. (2015, May 22). Weimar Republic And The Great Depression. Retrieved from History Learning Site: http://www.historylearningsite.co.uk/modern-world-history-1918-to-1980/weimar-germany/weimar-republic-and-the-great-depression/

U.S. Census Bureau. (n.d.). Current Population Survey Annual Social and Economic Supplement (CPS-ASEC). Retrieved from census.gov: https://www.census.gov/topics/health/health-insurance/guidance/cps-asec.html

U.S. Department of Commerce; U.S. Census Bureau. (2009, September). Income, Poverty and Health Insurance in the United States: 2008. Retrieved from census.gov: https://www.census.gov/prod/2009pubs/p60-236.pdf

U.S. Government Accountability Office. (n.d.). Antideficiency Act. Retrieved from GAO.gov: https://www.gao.gov/legal/anti-deficiency-act/about

U.S. News and World Report. (2012, July 19). Medicare Beats Private Plans for Patient Satisfaction: Survey. Retrieved from U.S. News: http://health.usnews.com/health-news/news/articles/2012/07/19/medicare-beats-private-plans-for-patient-satisfaction-survey

Ungar, R. (2012, May 1). Georgia Cross-State Health Insurance Sales Law A Major Bust. Retrieved from Forbes: https://www.forbes.com/sites/rickungar/2012/05/01/georgia-cross-state-health-insurance-sales-law-a-major-bust

United States Census Bureau. (2016, September 1). Historical Poverty Tables: People and Families - 1959 to 2015, Tables 2-3. Retrieved from United States Census Bureau:

https://www.census.gov/data/tables/time-series/demo/income-poverty/historical-poverty-people.html

United States v. Lopez, 93-1260 (Supreme Court of the United States April 26, 1995).

VanderMay, A., & Rapp, N. (2017, March 30). Here's How Bad U.S. Infrastructure Has Become. Retrieved from Fortune: http://fortune.com/2017/03/30/infrastructure-spending-funding/

Vaughn, C., Bangia, S., Bridget Dou, S. G., & Mattingly, J. (n.d.). Quantifying Gerrymandering @Duke University. Retrieved from services.math.duke.edu: https://services.math.duke.edu/projects/gerrymandering/

Viro, O. Y., Ivanov, O. A., Netsvetaev, N. Y., & Kharlamov, V. M. (2008). Elementary Topology: Problem Textbook. Telangana: Orient BlackSwan.

Volokh, S. (2014, February 7). Are public-sector employees "overpaid"? The Washington Post.

von Neumann, J., & Morgenstern, O. (2007). Theory of Games and Economic Behavior: 60th Anniversary Commemorative Edition. Princeton: Princeton University Press.

Weir, A. (2014). The Martian. New York: Crown Publishers.

Wikipedia. (n.d.). Apollo Lunar Module. Retrieved from wikipedia.org: https://en.wikipedia.org/wiki/Apollo_Lunar_Module#Ascent_stage

Wikipedia. (n.d.). Apportionment paradox. Retrieved from wikipedia.org: https://en.wikipedia.org/wiki/Apportionment_paradox

Wikipedia. (n.d.). Saturn V. Retrieved from wikipedia.org: https://en.wikipedia.org/wiki/Saturn_V

Wikipedia. (n.d.). Thomas Bayes. Retrieved from www.wikipedia.org: https://en.wikipedia.org/wiki/Thomas_Bayes

Wikipedia. (n.d.). Topological property. Retrieved from wikipedia.org: https://en.wikipedia.org/wiki/Topological_property

Wikipedia. (n.d.). United States House of Representatives elections in Ohio, 2012. Retrieved from wikipedia.org: https://en.wikipedia.org/wiki/

United_States_House_of_Representatives_elections_in_Ohio,_
2012

Wikipedia. (n.d.). Weimar Constitution. Retrieved from
wikipedia.org: https://en.wikipedia.org/wiki/
Weimar_Constitution

World Bank Group. (n.d.). GDP growth (annual %). Retrieved from
data.worldbank.org: https://data.worldbank.org/indicator/
NY.GDP.MKTP.KD.ZG?locations=US

World Bank. (n.d.). Health expenditure, total (% of GDP).
Retrieved from data.worldbank.org:
https://data.worldbank.org/indicator/SH.XPD.TOTL.ZS

World Bank. (n.d.). Life expectancy at birth, total (years). Retrieved
from data.worldbank.org: http://data.worldbank.org/indicator/
SP.DYN.LE00.IN

World Bank. (n.d.). Mortality rate, adult, male (per 1,000 male
adults). Retrieved from data.worldbank.org:
https://data.worldbank.org/indicator/SP.DYN.AMRT.MA

World Health Organization. (2016, June 06). Life expectancy data
by country. Retrieved from apps.who.int: http://apps.who.int/
gho/data/view.main.SDG2016LEXv?lang=en

INDEX